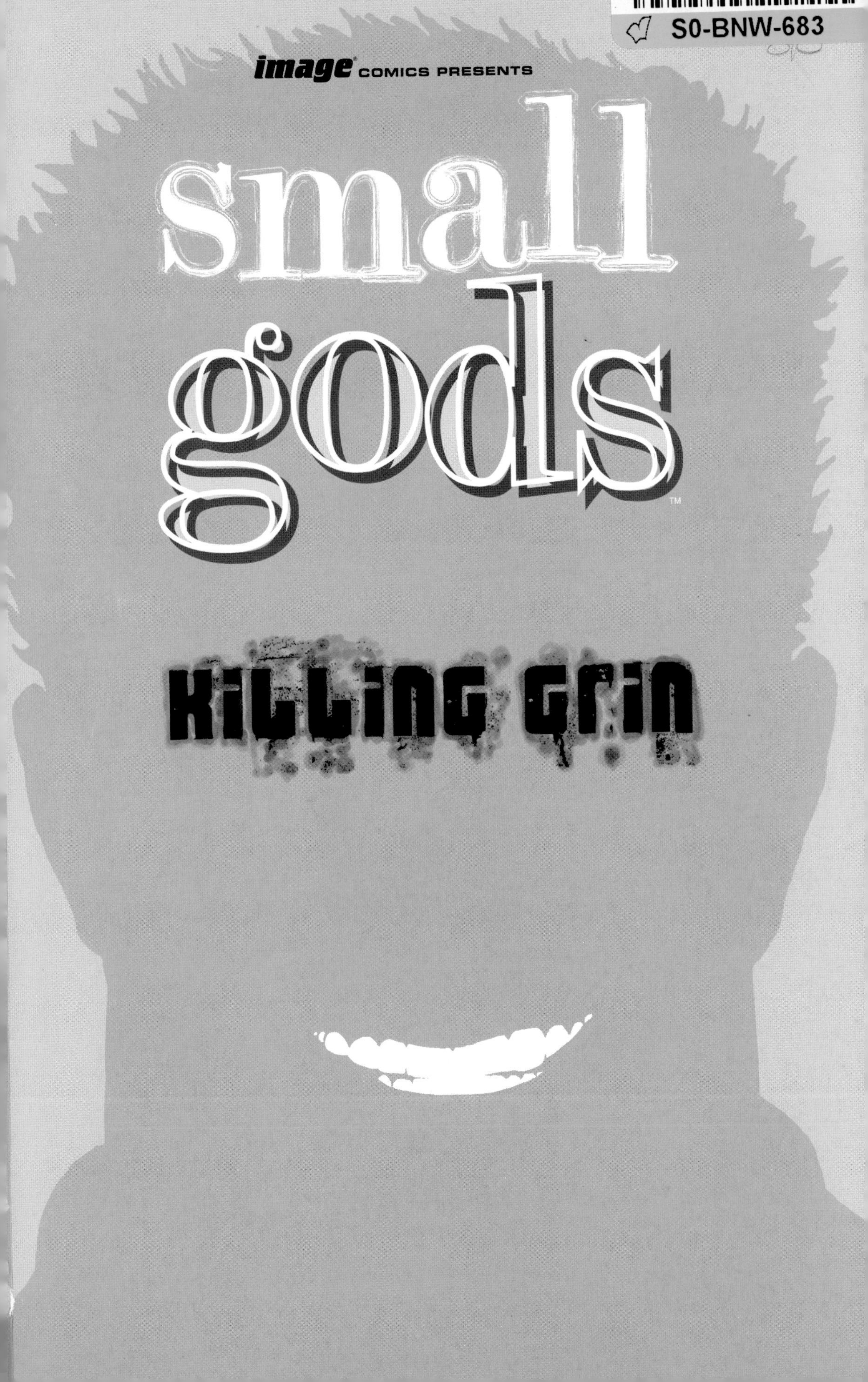
image COMICS PRESENTS
small gods™
KILLING GRIN

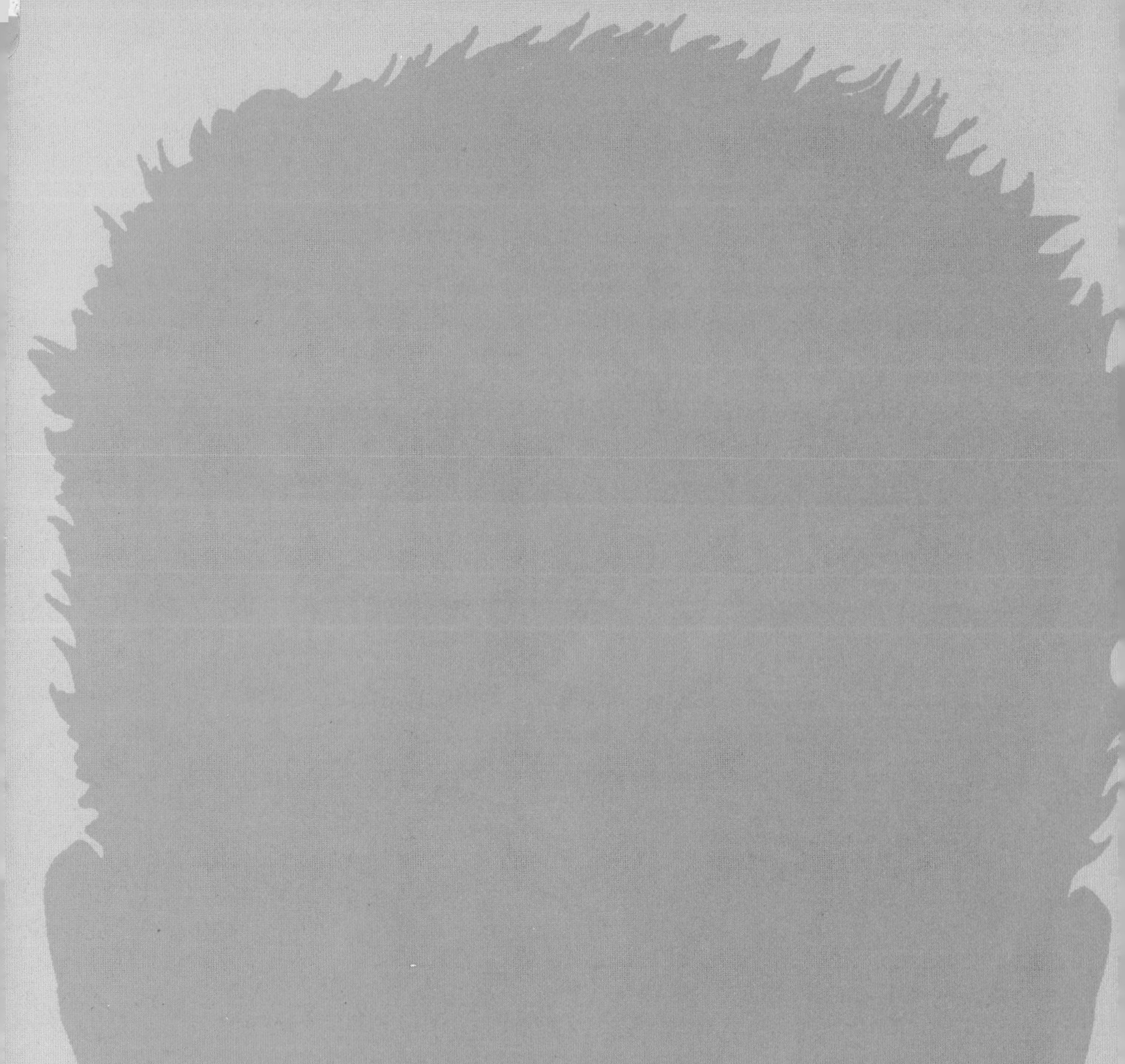

IMAGE COMICS, INC.

Erik Larsen - *Publisher*
Todd McFarlane - *President*
Marc Silvestri - *CEO*
Jim Valentino - *Vice-President*

Eric Stephenson - *Executive Director*
Missie Miranda - *Controller*
Brett Evans - *Production Manager*
B. Clay Moore - *PR & Marketing Coordinator*
Joe Keatinge - *Inventory Controller*
Allen Hui - *Production Artist*

www.imagecomics.com

MAN, I DON'T EVEN LIKE NORMAL COPS.

I hate the way they swagger around, with their guns, and tasers and billy clubs, and glare at me like they know something. Not that they do. Nosirree, officer. No convictions on my record. Nothin' to see here.

Granted, I've shoplifted just about everything I own, but I've never been caught. And yes, I did go through a Peeping Tom period, but I understand that is perfectly natural for lonely, 40-something males. Those letters and small tokens I kept sending to that trampy little pop singer? They were just jokes — mostly — and besides, I took great precautions to make sure none could be traced back to me.

But you might understand how I find the idea of cops knowing what I've done — or what I'm up to — a bit...terrifying. Knowing what I'm going to do next? That's a freaking nightmare.

And yet, I like the idea behind it. I'm intrigued by a world where freaky mental powers exist, even if it just happens to one in every hundred. And when it happens, it has real-world repercussions. This is the world of Small Gods. This is a world that, at least in this debut story arc, gives new meaning to the phrase "thought police".

I wouldn't mind living in a world like this, either, even if it gave more damn cops an edge against me. Wouldn't mind, assuming I could have some of those freaky psychic powers, too.

And, if I did, I know the first place I'd choose for my next bit of larceny: Jason Rand's head. You won't be too far into this book before you figure out he's got plenty of ideas and likely plenty more to spare, and all of 'em seem to be damn good ones. Just as important, he knows how to execute a good idea. He knows how to tell a story and how to make you care — and keep you on the edge of your seat — as he puts his lead character up to his neck in a rising tide of deep shit.

I'd be remiss if I didn't mention the contribution to the book of artist Juan Ferreyra. The guy's a real find and as part of my continuing crime spree, I'd be perfectly happy to steal him away from Jason. Clear storytelling and layouts, expressive characters and believable body language, and an uncanny ability to capture one very difficult and intangible element: suspense. Juan Ferreyra is the sort of artist any comic book writer would kill for. Not that I — ya know — think much about things like that.

I discovered the first two issues of Small Gods at last year's San Diego Comic Con. I devoured both issues and just as soon as I was done I read 'em again. They were that good. That smart. That taut. And I remember reading issue #3 at my house, halfway through when the doorbell rang, and literally not being able to put it down before I got through one more page, one more, one more.

You're about to discover that feeling. And I don't need to be a precog to see what's going to happen next, or a telepath to know what you're going to think of what you read. You're gonna like it. A lot.

Either that, or you're just simply not right in the head. And, at least in this world, there's not a cop around that's gonna know any better...as long as you play things straight and keep your big trap shut.

-- John Layman
Jackin' bustahs in the barrio
12.16.04

John Layman is a notorious comics lowlife, culpable for Puffed, Gambit, Thundercats, Bay City Jive, and assorted other crimes against humanity. Layman, incarcerated subsequent to writing this introduction, continues to send Jason Rand missives of fawning praise for Small Gods, but once Rand refused to pay Layman in cigarettes, the letters have taken a darker tone, and are now delivered with disturbing and obsessive frequency.

ACKNOWLEDGMENTS

JASON RAND

This one's for everyone who's helped me along the way. You know who you are, but there are just too many of you to name here, so I'd just like to single out a few of you. My family, who are always good for a more-or-less objective opinion on things; the team, as always, without whom this book simply wouldn't exist; and Jim Valentino, who said yes to my crazy idea and looked after us in so many ways throughout our grand journey.

JUAN FERREYRA

First of all I would like to thank my Dad for helping me out with the greyscales. I would have never dreamed that one day I would be working with the man who introduced me to comics, it's a dream come true.
To all my family, Ana, Michelle, Cande & Salva.
To my girlfriend Laura for all her support and help.
To all my friends for showing interest in the comic, that made me feel good, Diego, Coke, Joaquin, Gregorio, Clavo, Mateo, Esteban, both Victors, Ale, Gon, chelo, Fer León.
Special thanks to Justin who was the only one who actually bought the issues.
To Jim Hoffmann and his family, Cindy, Austin and off course Ian.
To Jim Valentino for accepting and giving us this opportunity.
And to all the people who bought the comic.

JIM KEPLINGER

For Lisa, Lynnsie, Camryn & Cole for all the usual reasons. I love you! A special thank you to Nate at Blambot for his amazing fonts... you make me look better than genetics alone. Without Ed at Digital Webbing none of this would be possible, thank you for keeping the small press world thriving and together. Finally, for the Small Gods team for letting me play on your field, it's an honor.

KRISTEN SIMON

For Jason, Juan and Kep! A truly fantastic team of professionals. And to the people who love me the most, I couldn't have accomplished any of it without your support.

CHAPTER ONE

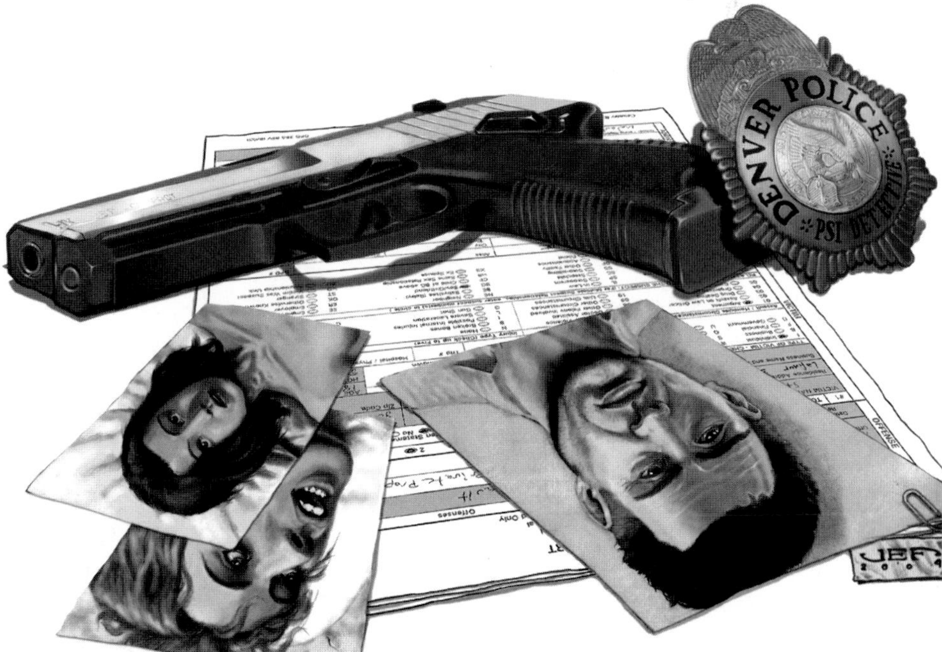
DENVER POLICE
PSI DETECTIVE

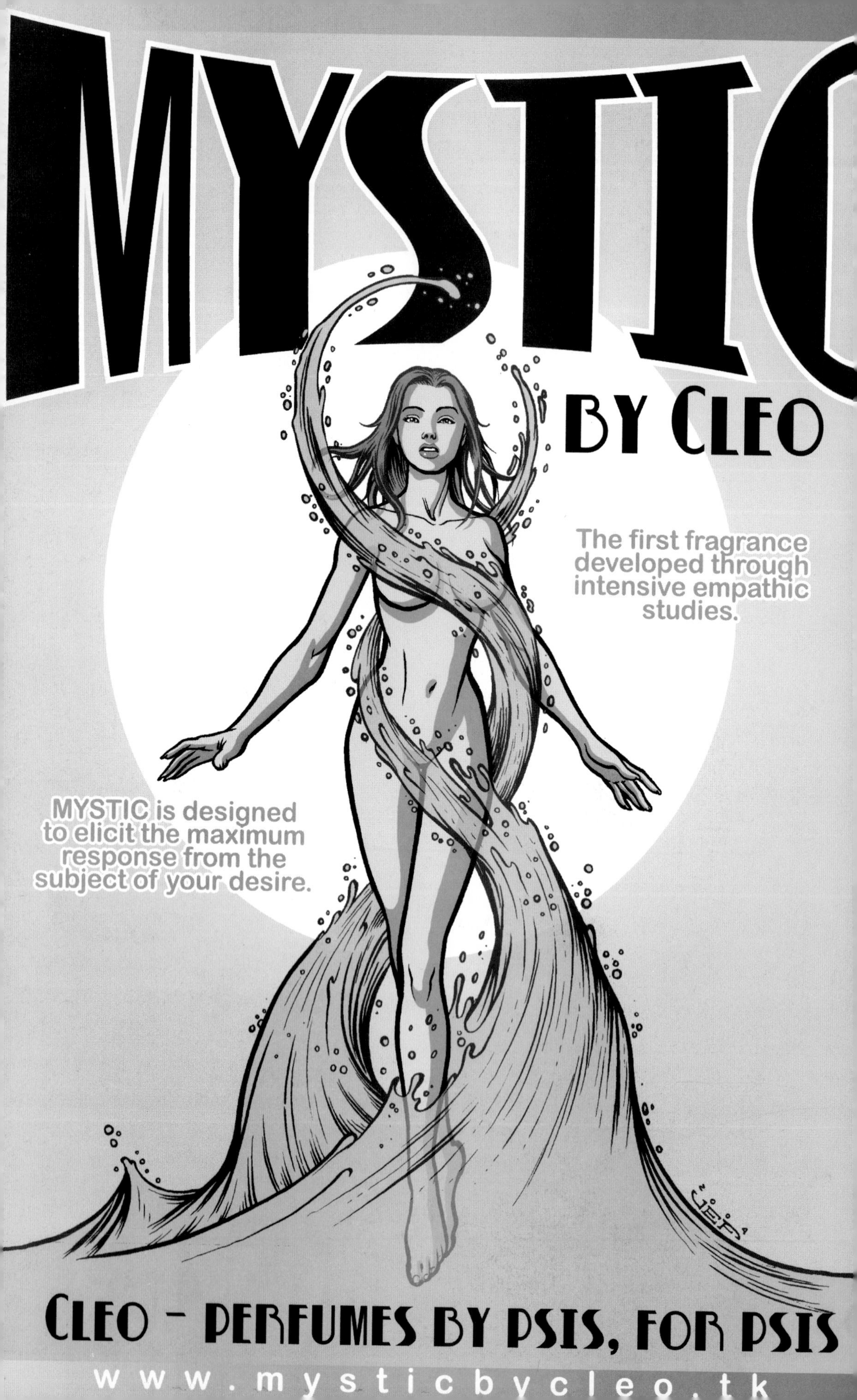
MYSTIC
BY CLEO
The first fragrance developed through intensive empathic studies.
MYSTIC is designed to elicit the maximum response from the subject of your desire.
CLEO - PERFUMES BY PSIS, FOR PSIS
www.mysticbycleo.tk

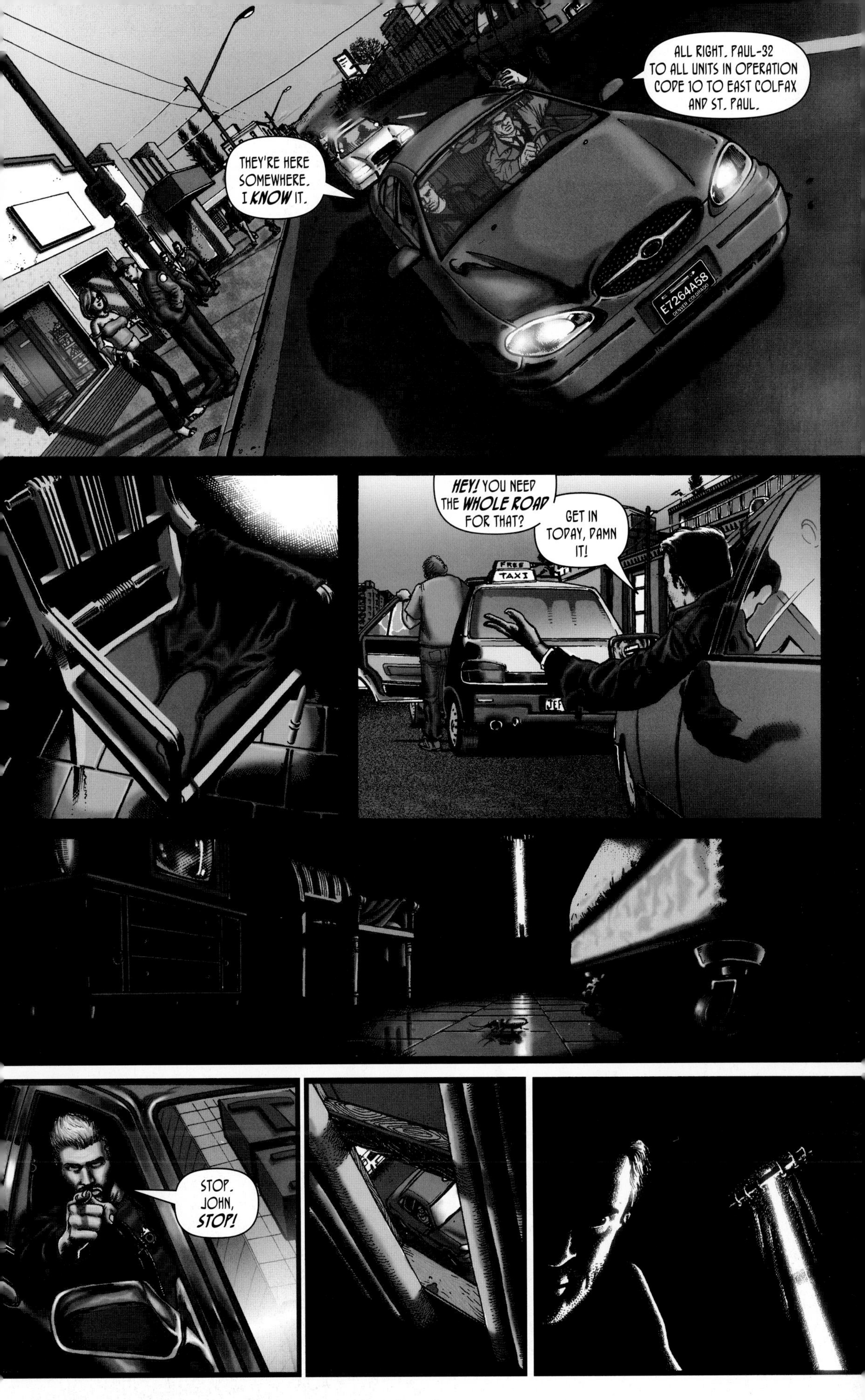
ALL RIGHT. PAUL-32 TO ALL UNITS IN OPERATION CODE 10 TO EAST COLFAX AND ST. PAUL.
THEY'RE HERE SOMEWHERE. I KNOW IT.
E7264A58
DENVER, COLORADO
HEY! YOU NEED THE WHOLE ROAD FOR THAT?
GET IN TODAY, DAMN IT!
FREE
TAXI
STOP. JOHN, STOP!

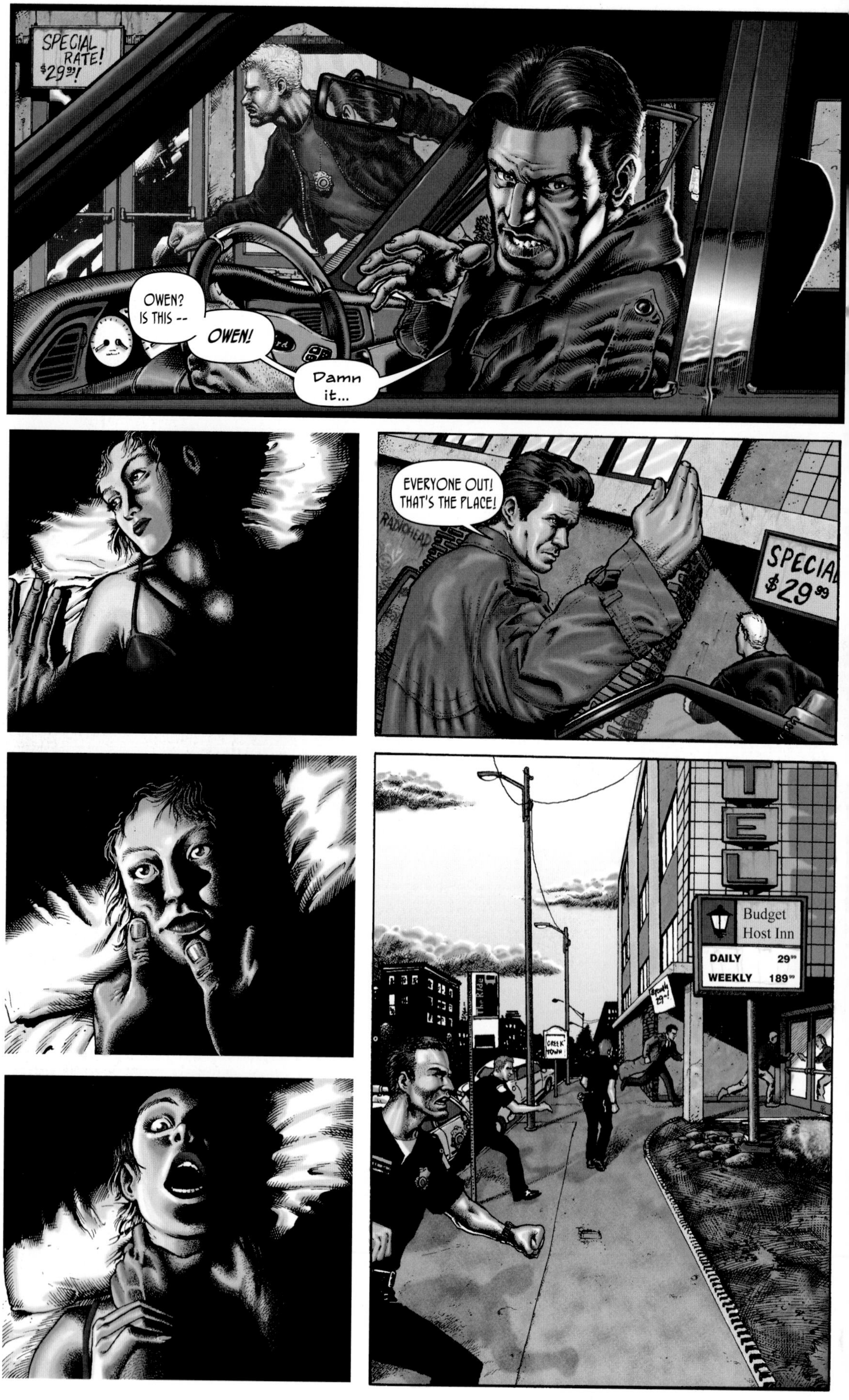
SPECIAL RATE! $29 99!
OWEN? IS THIS --
OWEN!
Damn it...
EVERYONE OUT! THAT'S THE PLACE!
RADIOHEAD
SPECIAL $29 99
TEL
Budget Host Inn
DAILY 29 99
WEEKLY 189 99

THIRD FLOOR. WE'LL MEET YOU UP THERE.

WHICH ROOM? HEY! WHICH - ROOM?

WHAT? *Nah*, DUDE, NEVER SEEN HIM BEFORE.

BULL- *SHIT!*

LET ME SPELL IT OUT. THIS MAN IS HERE, IN *THIS* HOTEL. HE HAS A GIRL WITH HIM. HE'S GOING TO *KILL HER* IF WE DON'T FIND THEM.

AND IF THAT HAPPENS WHILE YOU'RE *FUCKING* US AROUND...

...YOU'LL BE AN ACCESSORY TO *MURDER.* *IS THAT WHAT YOU WANT?!*

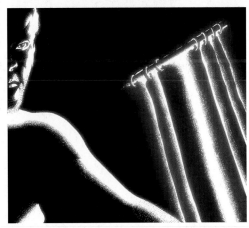

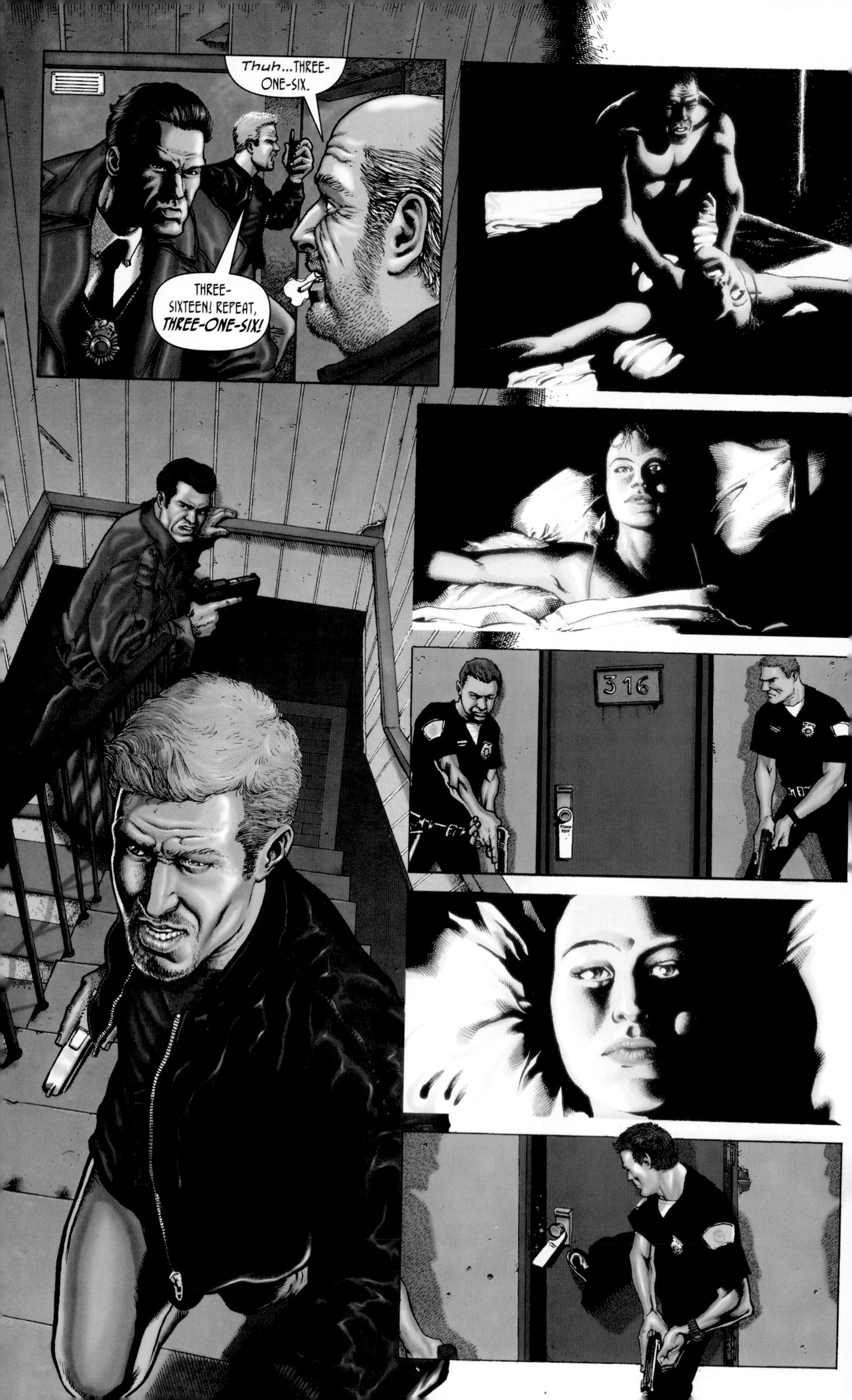
Thuh...THREE-ONE-SIX.
THREE-SIXTEEN! REPEAT, THREE-ONE-SIX!
316

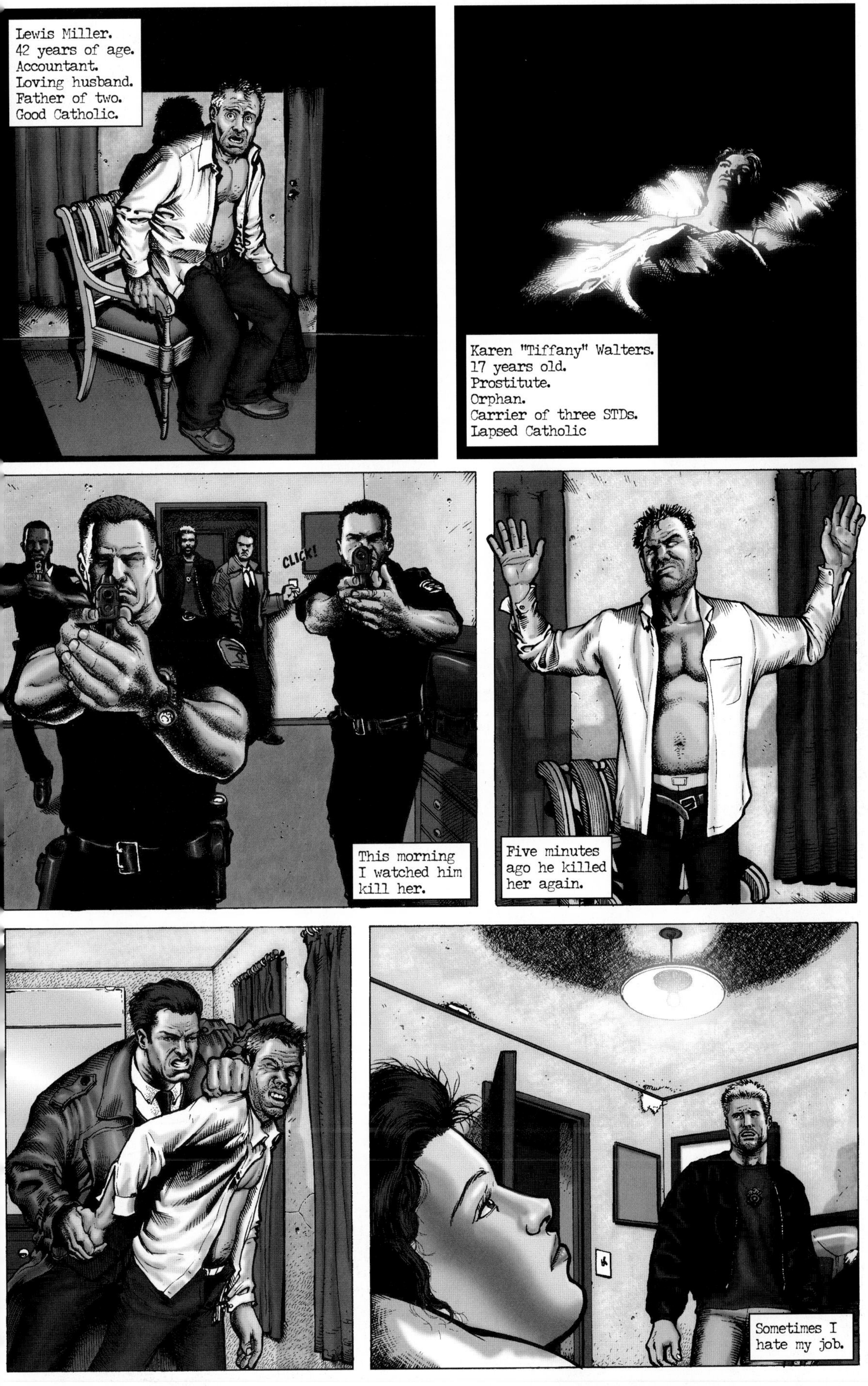
Lewis Miller.
42 years of age.
Accountant.
Loving husband.
Father of two.
Good Catholic.
Karen "Tiffany" Walters.
17 years old.
Prostitute.
Orphan.
Carrier of three STDs.
Lapsed Catholic
CLICK!
This morning I watched him kill her.
Five minutes ago he killed her again.
Sometimes I hate my job.

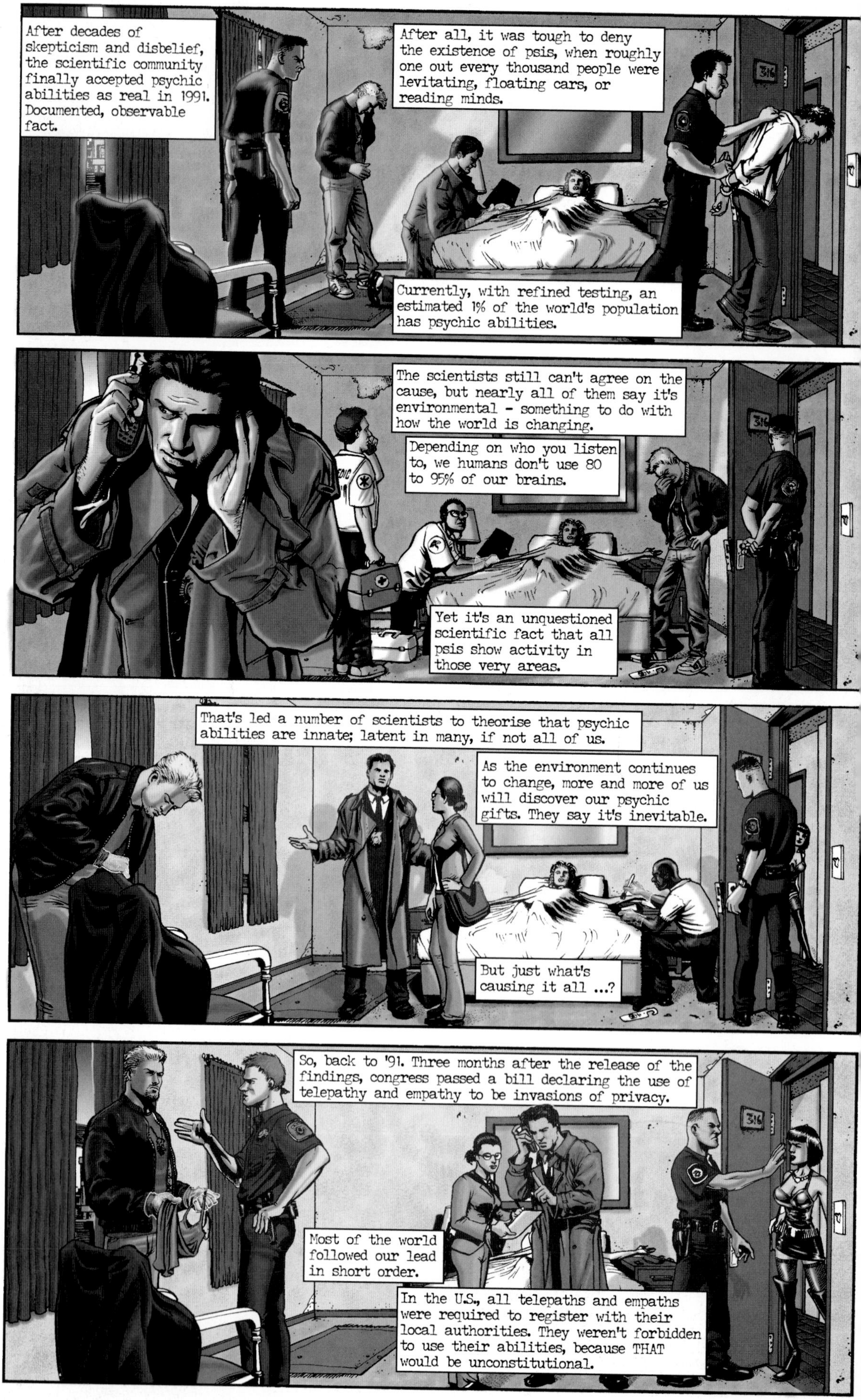

After decades of skepticism and disbelief, the scientific community finally accepted psychic abilities as real in 1991. Documented, observable fact.
After all, it was tough to deny the existence of psis, when roughly one out every thousand people were levitating, floating cars, or reading minds.
316
Currently, with refined testing, an estimated 1% of the world's population has psychic abilities.
The scientists still can't agree on the cause, but nearly all of them say it's environmental - something to do with how the world is changing.
Depending on who you listen to, we humans don't use 80 to 95% of our brains.
Yet it's an unquestioned scientific fact that all psis show activity in those very areas.
That's led a number of scientists to theorise that psychic abilities are innate; latent in many, if not all of us.
As the environment continues to change, more and more of us will discover our psychic gifts. They say it's inevitable.
But just what's causing it all ...?
So, back to '91. Three months after the release of the findings, congress passed a bill declaring the use of telepathy and empathy to be invasions of privacy.
316
Most of the world followed our lead in short order.
In the U.S., all telepaths and empaths were required to register with their local authorities. They weren't forbidden to use their abilities, because THAT would be unconstitutional.

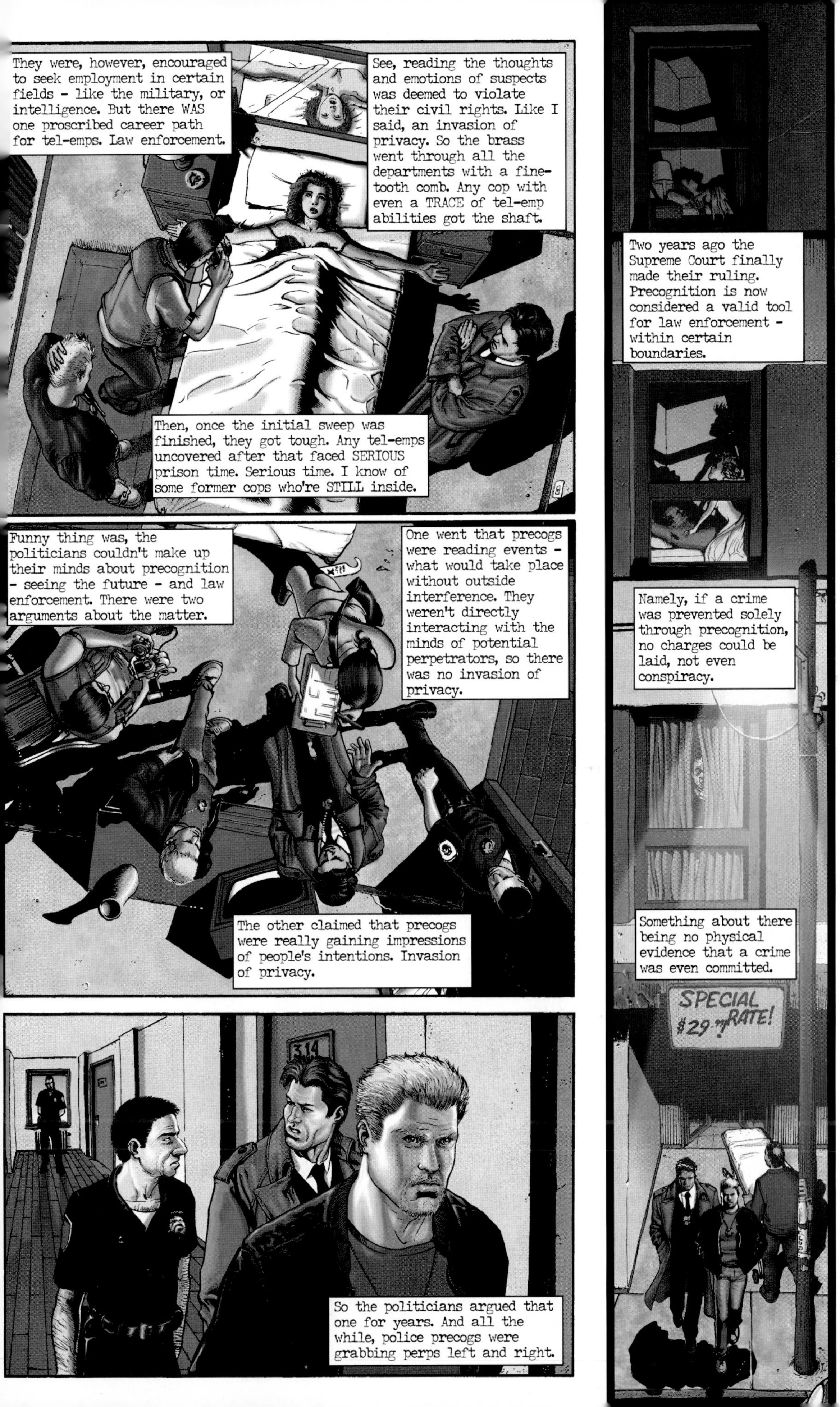
They were, however, encouraged to seek employment in certain fields - like the military, or intelligence. But there WAS one proscribed career path for tel-emps. Law enforcement.
See, reading the thoughts and emotions of suspects was deemed to violate their civil rights. Like I said, an invasion of privacy. So the brass went through all the departments with a fine-tooth comb. Any cop with even a TRACE of tel-emp abilities got the shaft.
Then, once the initial sweep was finished, they got tough. Any tel-emps uncovered after that faced SERIOUS prison time. Serious time. I know of some former cops who're STILL inside.
Funny thing was, the politicians couldn't make up their minds about precognition - seeing the future - and law enforcement. There were two arguments about the matter.
One went that precogs were reading events - what would take place without outside interference. They weren't directly interacting with the minds of potential perpetrators, so there was no invasion of privacy.
The other claimed that precogs were really gaining impressions of people's intentions. Invasion of privacy.
So the politicians argued that one for years. And all the while, police precogs were grabbing perps left and right.
Two years ago the Supreme Court finally made their ruling. Precognition is now considered a valid tool for law enforcement - within certain boundaries.
Namely, if a crime was prevented solely through precognition, no charges could be laid, not even conspiracy.
Something about there being no physical evidence that a crime was even committed.
SPECIAL $29.99 RATE!

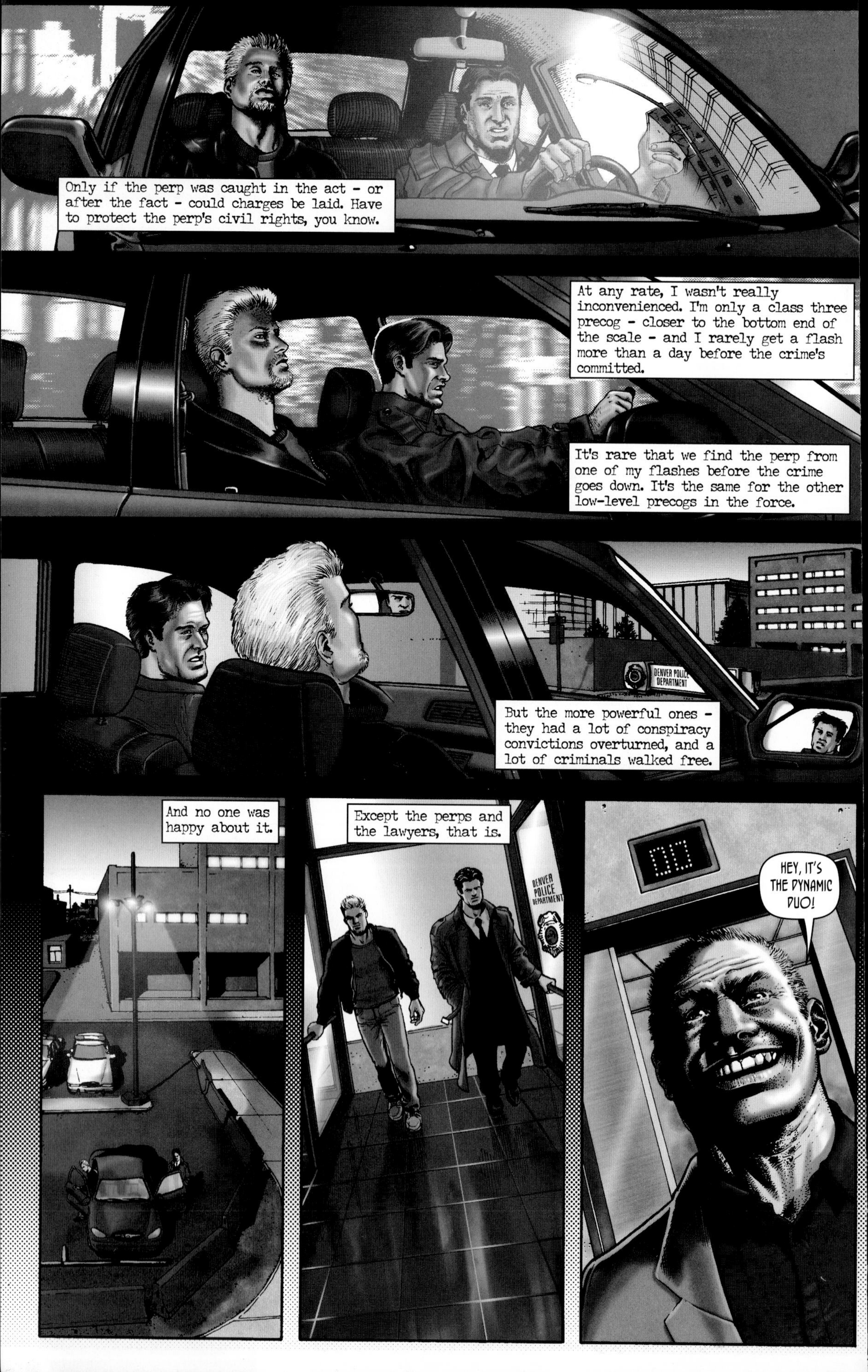
Only if the perp was caught in the act - or after the fact - could charges be laid. Have to protect the perp's civil rights, you know.
At any rate, I wasn't really inconvenienced. I'm only a class three precog - closer to the bottom end of the scale - and I rarely get a flash more than a day before the crime's committed.
It's rare that we find the perp from one of my flashes before the crime goes down. It's the same for the other low-level precogs in the force.
DENVER POLICE DEPARTMENT
But the more powerful ones - they had a lot of conspiracy convictions overturned, and a lot of criminals walked free.
And no one was happy about it.
Except the perps and the lawyers, that is.
DENVER POLICE DEPARTMENT
HEY, IT'S THE DYNAMIC DUO!

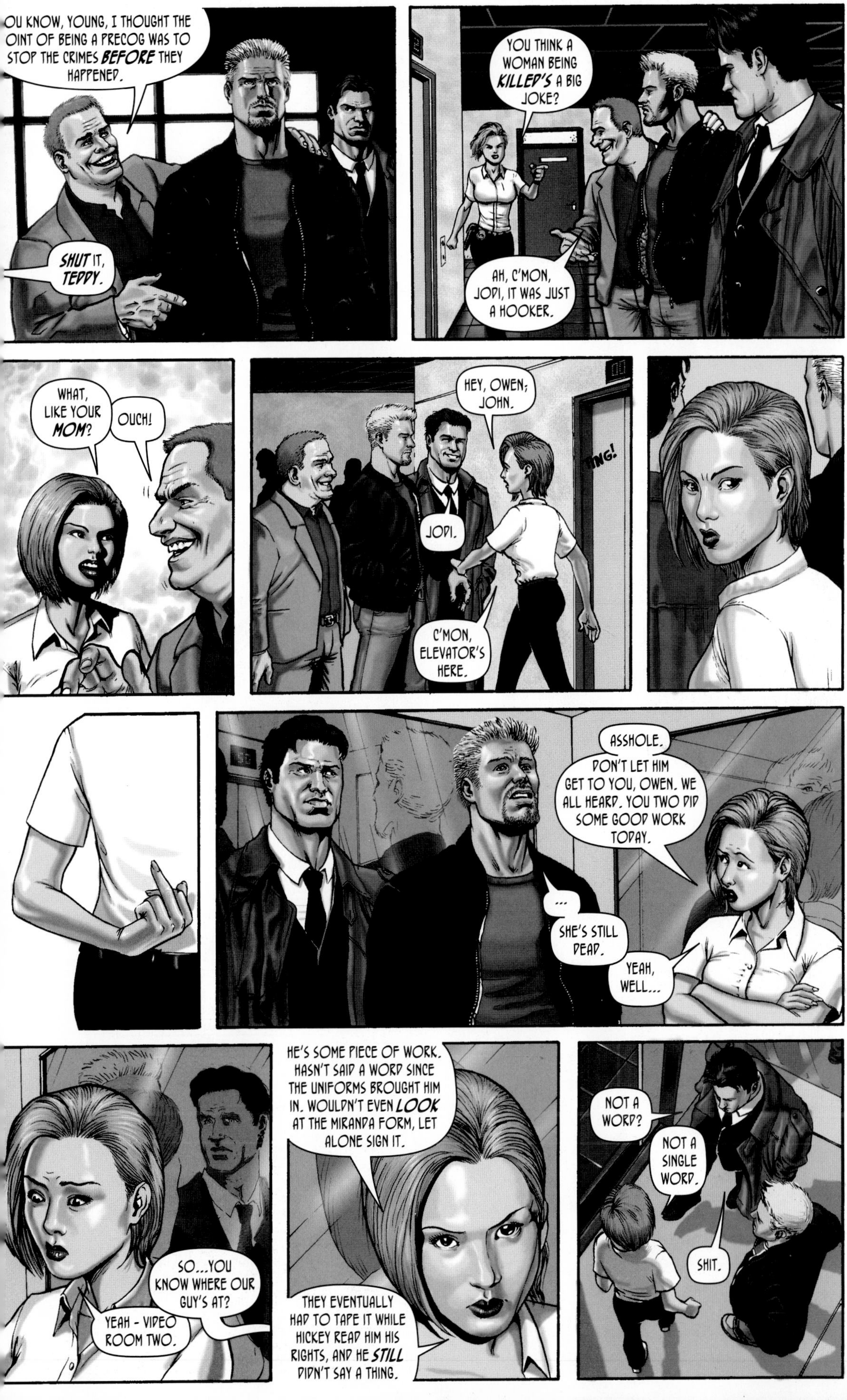
OU KNOW, YOUNG, I THOUGHT THE OINT OF BEING A PRECOG WAS TO STOP THE CRIMES *BEFORE* THEY HAPPENED.
SHUT IT, *TEDDY*.
YOU THINK A WOMAN BEING *KILLED'S* A BIG JOKE?
AH, C'MON, JODI, IT WAS JUST A HOOKER.
WHAT, LIKE YOUR *MOM*?
OUCH!
HEY, OWEN; JOHN.
ING!
JODI.
C'MON, ELEVATOR'S HERE.
ASSHOLE.
DON'T LET HIM GET TO YOU, OWEN. WE ALL HEARD. YOU TWO DID SOME GOOD WORK TODAY.
...
SHE'S STILL DEAD.
YEAH, WELL...
SO...YOU KNOW WHERE OUR GUY'S AT?
YEAH - VIDEO ROOM TWO.
HE'S SOME PIECE OF WORK. HASN'T SAID A WORD SINCE THE UNIFORMS BROUGHT HIM IN. WOULDN'T EVEN *LOOK* AT THE MIRANDA FORM, LET ALONE SIGN IT.
THEY EVENTUALLY HAD TO TAPE IT WHILE HICKEY READ HIM HIS RIGHTS, AND HE *STILL* DIDN'T SAY A THING.
NOT A WORD?
NOT A SINGLE WORD.
SHIT.

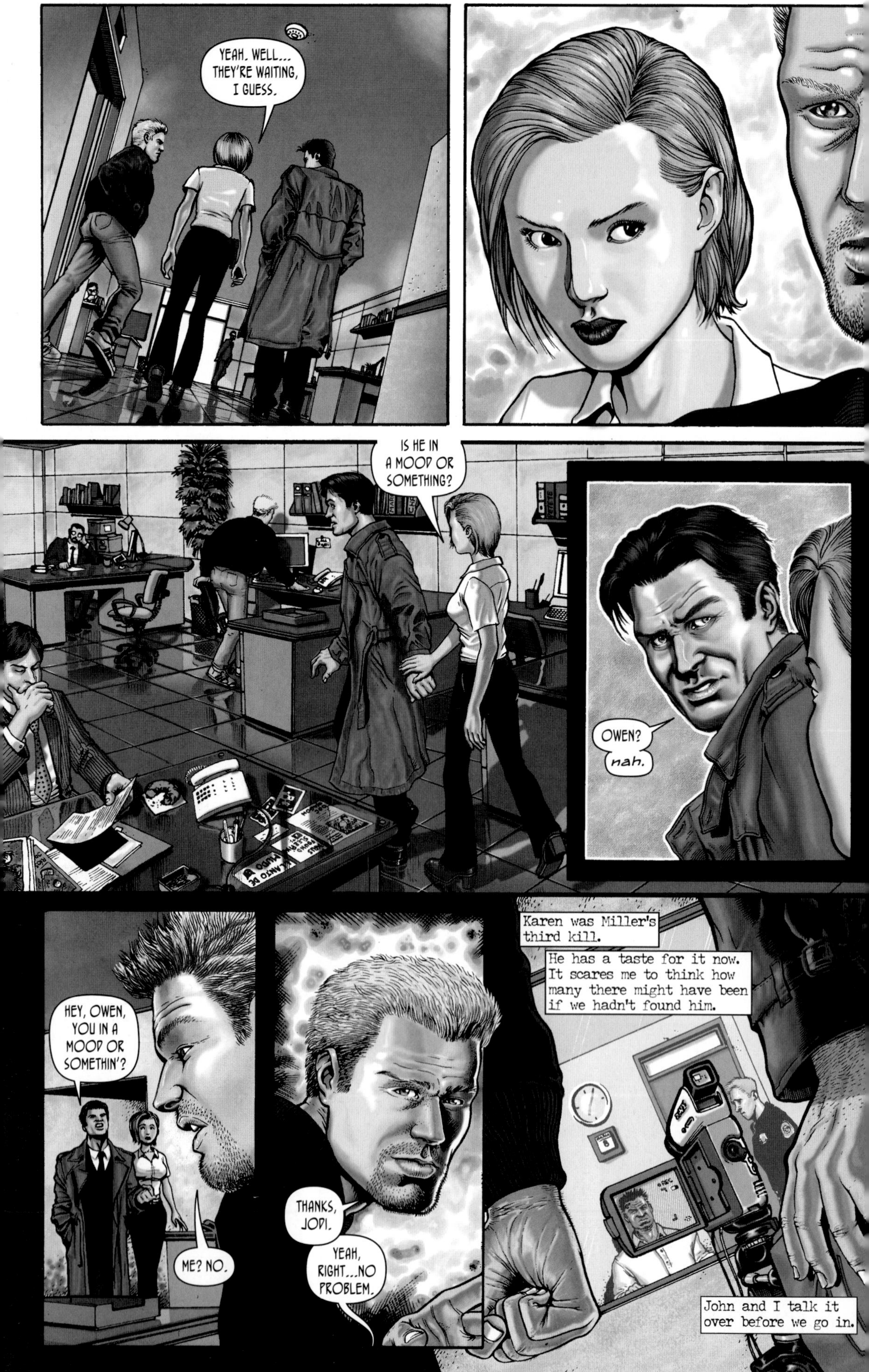
YEAH. WELL... THEY'RE WAITING, I GUESS.
IS HE IN A MOOD OR SOMETHING?
OWEN?
nah.
HEY, OWEN, YOU IN A MOOD OR SOMETHIN'?
ME? NO.
THANKS, JODI.
YEAH, RIGHT...NO PROBLEM.
Karen was Miller's third kill.
He has a taste for it now. It scares me to think how many there might have been if we hadn't found him.
John and I talk it over before we go in.

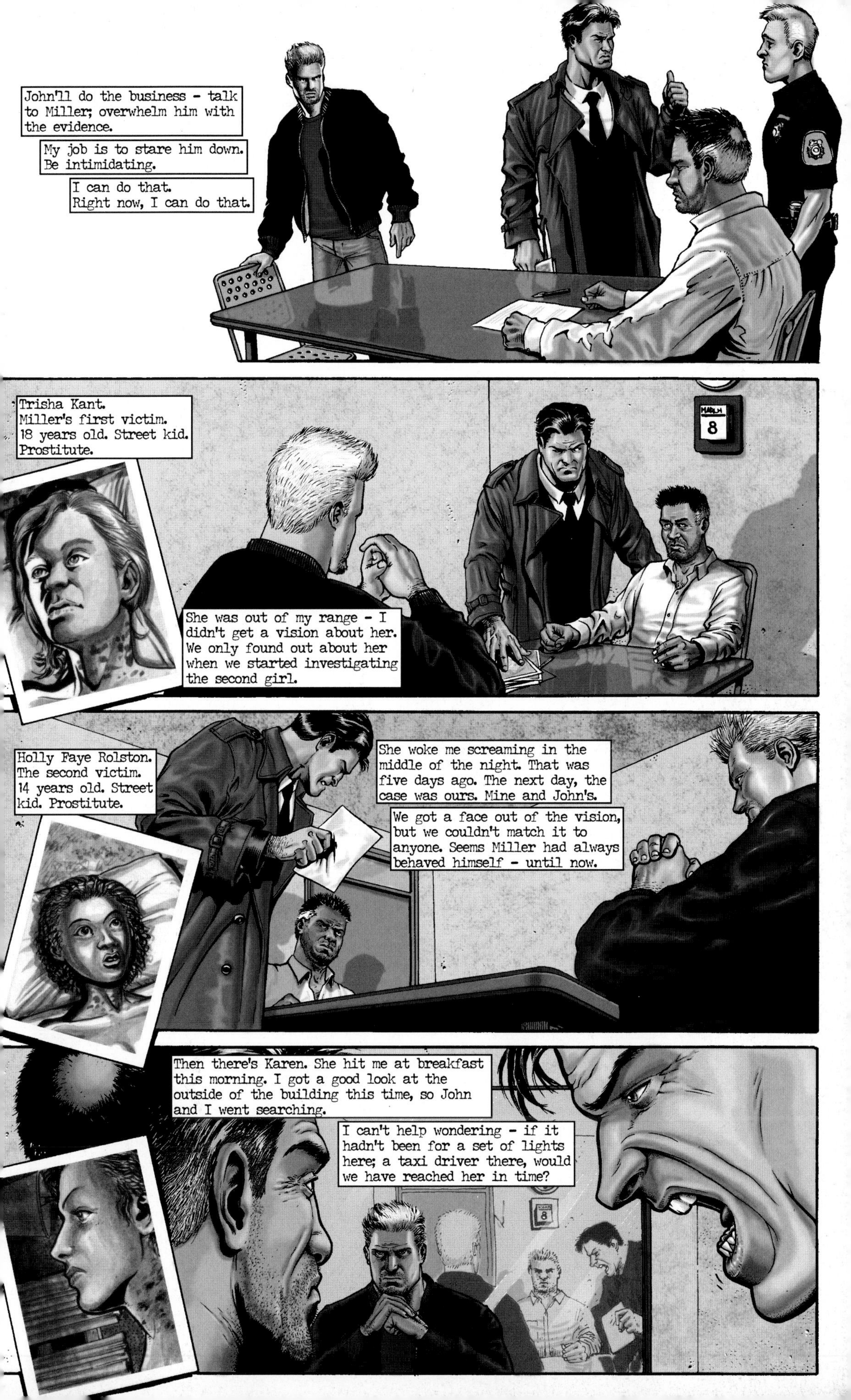
John'll do the business - talk to Miller; overwhelm him with the evidence.
My job is to stare him down. Be intimidating.
I can do that. Right now, I can do that.
Trisha Kant. Miller's first victim. 18 years old. Street kid. Prostitute.
She was out of my range - I didn't get a vision about her. We only found out about her when we started investigating the second girl.
Holly Faye Rolston. The second victim. 14 years old. Street kid. Prostitute.
She woke me screaming in the middle of the night. That was five days ago. The next day, the case was ours. Mine and John's.
We got a face out of the vision, but we couldn't match it to anyone. Seems Miller had always behaved himself - until now.
Then there's Karen. She hit me at breakfast this morning. I got a good look at the outside of the building this time, so John and I went searching.
I can't help wondering - if it hadn't been for a set of lights here; a taxi driver there, would we have reached her in time?

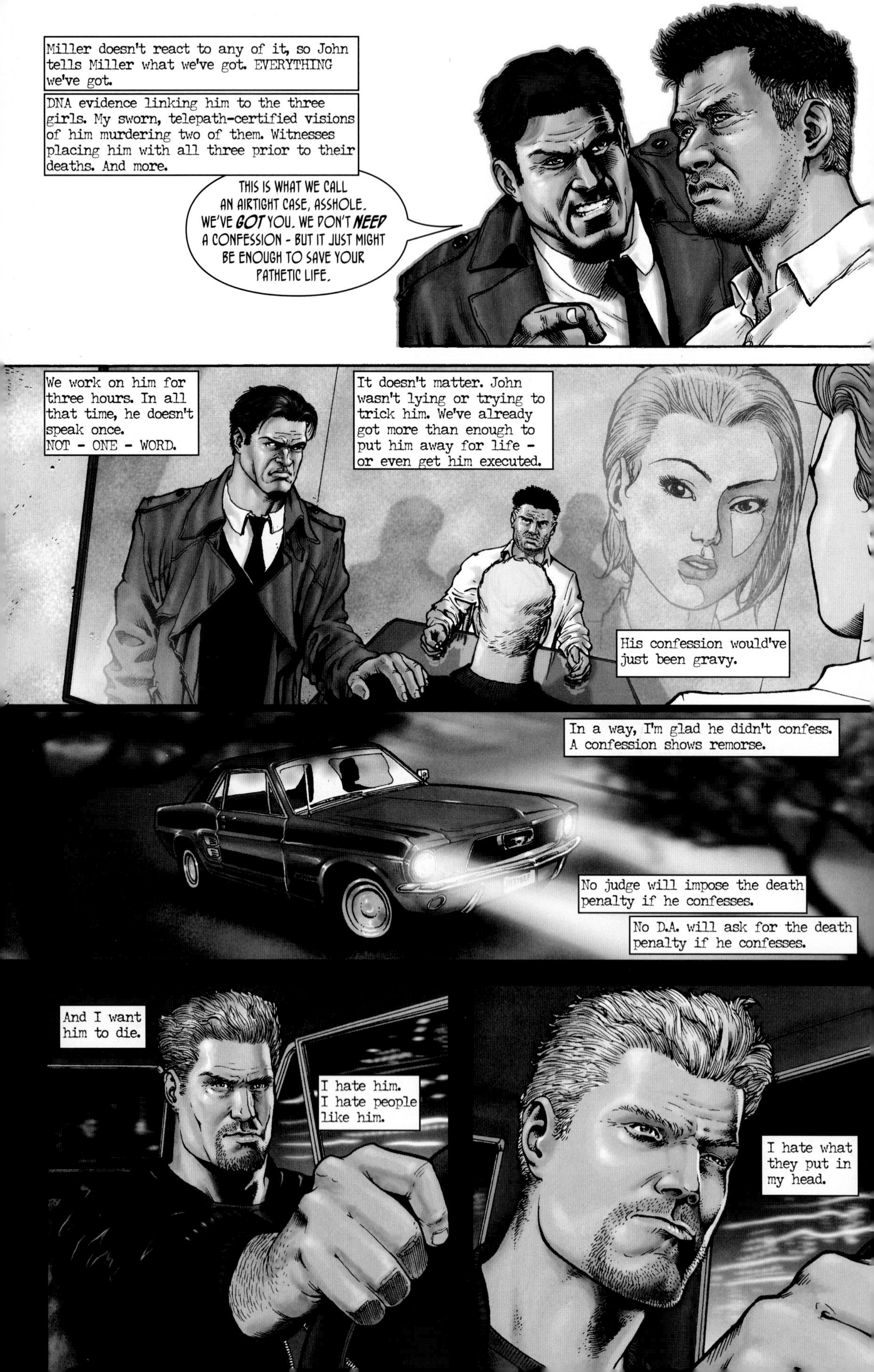

Miller doesn't react to any of it, so John tells Miller what we've got. EVERYTHING we've got.
DNA evidence linking him to the three girls. My sworn, telepath-certified visions of him murdering two of them. Witnesses placing him with all three prior to their deaths. And more.
THIS IS WHAT WE CALL AN AIRTIGHT CASE, ASSHOLE. WE'VE GOT YOU. WE DON'T NEED A CONFESSION - BUT IT JUST MIGHT BE ENOUGH TO SAVE YOUR PATHETIC LIFE.
We work on him for three hours. In all that time, he doesn't speak once. NOT - ONE - WORD.
It doesn't matter. John wasn't lying or trying to trick him. We've already got more than enough to put him away for life - or even get him executed.
His confession would've just been gravy.
In a way, I'm glad he didn't confess. A confession shows remorse.
No judge will impose the death penalty if he confesses.
No D.A. will ask for the death penalty if he confesses.
And I want him to die.
I hate him. I hate people like him.
I hate what they put in my head.

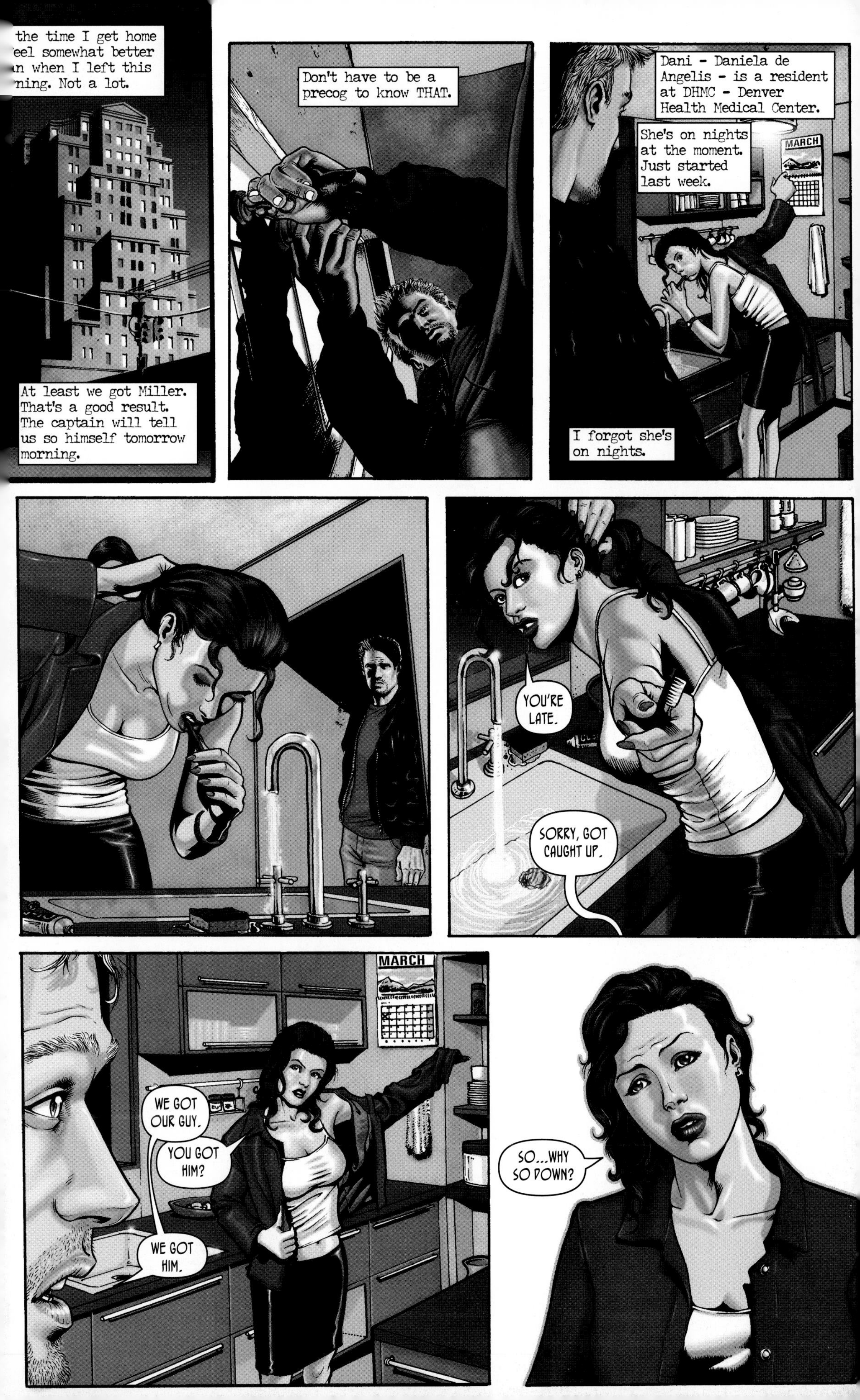
the time I get home
eel somewhat better
n when I left this
ning. Not a lot.
At least we got Miller. That's a good result. The captain will tell us so himself tomorrow morning.
Don't have to be a precog to know THAT.
Dani - Daniela de Angelis - is a resident at DHMC - Denver Health Medical Center.
She's on nights at the moment. Just started last week.
MARCH
I forgot she's on nights.
YOU'RE LATE.
SORRY, GOT CAUGHT UP.
MARCH
WE GOT OUR GUY.
YOU GOT HIM?
WE GOT HIM.
SO...WHY SO DOWN?

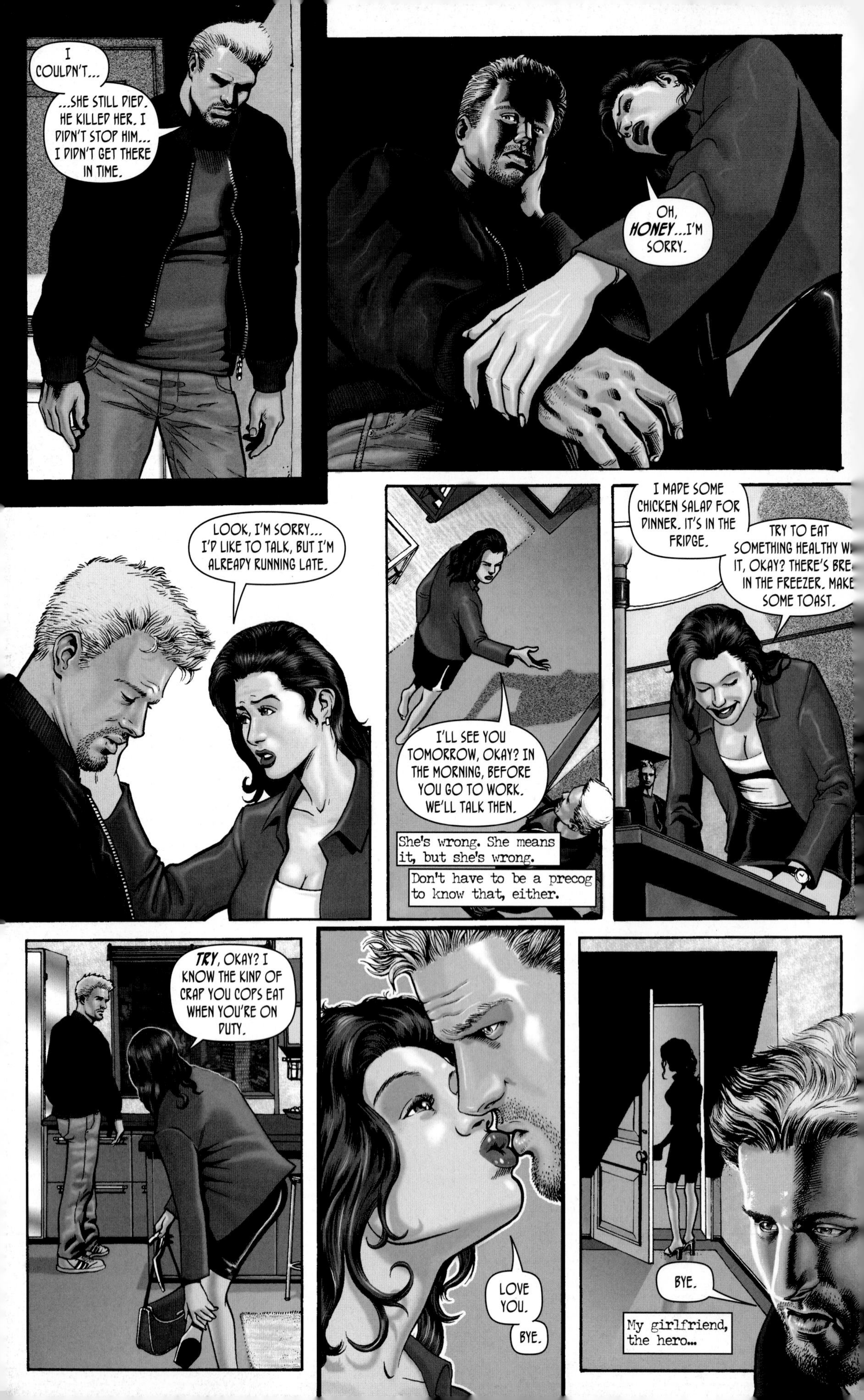
I COULDN'T...
...SHE STILL DIED. HE KILLED HER. I DIDN'T STOP HIM... I DIDN'T GET THERE IN TIME.
OH, HONEY...I'M SORRY.
LOOK, I'M SORRY... I'D LIKE TO TALK, BUT I'M ALREADY RUNNING LATE.
I'LL SEE YOU TOMORROW, OKAY? IN THE MORNING, BEFORE YOU GO TO WORK. WE'LL TALK THEN.
She's wrong. She means it, but she's wrong.
Don't have to be a precog to know that, either.
I MADE SOME CHICKEN SALAD FOR DINNER. IT'S IN THE FRIDGE.
TRY TO EAT SOMETHING HEALTHY W IT, OKAY? THERE'S BRE IN THE FREEZER. MAKE SOME TOAST.
TRY, OKAY? I KNOW THE KIND OF CRAP YOU COPS EAT WHEN YOU'RE ON DUTY.
LOVE YOU.
BYE.
BYE.
My girlfriend, the hero...

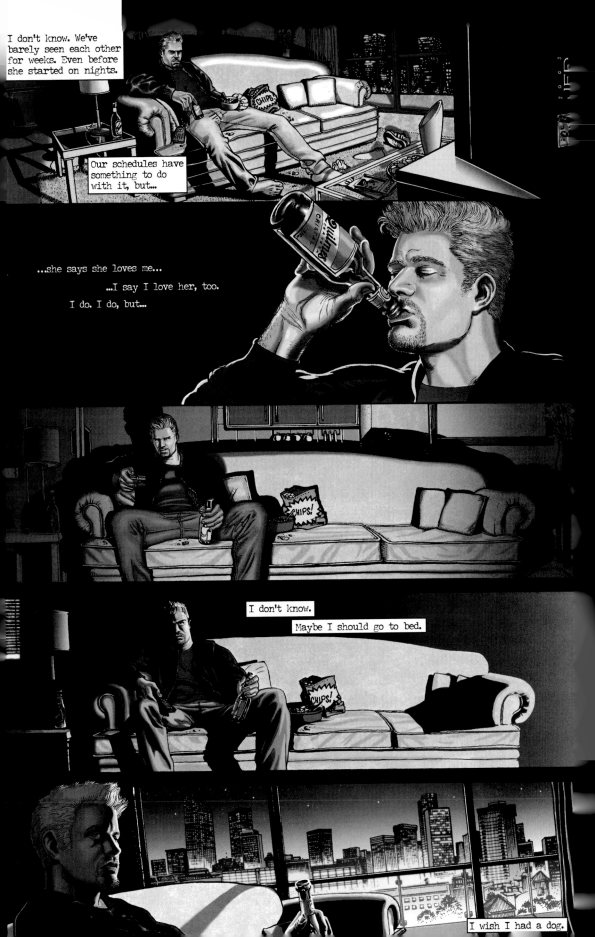

I don't know. We've barely seen each other for weeks. Even before she started on nights.

Our schedules have something to do with it, but...

...she says she loves me...

...I say I love her, too.

I do. I do, but...

I don't know.

Maybe I should go to bed.

I wish I had a dog.

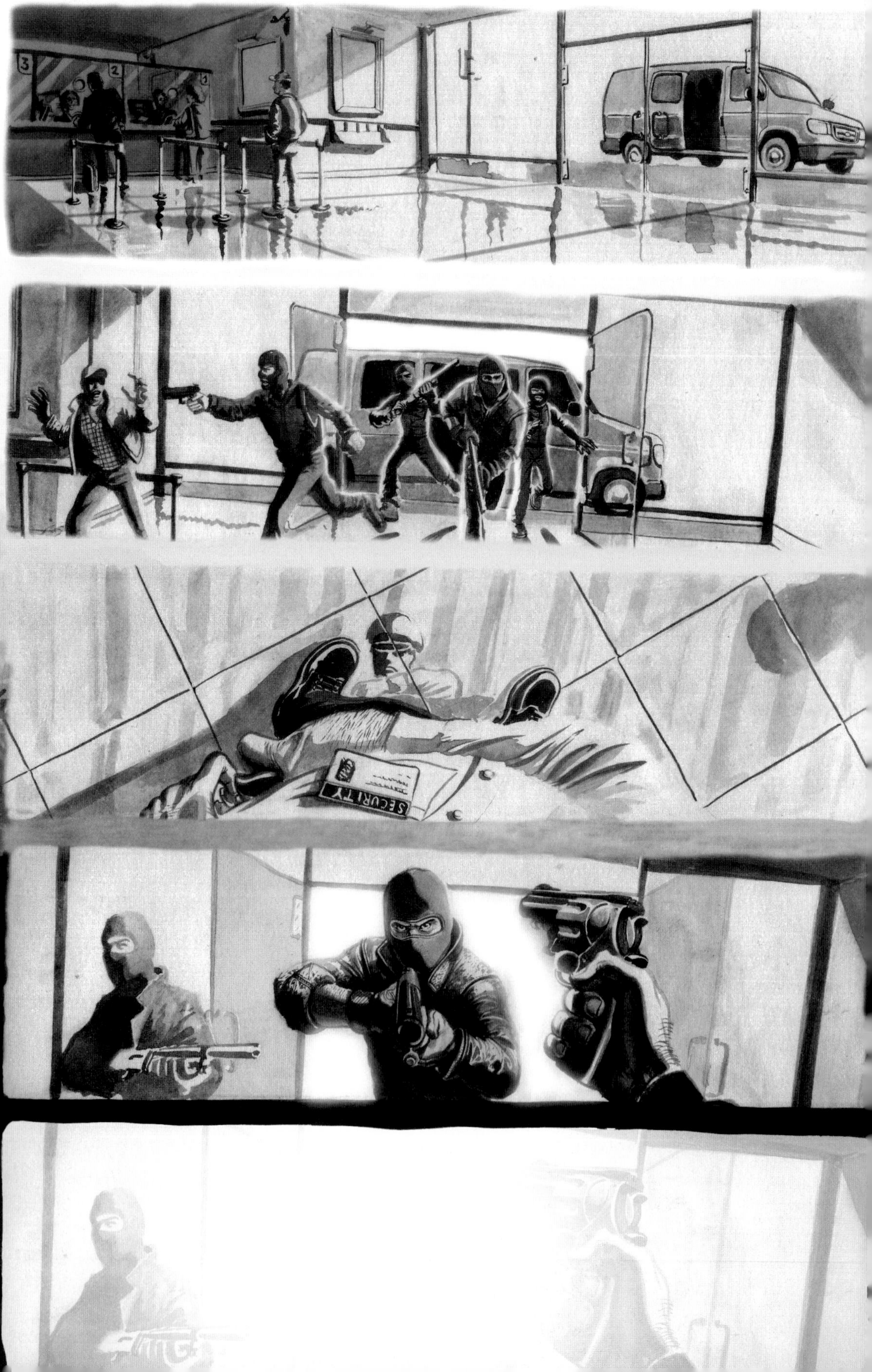
SECURITY

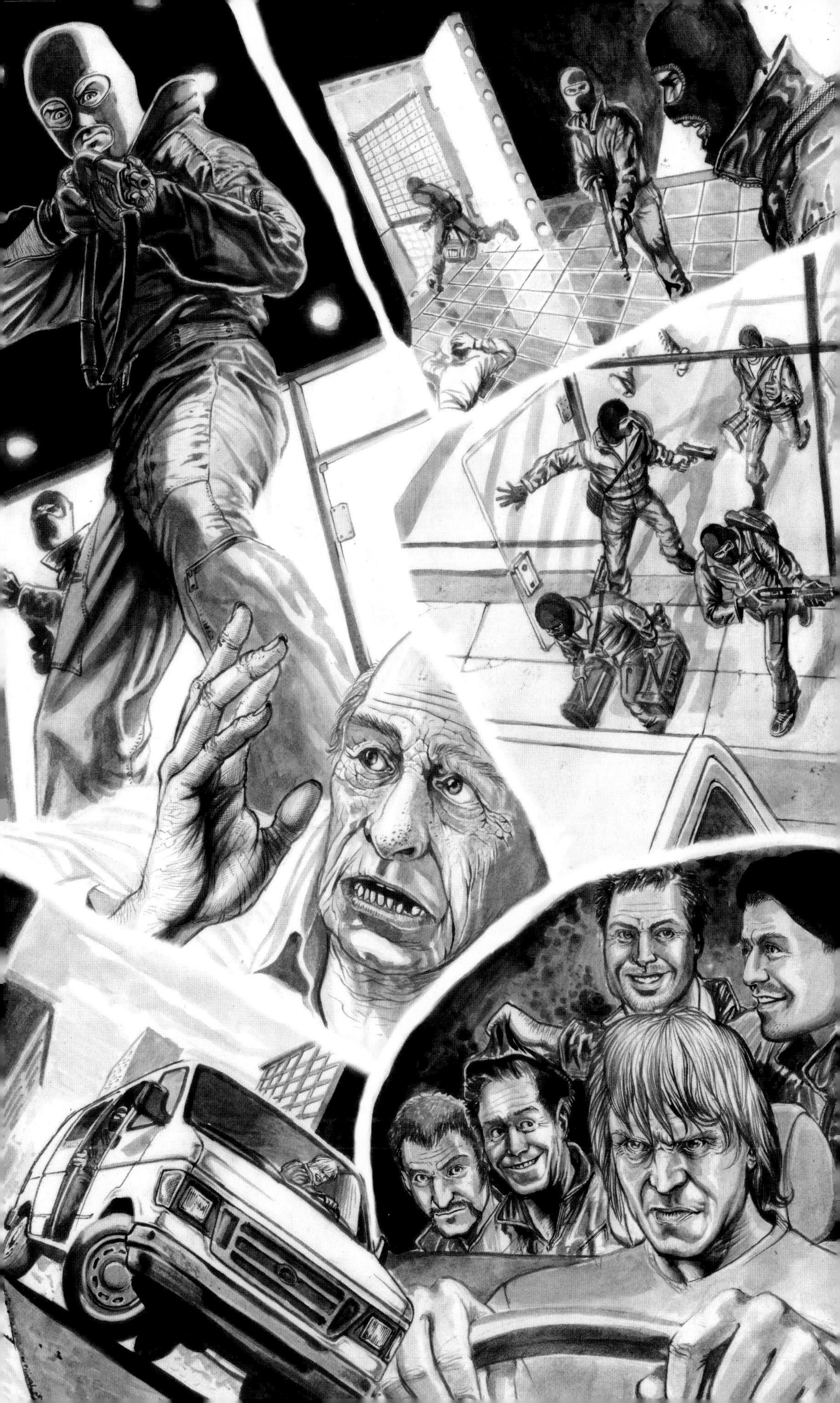

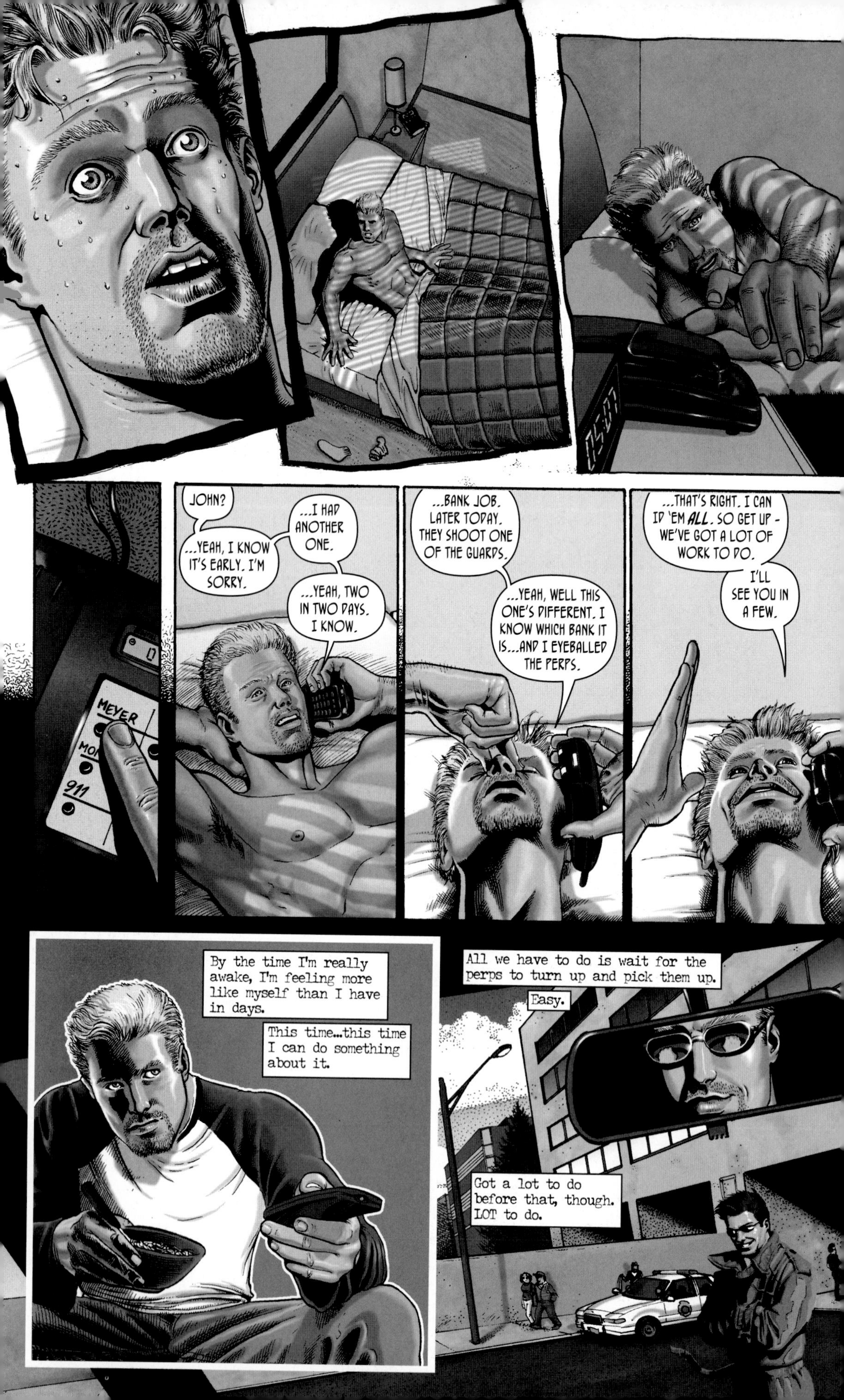

MEYER
911
JOHN?
...YEAH, I KNOW IT'S EARLY. I'M SORRY.
...I HAD ANOTHER ONE.
...YEAH, TWO IN TWO DAYS. I KNOW.
...BANK JOB. LATER TODAY. THEY SHOOT ONE OF THE GUARDS.
...YEAH, WELL THIS ONE'S DIFFERENT. I KNOW WHICH BANK IT IS...AND I EYEBALLED THE PERPS.
...THAT'S RIGHT. I CAN ID 'EM ALL. SO GET UP - WE'VE GOT A LOT OF WORK TO DO.
I'LL SEE YOU IN A FEW.
By the time I'm really awake, I'm feeling more like myself than I have in days.
This time...this time I can do something about it.
All we have to do is wait for the perps to turn up and pick them up.
Easy.
Got a lot to do before that, though. LOT to do.

It doesn't take long to find them. They're all career losers.

...YEAH, HIM TOO. THAT'S ALL OF THEM.

MALCOLM CREAN... ARMED ROBBERY... ARMED ROBBERY... ASSAULT WITH A DEADLY WEAPON... ARMED ROBBERY... SOUNDS ABOUT RIGHT, DOESN'T IT?

ANY PSIS IN THE BUNCH?

...mmm... NO. NO ARTIFICIAL ADDITIVES HERE - JUST LIKE MOTHER NATURE INTENDED.

err... NO OFFENSE, DETECTIVE.

NONE TAKEN.

SEND THOSE UP TO HOMICIDE, ROBBERY AND SWAT, ALL RIGHT?

SURE THING, DETECTIVE.

We brief SWAT on the takedown. Stephenson and Gonzo from robbery sit in. As the case overlaps our units, they'll be helping with the investigation.

Meanwhile, Lieutenant Scotney's talking to the captain, getting clearance for the operation.

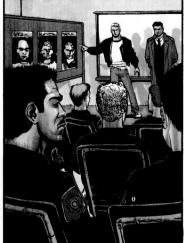

I take a Simons-Krueger test and my vision is verified as genuine. Now I can testify about the vision in court, if it comes to that.

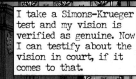

We convince the bank manager to cooperate with the operation. Not an easy sell.

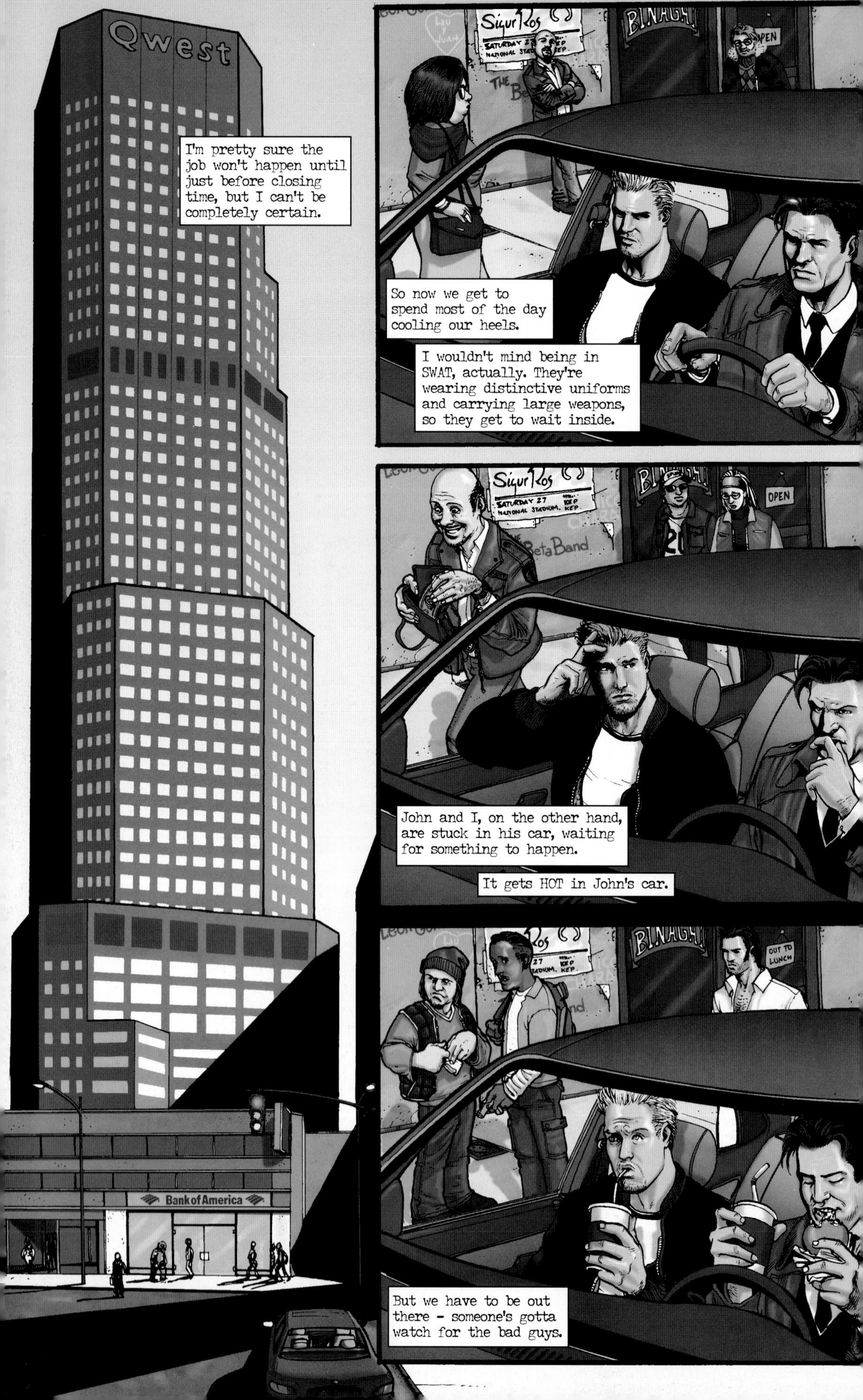
Qwest
I'm pretty sure the job won't happen until just before closing time, but I can't be completely certain.
Bank of America
Sigur Ros
BINAGH!
OPEN
So now we get to spend most of the day cooling our heels.
I wouldn't mind being in SWAT, actually. They're wearing distinctive uniforms and carrying large weapons, so they get to wait inside.
Sigur Ros
SATURDAY 27
NATIONAL STADIUM.
OPEN
Beta Band
John and I, on the other hand, are stuck in his car, waiting for something to happen.
It gets HOT in John's car.
BINAGH!
OUT TO LUNCH
But we have to be out there - someone's gotta watch for the bad guys.

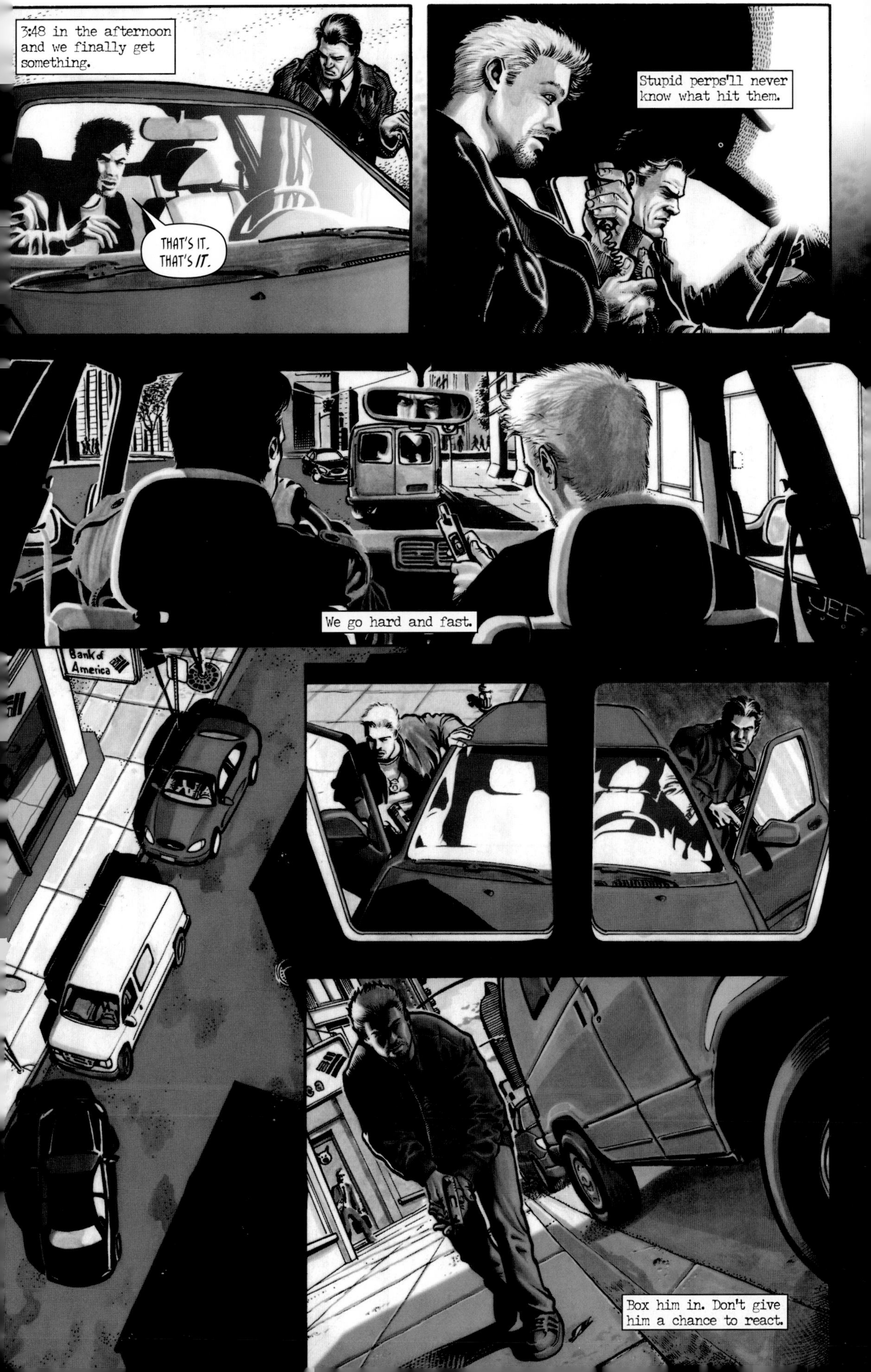
3:48 in the afternoon and we finally get something.
THAT'S IT. THAT'S *IT*.
Stupid perps'll never know what hit them.
We go hard and fast.
Bank of America
Box him in. Don't give him a chance to react.

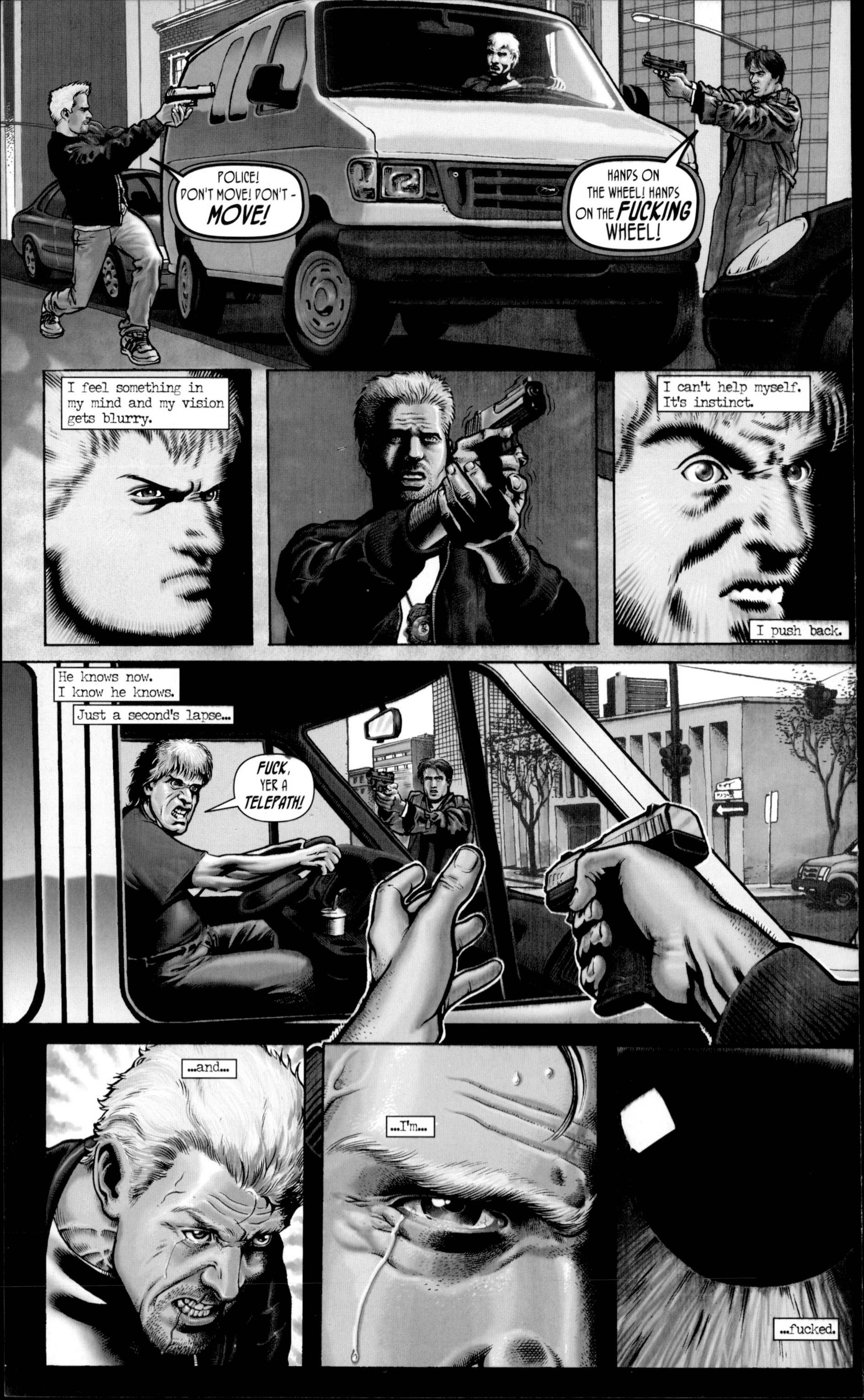
POLICE! DON'T MOVE! DON'T - MOVE!
HANDS ON THE WHEEL! HANDS ON THE FUCKING WHEEL!
I feel something in my mind and my vision gets blurry.
I can't help myself. It's instinct.
I push back.
He knows now. I know he knows.
Just a second's lapse...
FUCK, YER A TELEPATH!
...and...
...I'm...
...fucked.

CHAPTER TWO

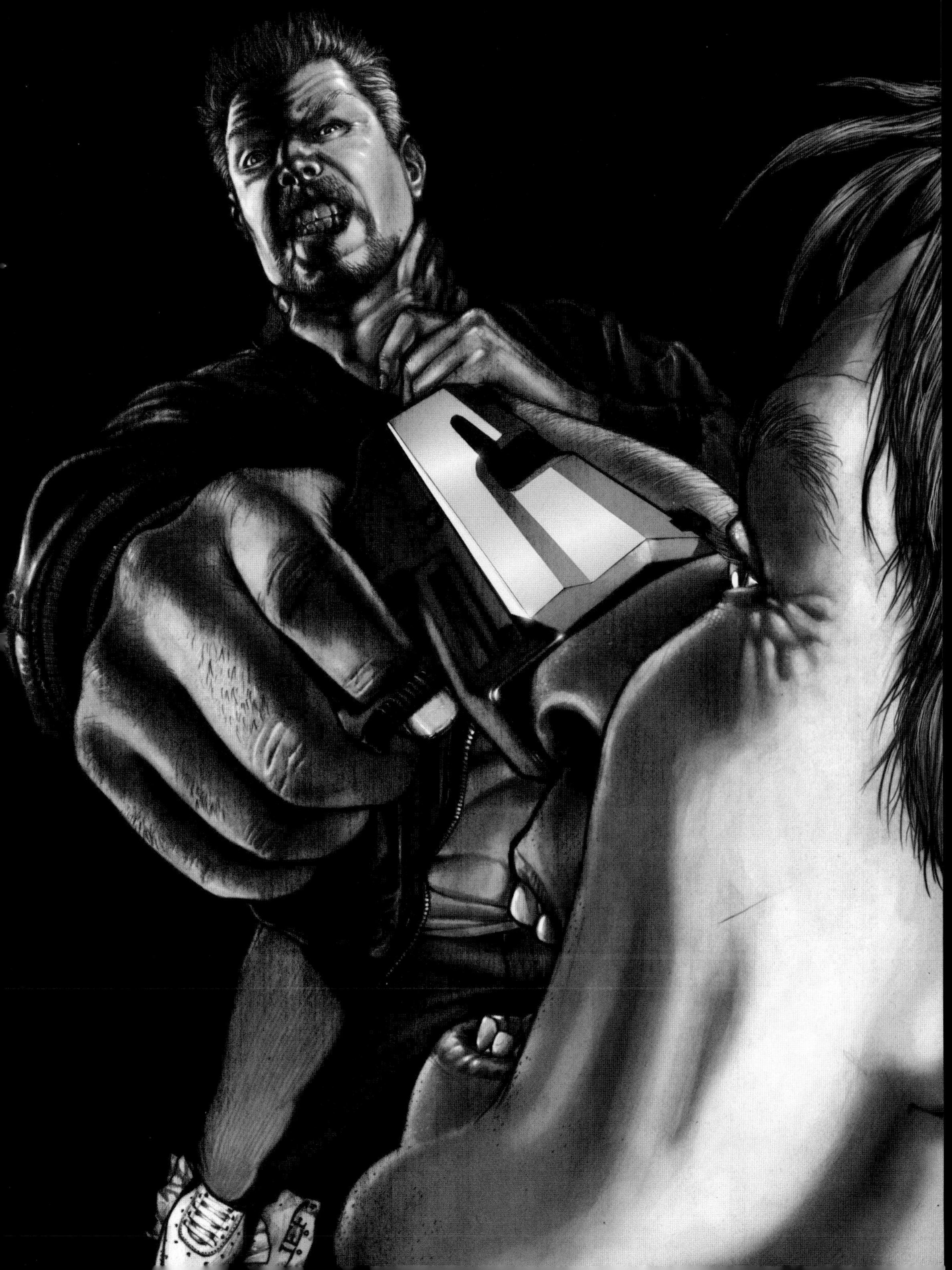

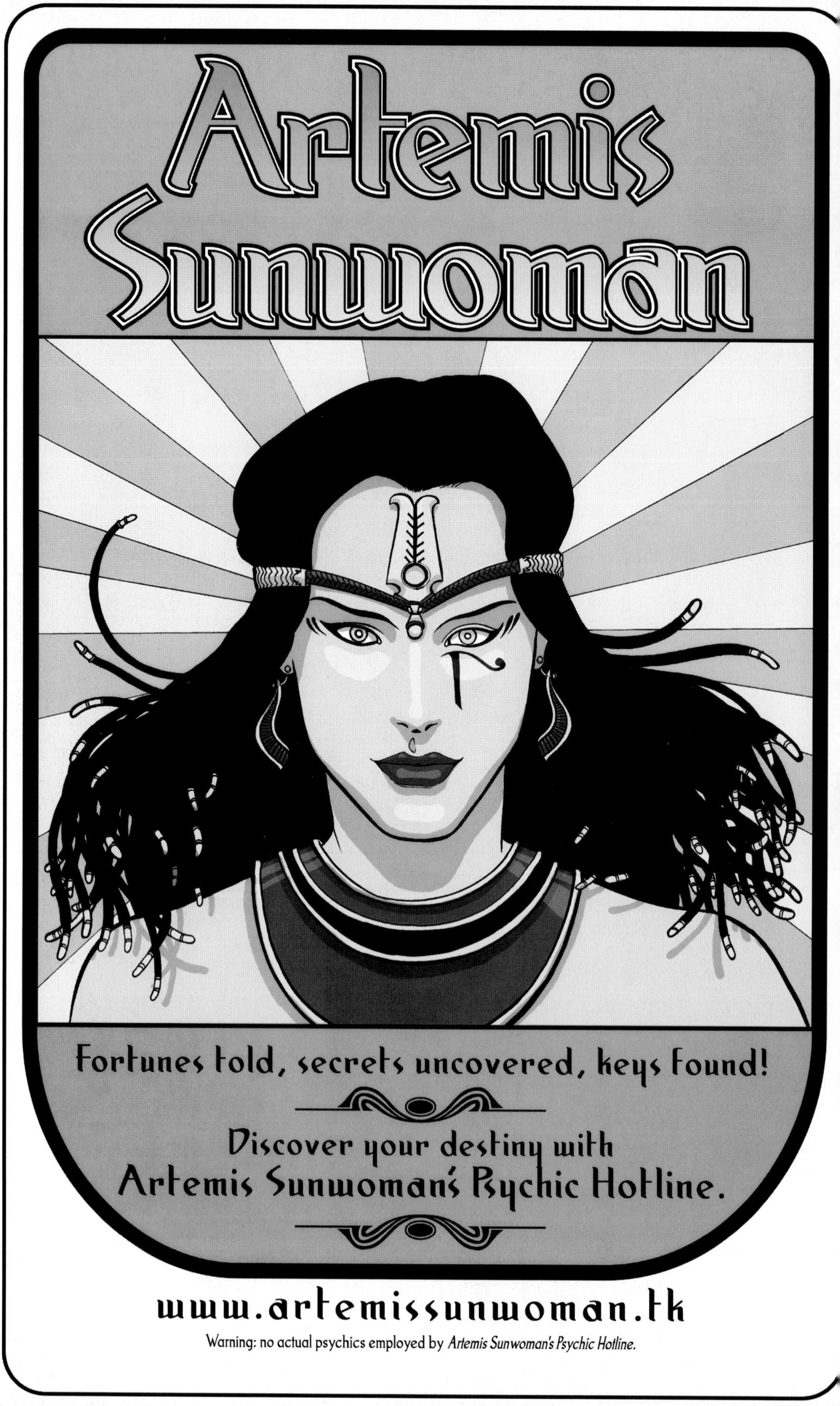
Artemis Sunwoman
Fortunes told, secrets uncovered, keys found!
Discover your destiny with Artemis Sunwoman's Psychic Hotline.
www.artemissunwoman.tk
Warning: no actual psychics employed by *Artemis Sunwoman's Psychic Hotline.*

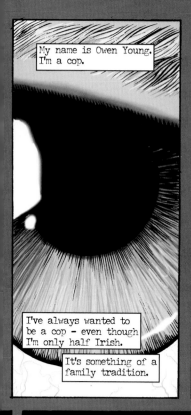

My name is Owen Young. I'm a cop.

I've always wanted to be a cop - even though I'm only half Irish.

It's something of a family tradition.

I'm a cop, but more than that, I'm a PSI. A precog. I can see the future. And no question, that's a big help in my line of work.

But don't let that fool you. It's not all good.

But I have to wonder... would I be tuned into the same frequency if I wasn't a cop? Would I see different things if my LIFE wasn't all about DEATH?

Or did I end up here BECAUSE of what I see?

Chicken or the egg?

I don't know. I don't really remember WHEN it all started. But I can live with that. I have, for as long as I CAN remember.

But I don't know if I can live with my secret.

My secret...

...I always knew that one day it'd get me into trouble.

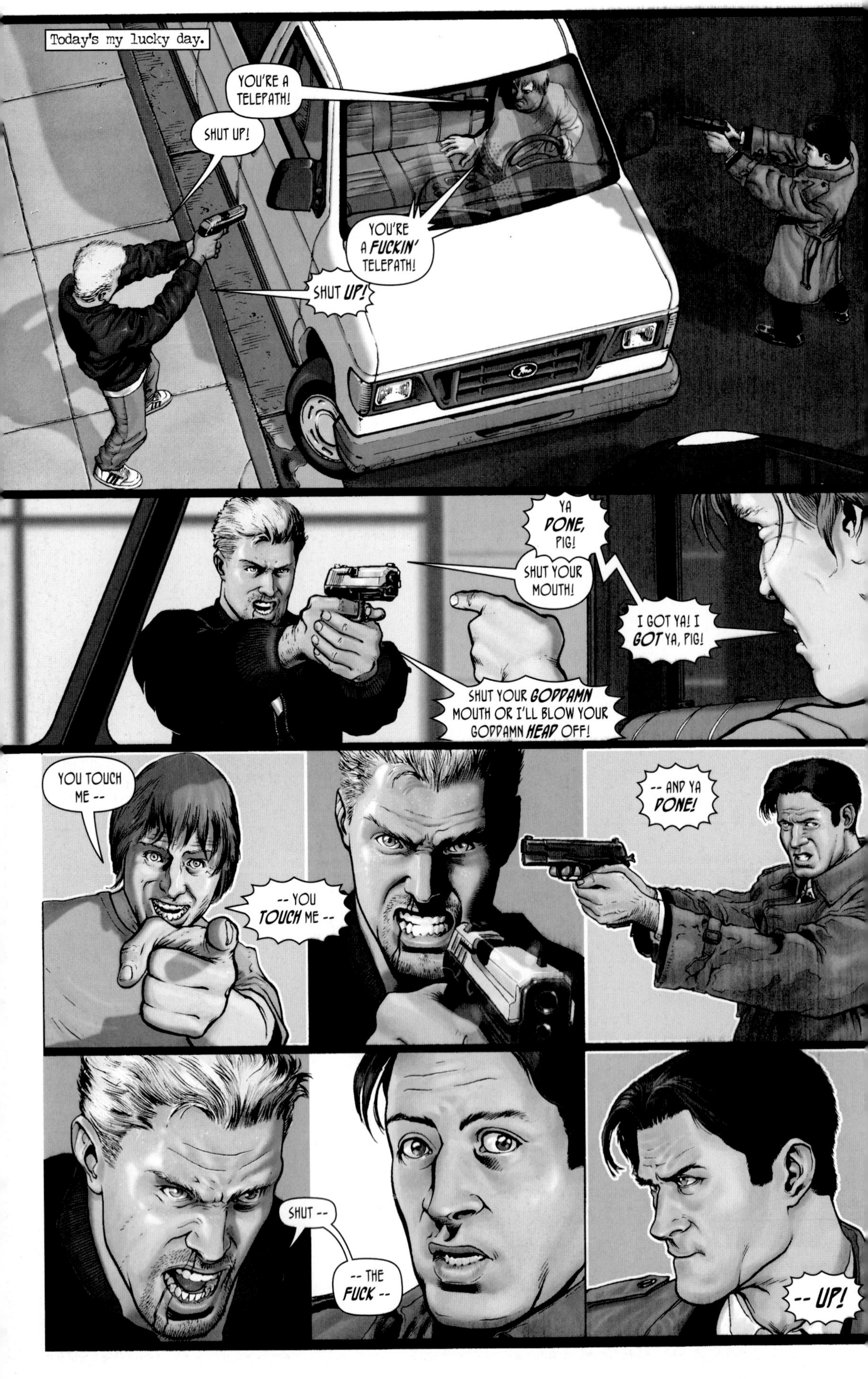
Today's my lucky day.
YOU'RE A TELEPATH!
SHUT UP!
YOU'RE A FUCKIN' TELEPATH!
SHUT UP!
YA DONE, PIG!
SHUT YOUR MOUTH!
I GOT YA! I GOT YA, PIG!
SHUT YOUR GODDAMN MOUTH OR I'LL BLOW YOUR GODDAMN HEAD OFF!
YOU TOUCH ME --
-- YOU TOUCH ME --
-- AND YA DONE!
SHUT --
-- THE FUCK --
-- UP!

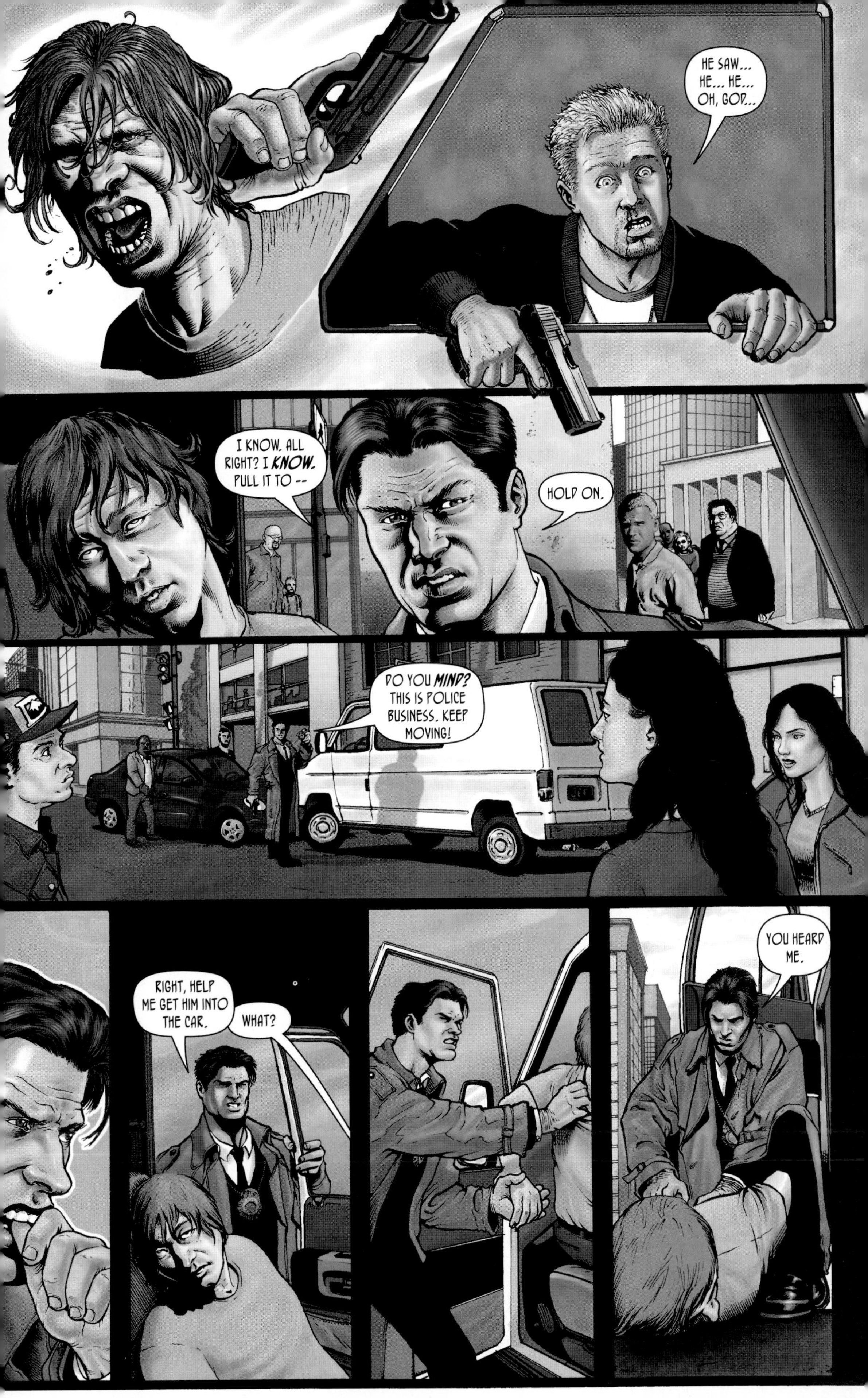
HE SAW... HE... HE... OH, GOD...
I KNOW. ALL RIGHT? I KNOW. PULL IT TO --
HOLD ON.
DO YOU MIND? THIS IS POLICE BUSINESS. KEEP MOVING!
RIGHT, HELP ME GET HIM INTO THE CAR.
WHAT?
YOU HEARD ME.

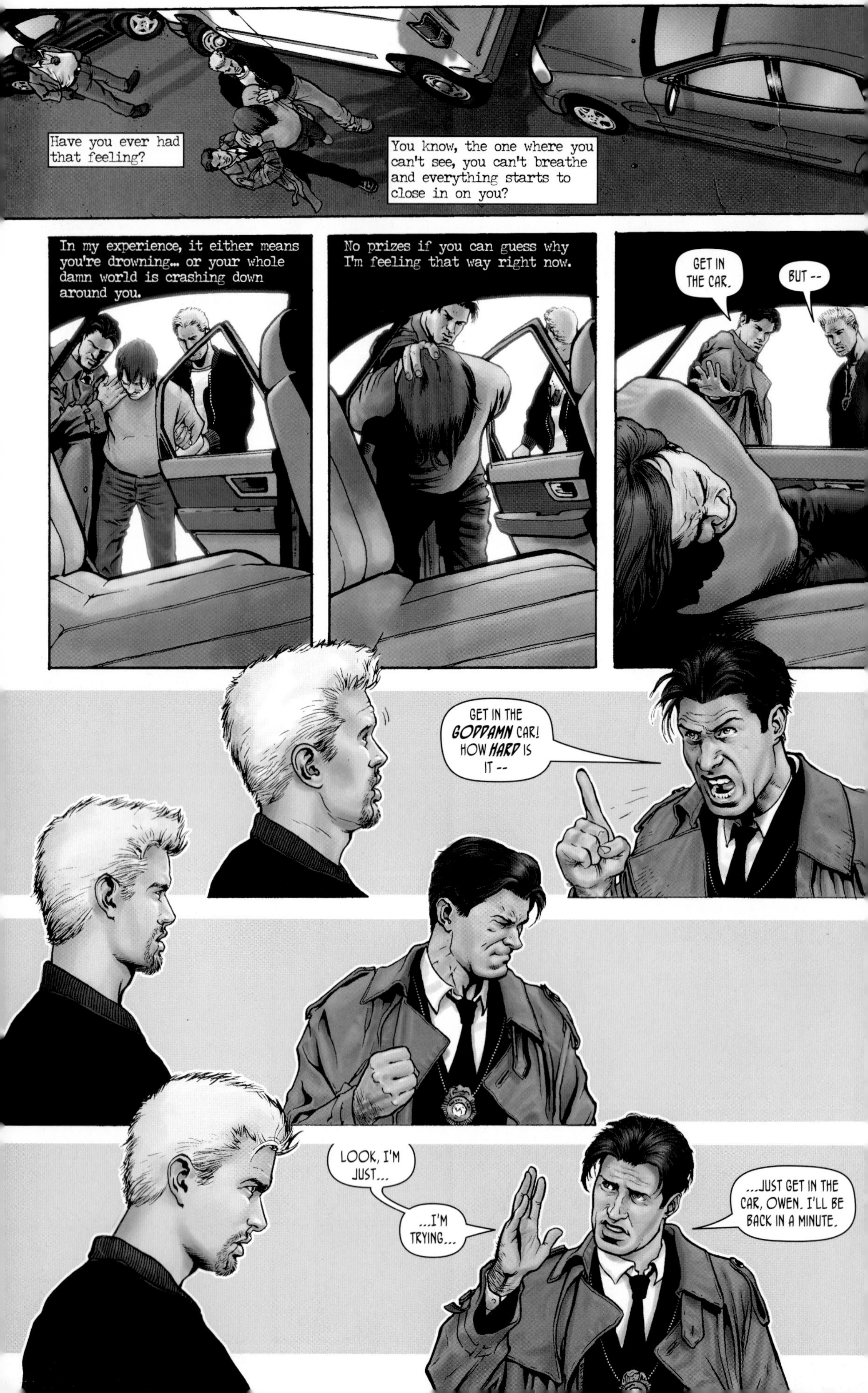

Have you ever had that feeling?
You know, the one where you can't see, you can't breathe and everything starts to close in on you?
In my experience, it either means you're drowning... or your whole damn world is crashing down around you.
No prizes if you can guess why I'm feeling that way right now.
GET IN THE CAR.
BUT --
GET IN THE GODDAMN CAR! HOW HARD IS IT --
LOOK, I'M JUST...
...I'M TRYING...
...JUST GET IN THE CAR, OWEN. I'LL BE BACK IN A MINUTE.

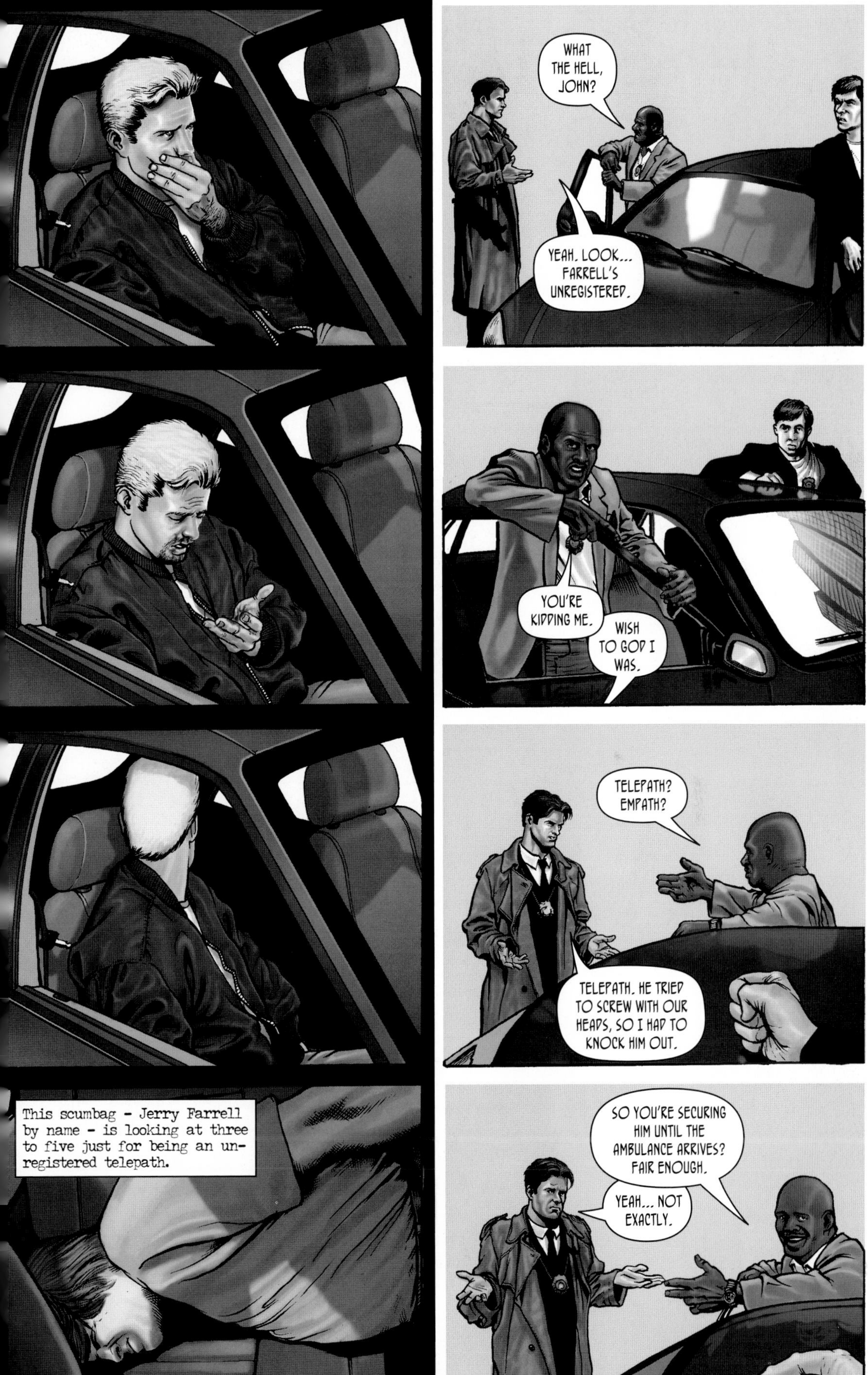
WHAT THE HELL, JOHN?
YEAH. LOOK... FARRELL'S UNREGISTERED.
YOU'RE KIDDING ME.
WISH TO GOD I WAS.
TELEPATH? EMPATH?
TELEPATH. HE TRIED TO SCREW WITH OUR HEADS, SO I HAD TO KNOCK HIM OUT.
This scumbag - Jerry Farrell by name - is looking at three to five just for being an unregistered telepath.
SO YOU'RE SECURING HIM UNTIL THE AMBULANCE ARRIVES? FAIR ENOUGH.
YEAH... NOT EXACTLY.

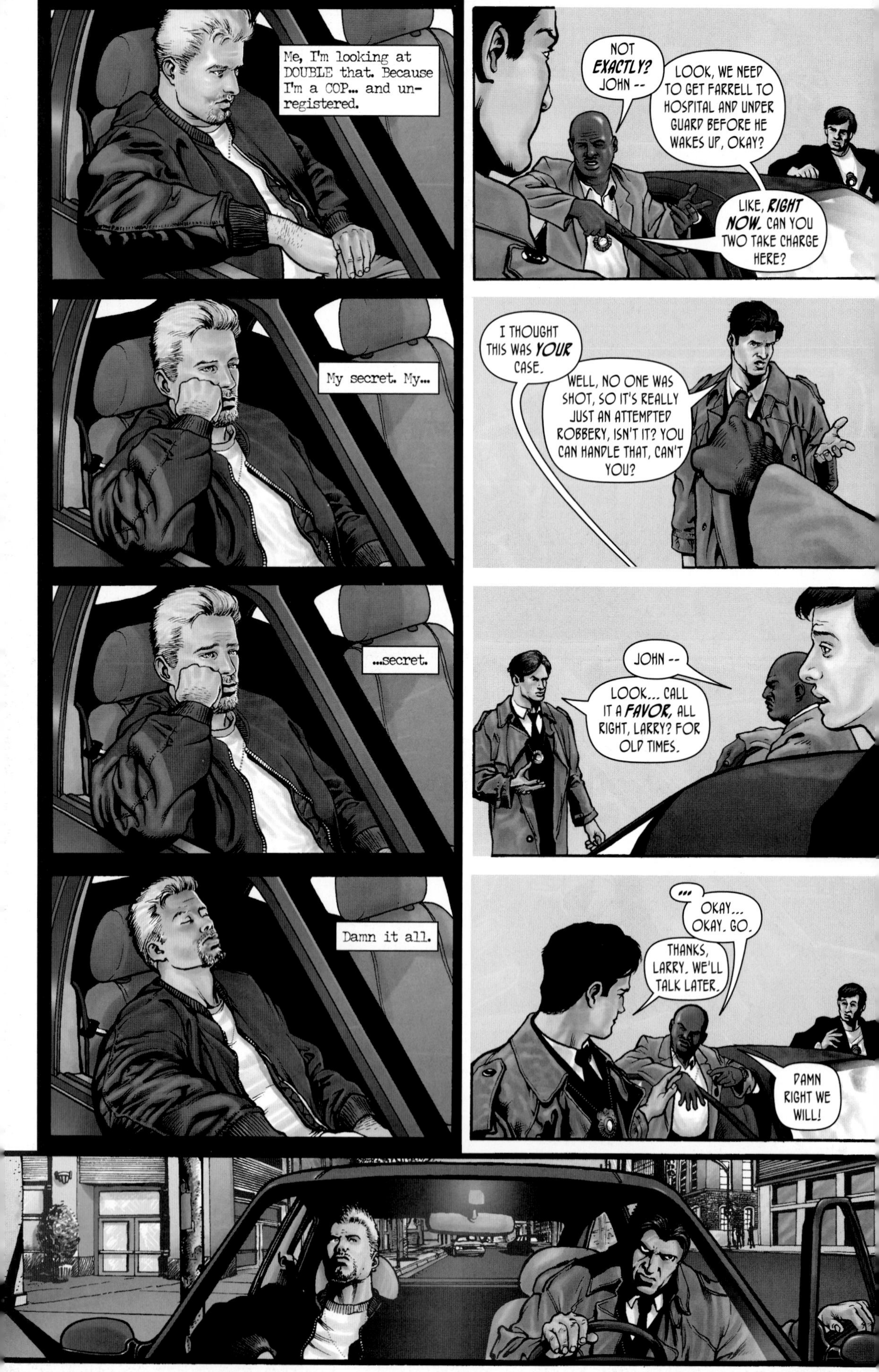

Me, I'm looking at DOUBLE that. Because I'm a COP... and unregistered.
NOT EXACTLY? JOHN --
LOOK, WE NEED TO GET FARRELL TO HOSPITAL AND UNDER GUARD BEFORE HE WAKES UP, OKAY?
LIKE, RIGHT NOW. CAN YOU TWO TAKE CHARGE HERE?
My secret. My...
I THOUGHT THIS WAS YOUR CASE.
WELL, NO ONE WAS SHOT, SO IT'S REALLY JUST AN ATTEMPTED ROBBERY, ISN'T IT? YOU CAN HANDLE THAT, CAN'T YOU?
...secret.
JOHN --
LOOK... CALL IT A FAVOR, ALL RIGHT, LARRY? FOR OLD TIMES.
Damn it all.
...
OKAY... OKAY. GO.
THANKS, LARRY. WE'LL TALK LATER.
DAMN RIGHT WE WILL!

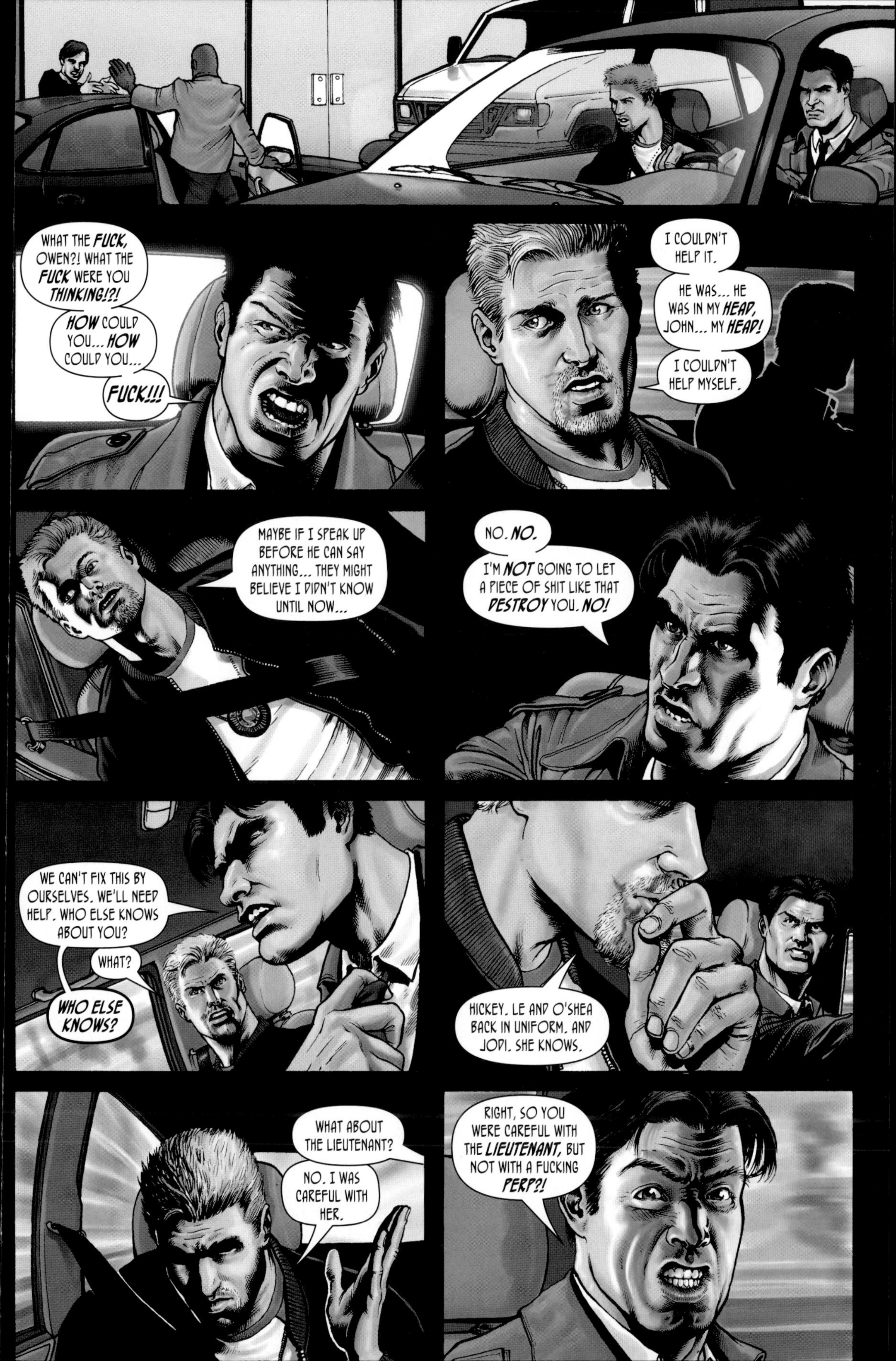
WHAT THE FUCK, OWEN?! WHAT THE FUCK WERE YOU THINKING!?!
HOW COULD YOU... HOW COULD YOU...
FUCK!!!
I COULDN'T HELP IT.
HE WAS... HE WAS IN MY HEAD, JOHN... MY HEAD!
I COULDN'T HELP MYSELF.
MAYBE IF I SPEAK UP BEFORE HE CAN SAY ANYTHING... THEY MIGHT BELIEVE I DIDN'T KNOW UNTIL NOW...
NO. NO.
I'M NOT GOING TO LET A PIECE OF SHIT LIKE THAT DESTROY YOU. NO!
WE CAN'T FIX THIS BY OURSELVES. WE'LL NEED HELP. WHO ELSE KNOWS ABOUT YOU?
WHAT?
WHO ELSE KNOWS?
HICKEY. LE AND O'SHEA BACK IN UNIFORM. AND JODI. SHE KNOWS.
WHAT ABOUT THE LIEUTENANT?
NO. I WAS CAREFUL WITH HER.
RIGHT, SO YOU WERE CAREFUL WITH THE LIEUTENANT, BUT NOT WITH A FUCKING PERP?!

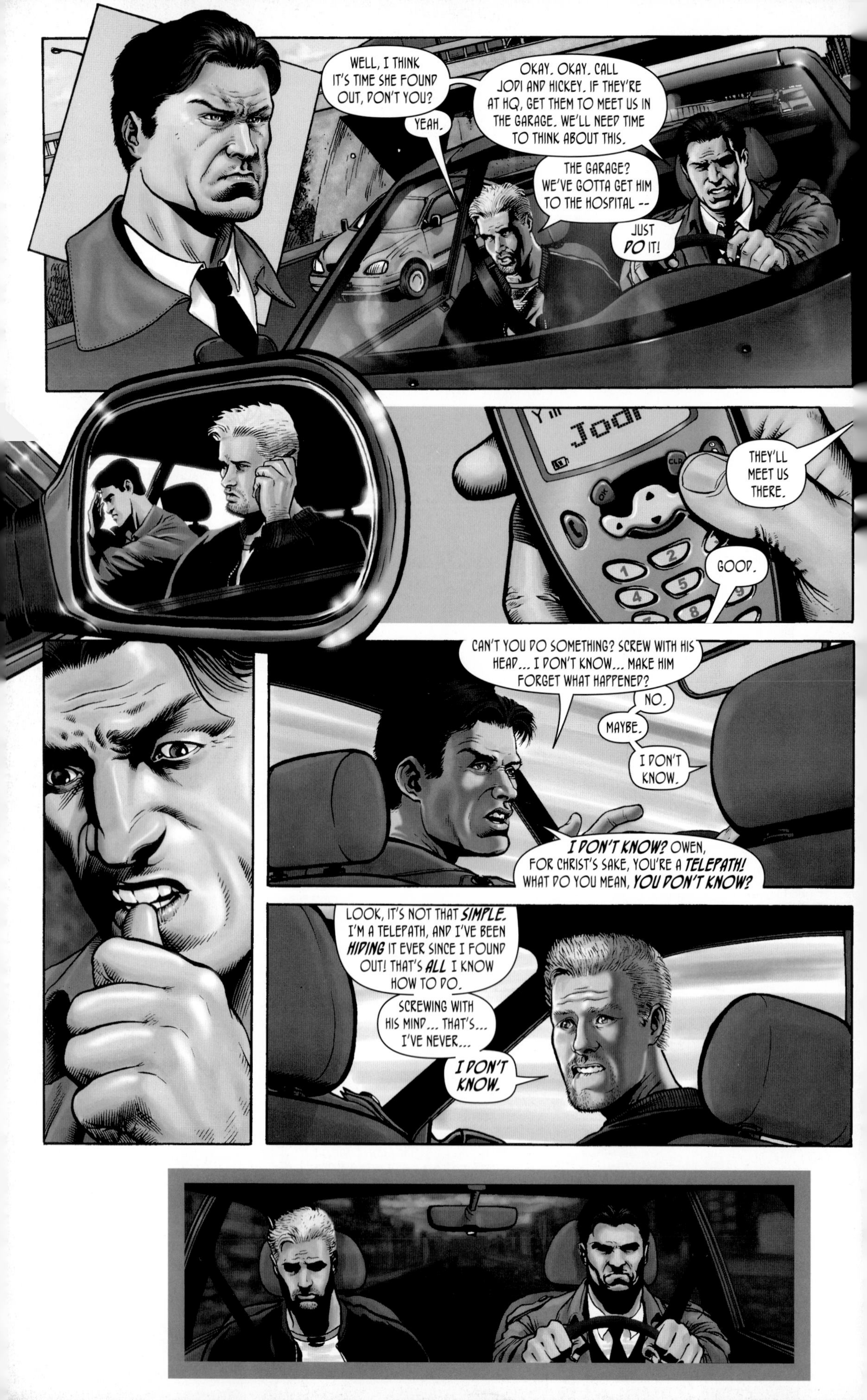
WELL, I THINK IT'S TIME SHE FOUND OUT, DON'T YOU?
YEAH.
OKAY. OKAY. CALL JODI AND HICKEY. IF THEY'RE AT HQ, GET THEM TO MEET US IN THE GARAGE. WE'LL NEED TIME TO THINK ABOUT THIS.
THE GARAGE? WE'VE GOTTA GET HIM TO THE HOSPITAL --
JUST DO IT!
Jodi
THEY'LL MEET US THERE.
GOOD.
CAN'T YOU DO SOMETHING? SCREW WITH HIS HEAD... I DON'T KNOW... MAKE HIM FORGET WHAT HAPPENED?
NO.
MAYBE.
I DON'T KNOW.
I DON'T KNOW? OWEN, FOR CHRIST'S SAKE, YOU'RE A TELEPATH! WHAT DO YOU MEAN, YOU DON'T KNOW?
LOOK, IT'S NOT THAT SIMPLE. I'M A TELEPATH, AND I'VE BEEN HIDING IT EVER SINCE I FOUND OUT! THAT'S ALL I KNOW HOW TO DO.
SCREWING WITH HIS MIND... THAT'S... I'VE NEVER...
I DON'T KNOW.

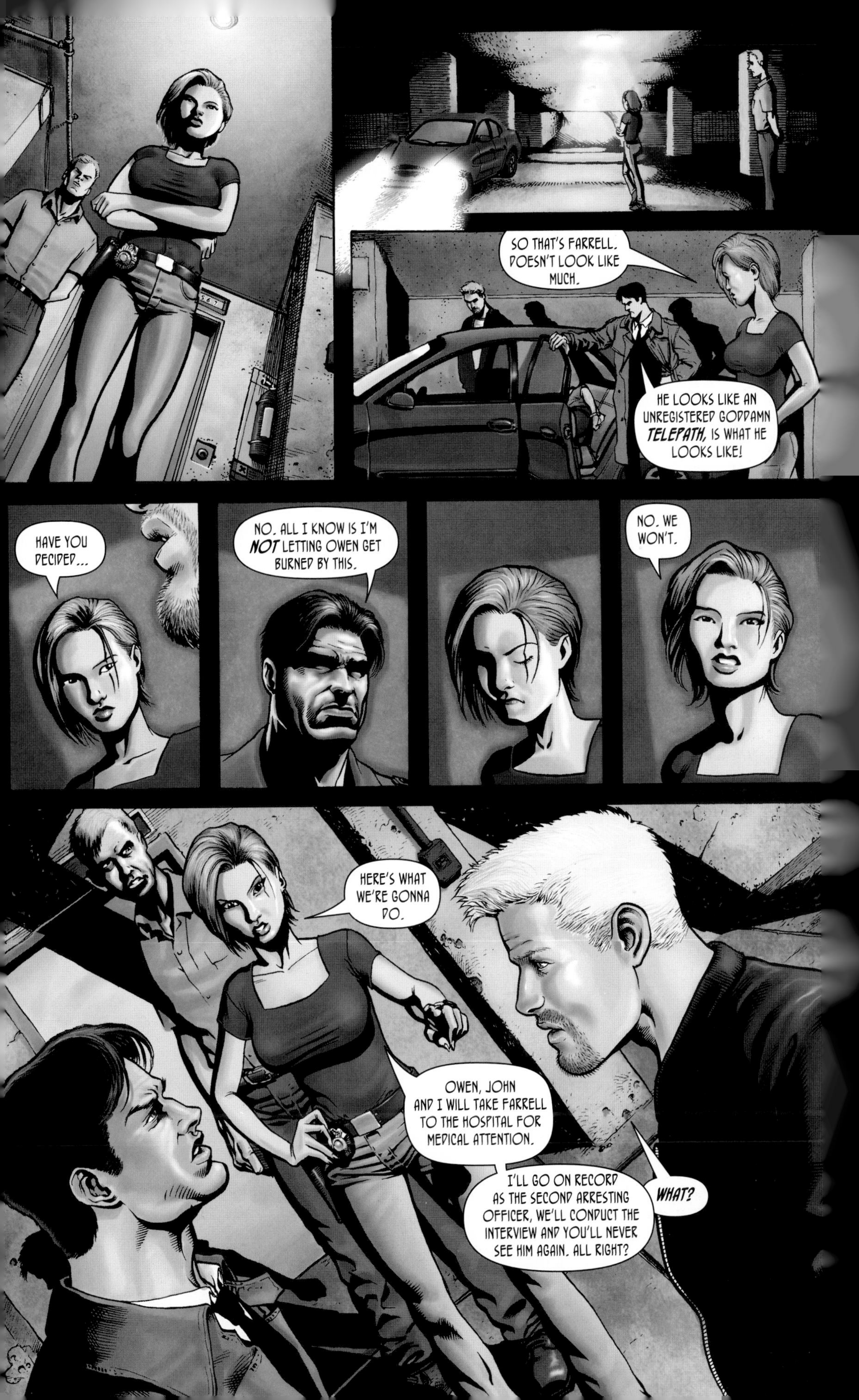

SO THAT'S FARRELL. DOESN'T LOOK LIKE MUCH.
HE LOOKS LIKE AN UNREGISTERED GODDAMN *TELEPATH,* IS WHAT HE LOOKS LIKE!
HAVE YOU DECIDED...
NO. ALL I KNOW IS I'M *NOT* LETTING OWEN GET BURNED BY THIS.
NO. WE WON'T.
HERE'S WHAT WE'RE GONNA DO.
OWEN, JOHN AND I WILL TAKE FARRELL TO THE HOSPITAL FOR MEDICAL ATTENTION.
I'LL GO ON RECORD AS THE SECOND ARRESTING OFFICER, WE'LL CONDUCT THE INTERVIEW AND YOU'LL NEVER SEE HIM AGAIN. ALL RIGHT?
WHAT?

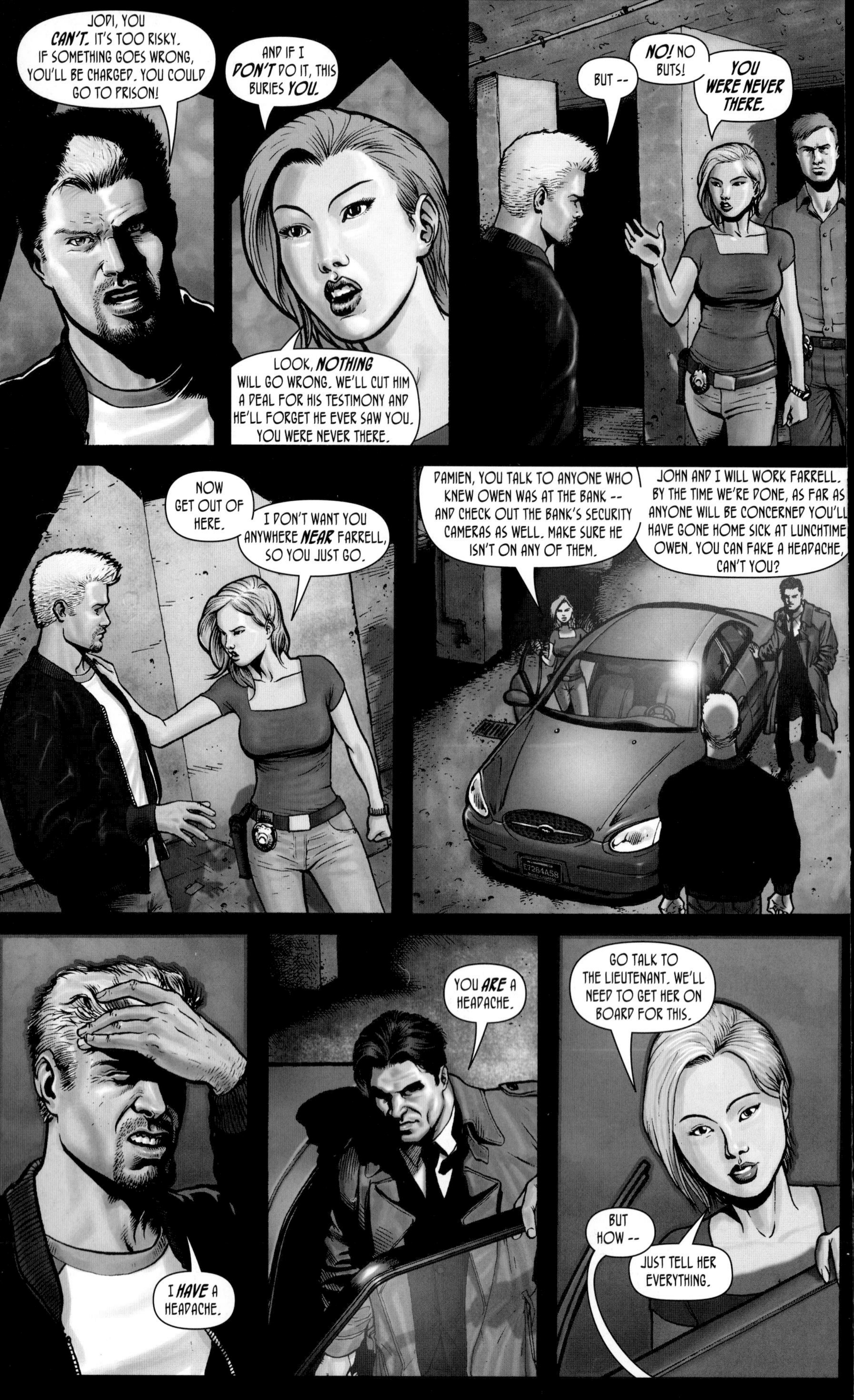
JODI, YOU CAN'T. IT'S TOO RISKY. IF SOMETHING GOES WRONG, YOU'LL BE CHARGED. YOU COULD GO TO PRISON!
AND IF I DON'T DO IT, THIS BURIES YOU.
LOOK, NOTHING WILL GO WRONG. WE'LL CUT HIM A DEAL FOR HIS TESTIMONY AND HE'LL FORGET HE EVER SAW YOU. YOU WERE NEVER THERE.
BUT --
NO! NO BUTS!
YOU WERE NEVER THERE.
NOW GET OUT OF HERE.
I DON'T WANT YOU ANYWHERE NEAR FARRELL, SO YOU JUST GO.
DAMIEN, YOU TALK TO ANYONE WHO KNEW OWEN WAS AT THE BANK -- AND CHECK OUT THE BANK'S SECURITY CAMERAS AS WELL. MAKE SURE HE ISN'T ON ANY OF THEM.
JOHN AND I WILL WORK FARRELL. BY THE TIME WE'RE DONE, AS FAR AS ANYONE WILL BE CONCERNED YOU'LL HAVE GONE HOME SICK AT LUNCHTIME OWEN. YOU CAN FAKE A HEADACHE, CAN'T YOU?
I HAVE A HEADACHE.
YOU ARE A HEADACHE.
GO TALK TO THE LIEUTENANT. WE'LL NEED TO GET HER ON BOARD FOR THIS.
BUT HOW --
JUST TELL HER EVERYTHING.

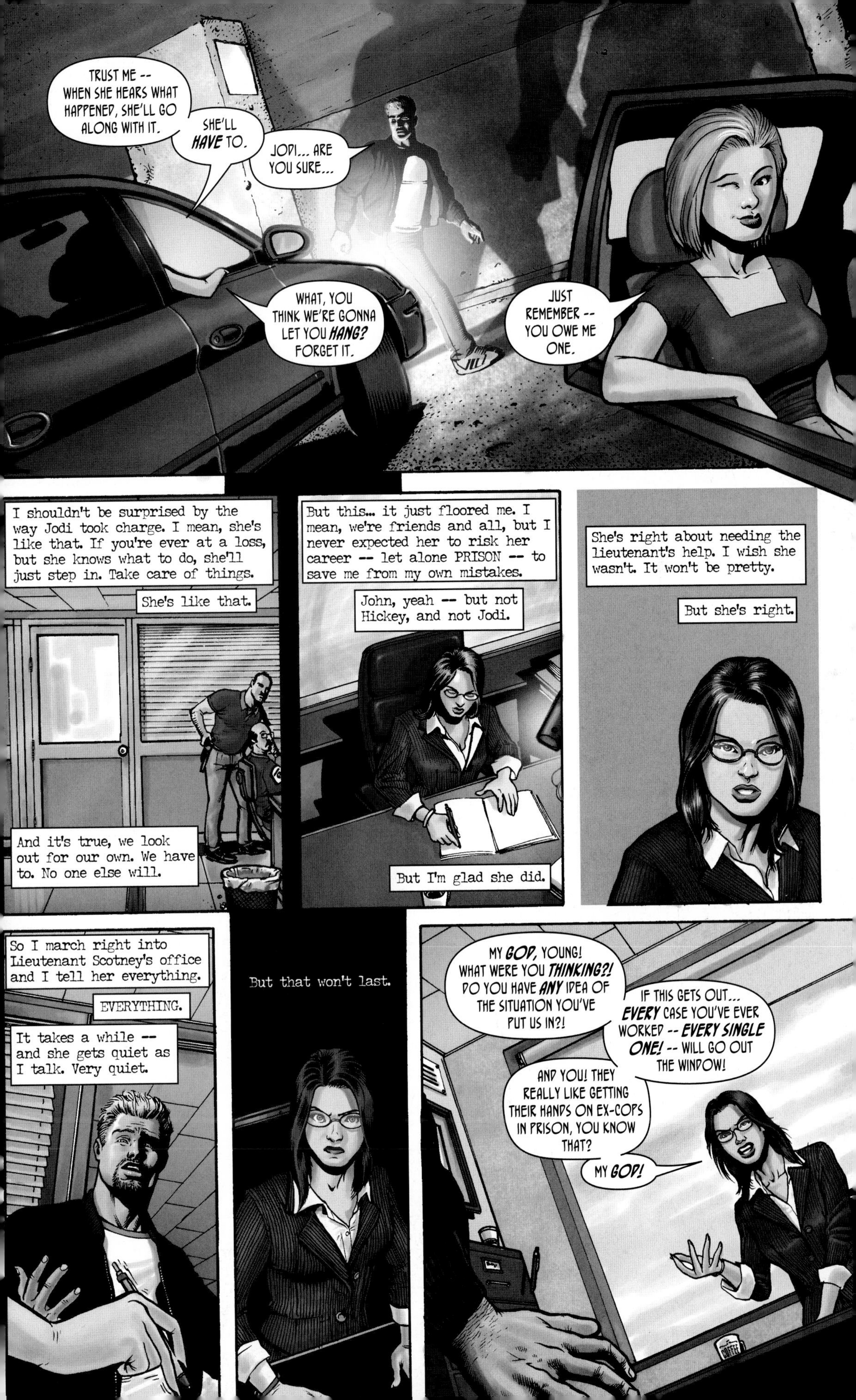
TRUST ME -- WHEN SHE HEARS WHAT HAPPENED, SHE'LL GO ALONG WITH IT.
SHE'LL HAVE TO.
JODI... ARE YOU SURE...
WHAT, YOU THINK WE'RE GONNA LET YOU HANG? FORGET IT.
JUST REMEMBER -- YOU OWE ME ONE.
I shouldn't be surprised by the way Jodi took charge. I mean, she's like that. If you're ever at a loss, but she knows what to do, she'll just step in. Take care of things.
She's like that.
And it's true, we look out for our own. We have to. No one else will.
But this... it just floored me. I mean, we're friends and all, but I never expected her to risk her career -- let alone PRISON -- to save me from my own mistakes.
John, yeah -- but not Hickey, and not Jodi.
But I'm glad she did.
She's right about needing the lieutenant's help. I wish she wasn't. It won't be pretty.
But she's right.
So I march right into Lieutenant Scotney's office and I tell her everything.
EVERYTHING.
It takes a while -- and she gets quiet as I talk. Very quiet.
But that won't last.
MY GOD, YOUNG! WHAT WERE YOU THINKING?! DO YOU HAVE ANY IDEA OF THE SITUATION YOU'VE PUT US IN?!
IF THIS GETS OUT... EVERY CASE YOU'VE EVER WORKED -- EVERY SINGLE ONE! -- WILL GO OUT THE WINDOW!
AND YOU! THEY REALLY LIKE GETTING THEIR HANDS ON EX-COPS IN PRISON, YOU KNOW THAT?
MY GOD!

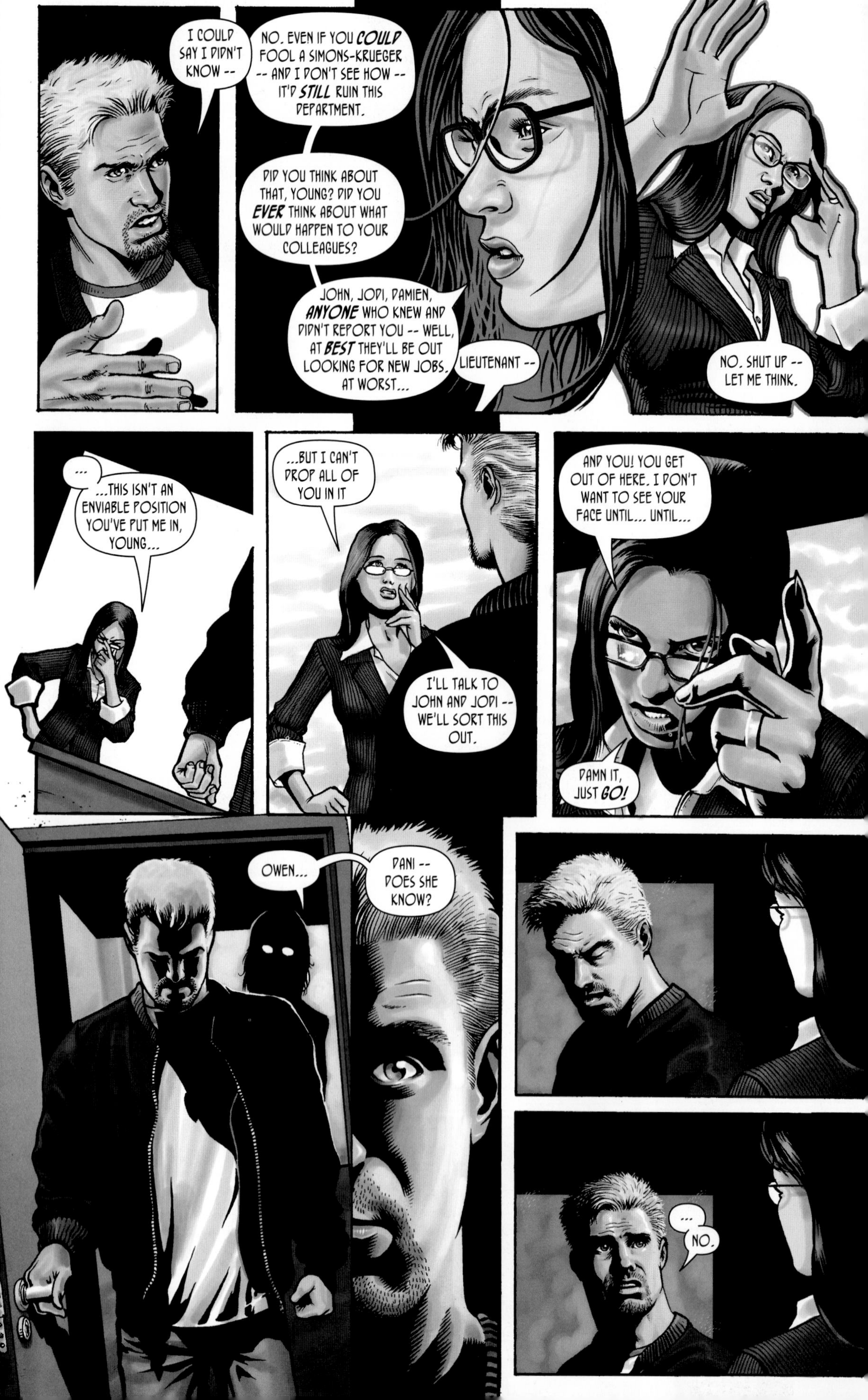
I COULD SAY I DIDN'T KNOW --
NO. EVEN IF YOU COULD FOOL A SIMONS-KRUEGER -- AND I DON'T SEE HOW -- IT'D STILL RUIN THIS DEPARTMENT.
DID YOU THINK ABOUT THAT, YOUNG? DID YOU EVER THINK ABOUT WHAT WOULD HAPPEN TO YOUR COLLEAGUES?
JOHN, JODI, DAMIEN, ANYONE WHO KNEW AND DIDN'T REPORT YOU -- WELL, AT BEST THEY'LL BE OUT LOOKING FOR NEW JOBS. AT WORST...
LIEUTENANT --
NO. SHUT UP -- LET ME THINK.
...
...THIS ISN'T AN ENVIABLE POSITION YOU'VE PUT ME IN, YOUNG...
...BUT I CAN'T DROP ALL OF YOU IN IT
I'LL TALK TO JOHN AND JODI -- WE'LL SORT THIS OUT.
AND YOU! YOU GET OUT OF HERE. I DON'T WANT TO SEE YOUR FACE UNTIL... UNTIL...
DAMN IT, JUST GO!
OWEN...
DANI -- DOES SHE KNOW?
...
NO.

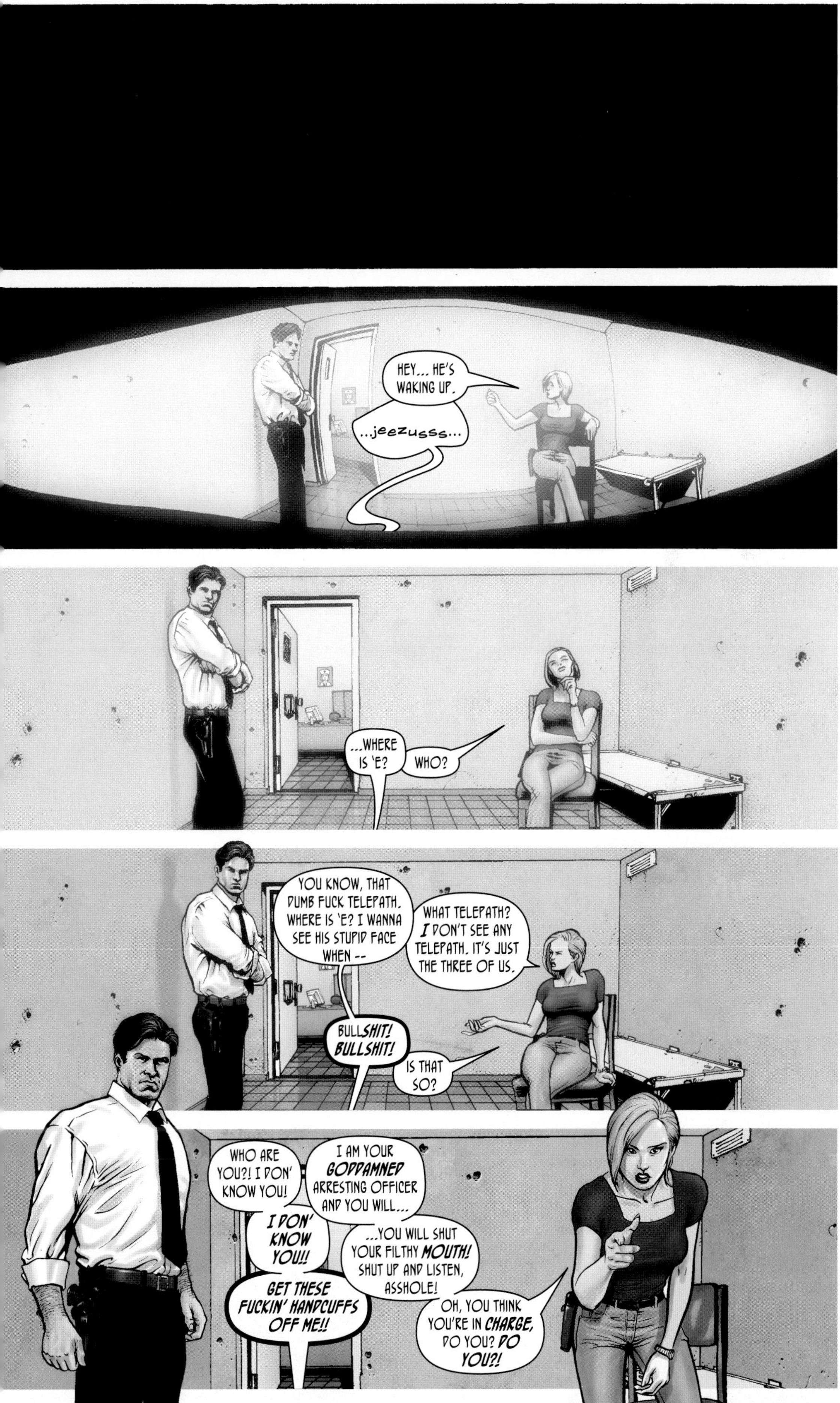
HEY... HE'S WAKING UP.
...jeezusss...
...WHERE IS 'E?
WHO?
YOU KNOW, THAT DUMB FUCK TELEPATH. WHERE IS 'E? I WANNA SEE HIS STUPID FACE WHEN --
WHAT TELEPATH? I DON'T SEE ANY TELEPATH. IT'S JUST THE THREE OF US.
BULLSHIT! BULLSHIT!
IS THAT SO?
WHO ARE YOU?! I DON' KNOW YOU!
I AM YOUR GODDAMNED ARRESTING OFFICER AND YOU WILL...
I DON' KNOW YOU!!
...YOU WILL SHUT YOUR FILTHY MOUTH! SHUT UP AND LISTEN, ASSHOLE!
GET THESE FUCKIN' HANDCUFFS OFF ME!!
OH, YOU THINK YOU'RE IN CHARGE, DO YOU? DO YOU?!

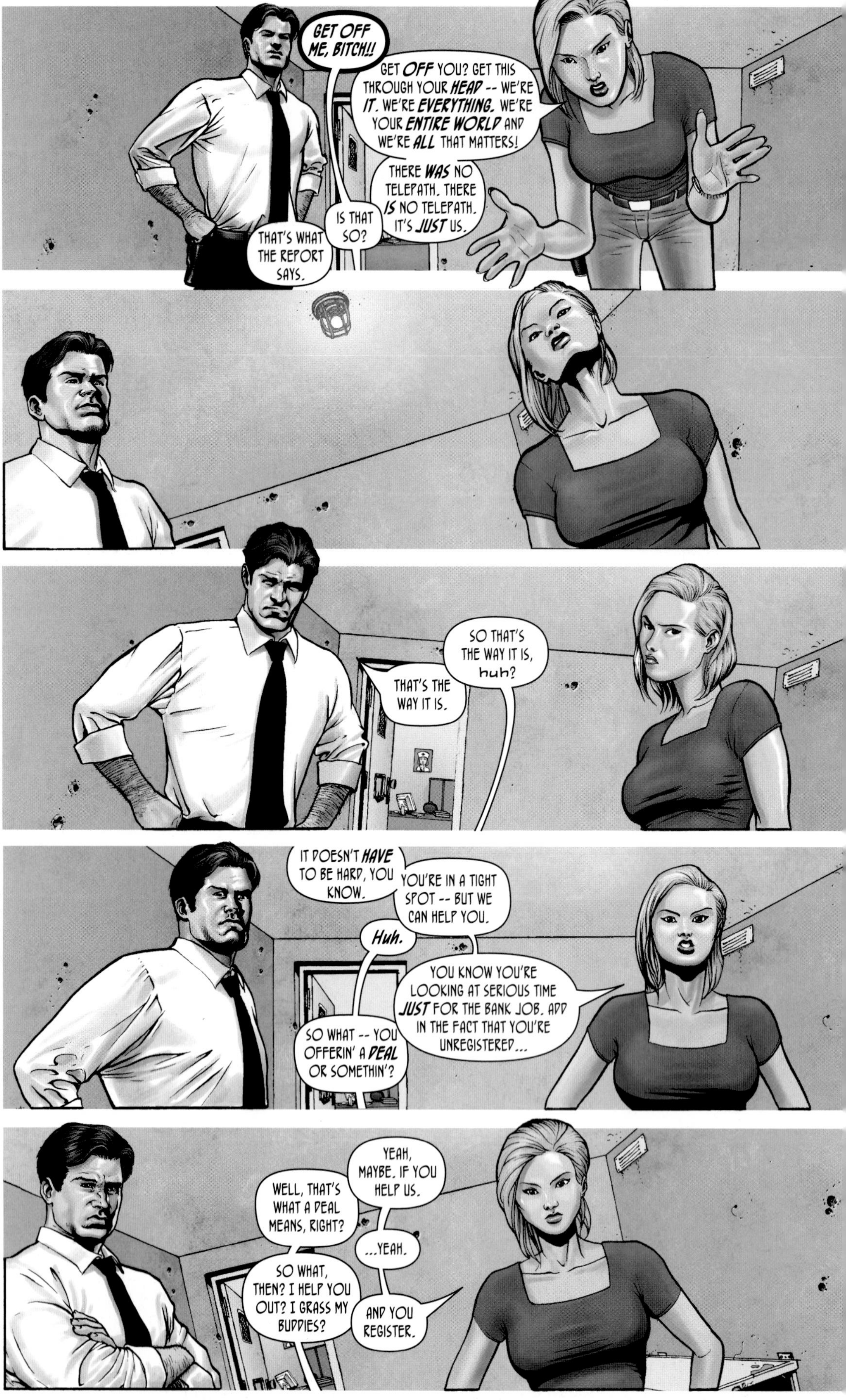
GET OFF ME, BITCH!!
GET OFF YOU? GET THIS THROUGH YOUR HEAD -- WE'RE IT. WE'RE EVERYTHING. WE'RE YOUR ENTIRE WORLD AND WE'RE ALL THAT MATTERS!
THERE WAS NO TELEPATH. THERE IS NO TELEPATH. IT'S JUST US.
IS THAT SO?
THAT'S WHAT THE REPORT SAYS.
SO THAT'S THE WAY IT IS, huh?
THAT'S THE WAY IT IS.
IT DOESN'T HAVE TO BE HARD, YOU KNOW.
YOU'RE IN A TIGHT SPOT -- BUT WE CAN HELP YOU.
Huh.
YOU KNOW YOU'RE LOOKING AT SERIOUS TIME JUST FOR THE BANK JOB. ADD IN THE FACT THAT YOU'RE UNREGISTERED...
SO WHAT -- YOU OFFERIN' A DEAL OR SOMETHIN'?
YEAH, MAYBE. IF YOU HELP US.
WELL, THAT'S WHAT A DEAL MEANS, RIGHT?
...YEAH.
SO WHAT, THEN? I HELP YOU OUT? I GRASS MY BUDDIES?
AND YOU REGISTER.

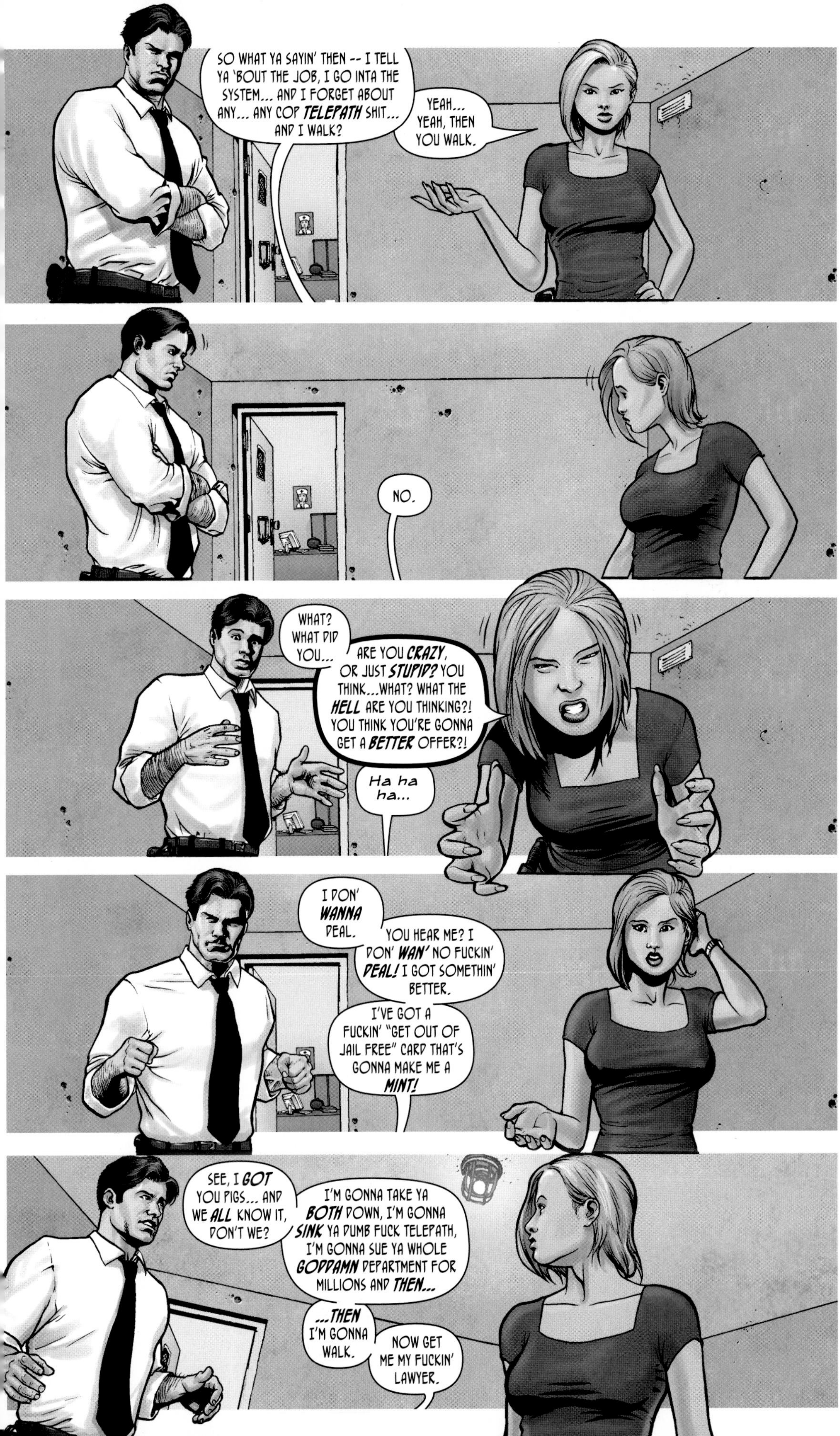
SO WHAT YA SAYIN' THEN -- I TELL YA 'BOUT THE JOB, I GO INTA THE SYSTEM... AND I FORGET ABOUT ANY... ANY COP TELEPATH SHIT... AND I WALK?
YEAH... YEAH, THEN YOU WALK.
NO.
WHAT? WHAT DID YOU...
ARE YOU CRAZY, OR JUST STUPID? YOU THINK...WHAT? WHAT THE HELL ARE YOU THINKING?! YOU THINK YOU'RE GONNA GET A BETTER OFFER?!
Ha ha ha...
I DON' WANNA DEAL.
YOU HEAR ME? I DON' WAN' NO FUCKIN' DEAL! I GOT SOMETHIN' BETTER.
I'VE GOT A FUCKIN' "GET OUT OF JAIL FREE" CARD THAT'S GONNA MAKE ME A MINT!
SEE, I GOT YOU PIGS... AND WE ALL KNOW IT, DON'T WE?
I'M GONNA TAKE YA BOTH DOWN, I'M GONNA SINK YA DUMB FUCK TELEPATH, I'M GONNA SUE YA WHOLE GODDAMN DEPARTMENT FOR MILLIONS AND THEN...
...THEN I'M GONNA WALK.
NOW GET ME MY FUCKIN' LAWYER.

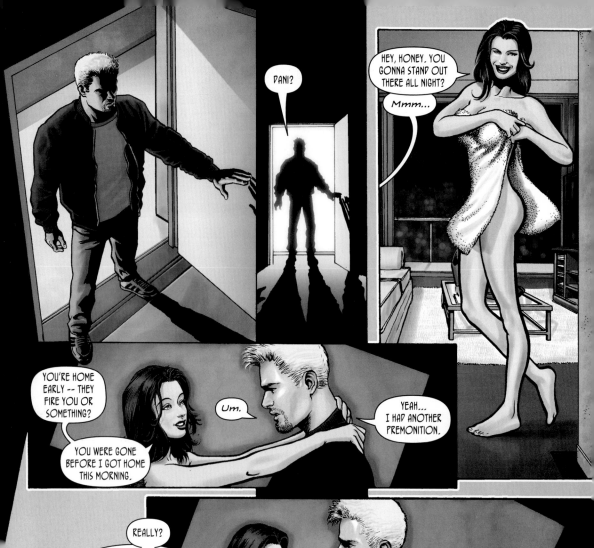

DANI?

HEY, HONEY. YOU GONNA STAND OUT THERE ALL NIGHT?

Mmm...

YOU'RE HOME EARLY -- THEY FIRE YOU OR SOMETHING?

Um.

YEAH... I HAD ANOTHER PREMONITION.

YOU WERE GONE BEFORE I GOT HOME THIS MORNING.

REALLY?

WELL, WE CAN TALK ABOUT IT LATER. RIGHT NOW, YOU'RE HOME EARLY, AND I DON'T HAVE TO LEAVE FOR HOURS YET.

WHY DON'T WE TALK ABOUT THAT?

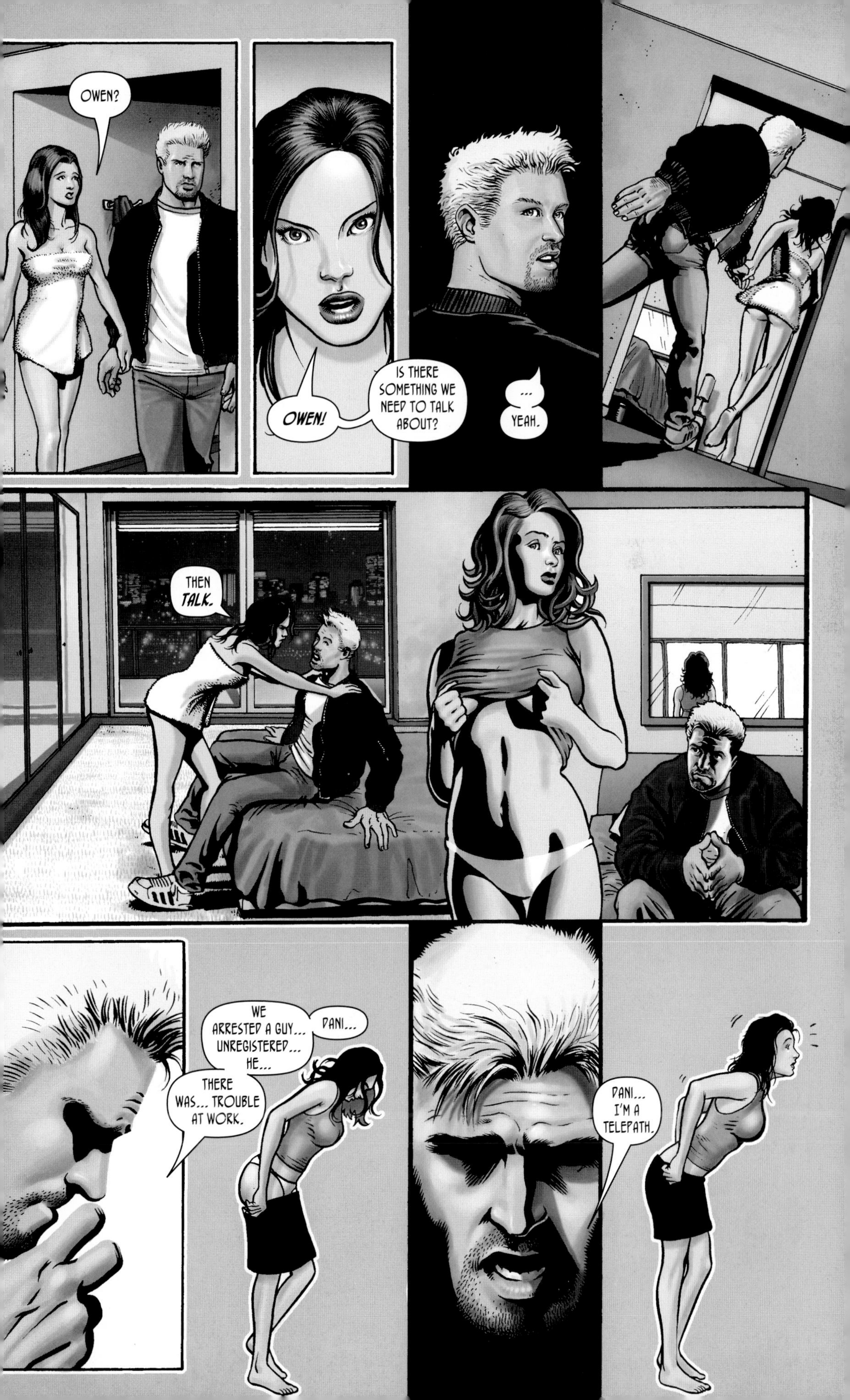
OWEN?
OWEN!
IS THERE SOMETHING WE NEED TO TALK ABOUT?
...
YEAH.
THEN TALK.
WE ARRESTED A GUY... UNREGISTERED... HE...
DANI...
THERE WAS... TROUBLE AT WORK.
DANI... I'M A TELEPATH.

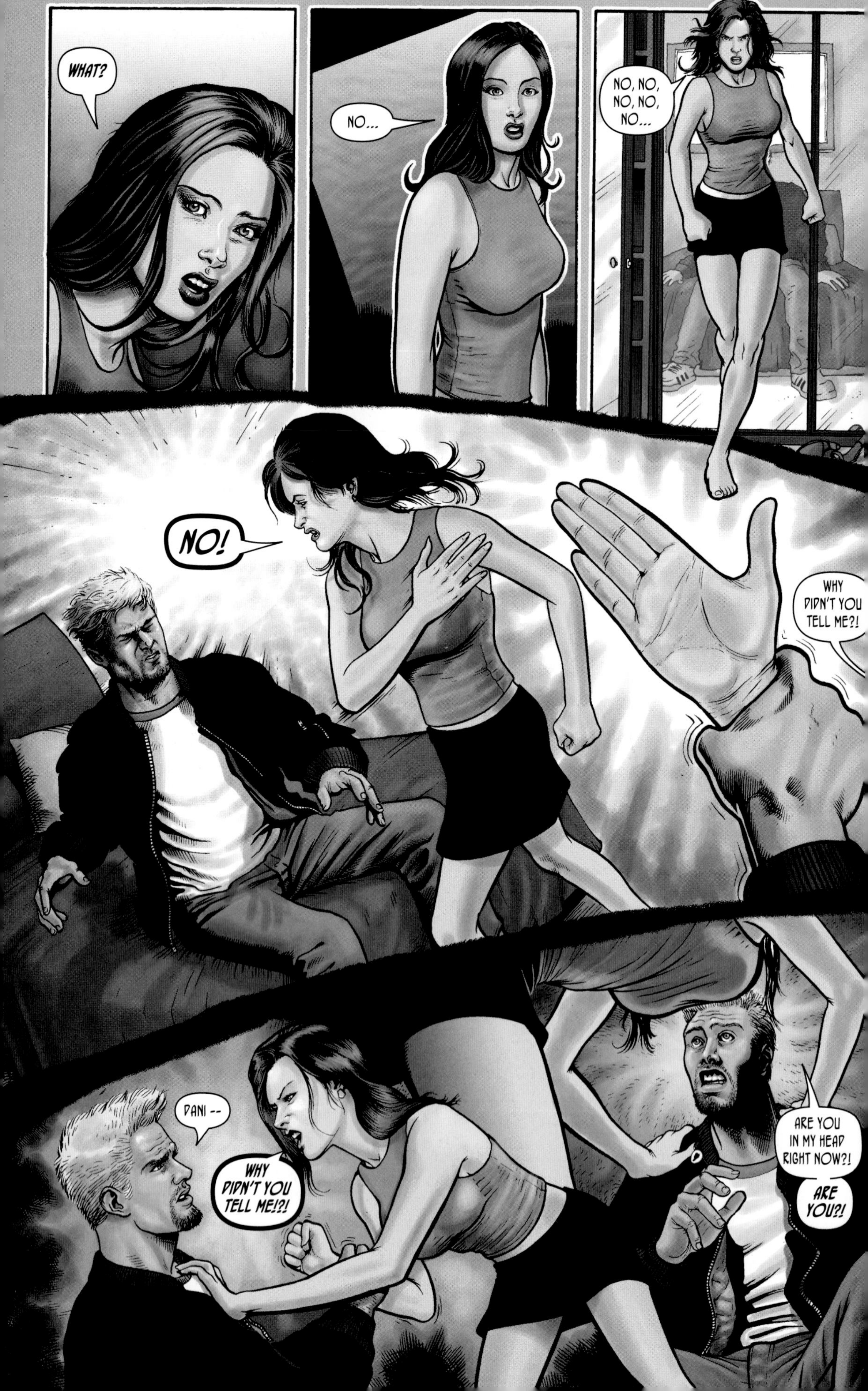
WHAT?
NO...
NO, NO, NO, NO, NO...
NO!
WHY DIDN'T YOU TELL ME?!
DANI --
WHY DIDN'T YOU TELL ME!?!
ARE YOU IN MY HEAD RIGHT NOW?!
ARE YOU?!

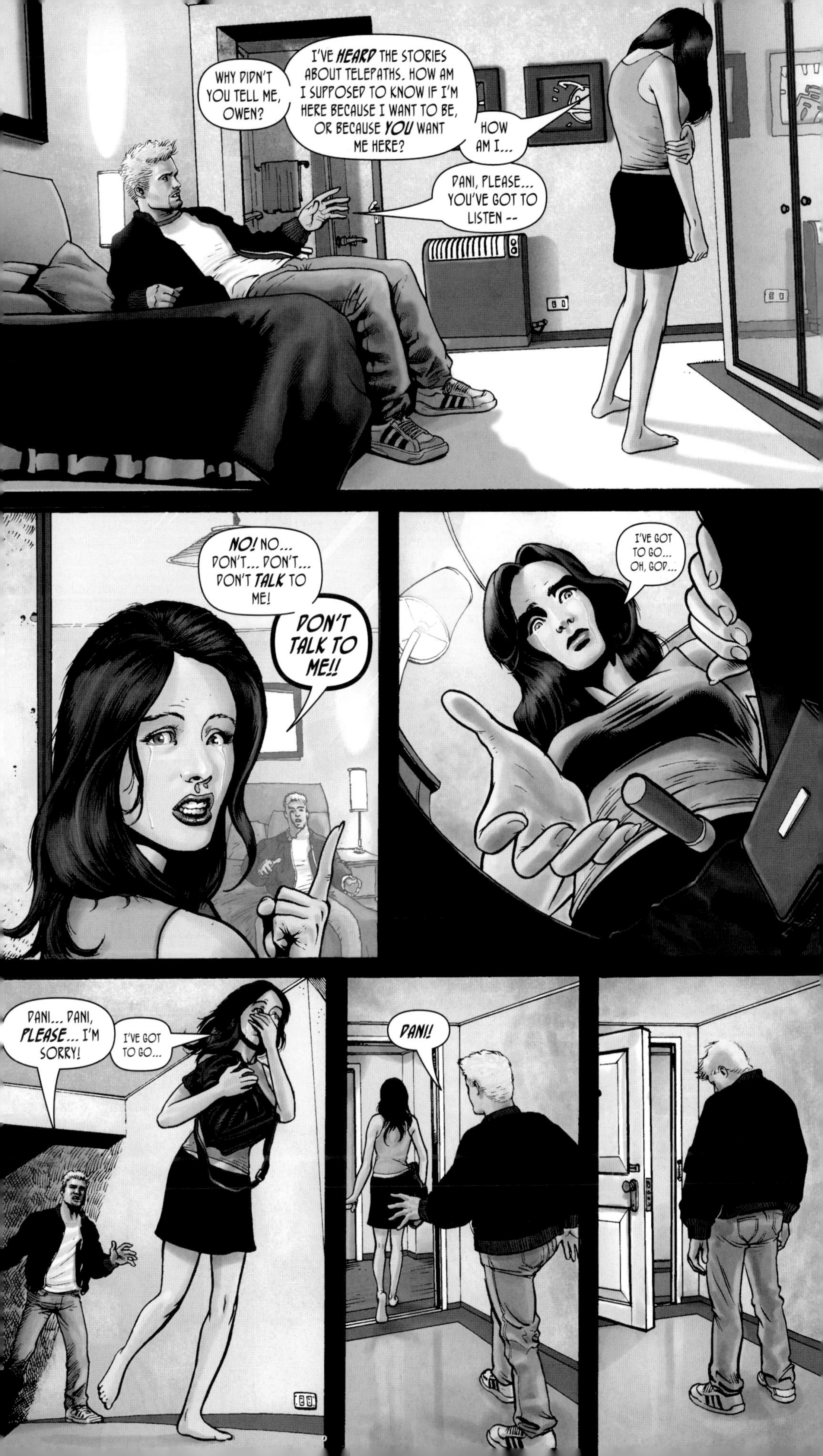

WHY DIDN'T YOU TELL ME, OWEN?
I'VE HEARD THE STORIES ABOUT TELEPATHS. HOW AM I SUPPOSED TO KNOW IF I'M HERE BECAUSE I WANT TO BE, OR BECAUSE YOU WANT ME HERE?
HOW AM I...
DANI, PLEASE... YOU'VE GOT TO LISTEN --
NO! NO... DON'T... DON'T... DON'T TALK TO ME!
DON'T TALK TO ME!!
I'VE GOT TO GO... OH, GOD...
DANI... DANI, PLEASE... I'M SORRY!
I'VE GOT TO GO...
DANI!

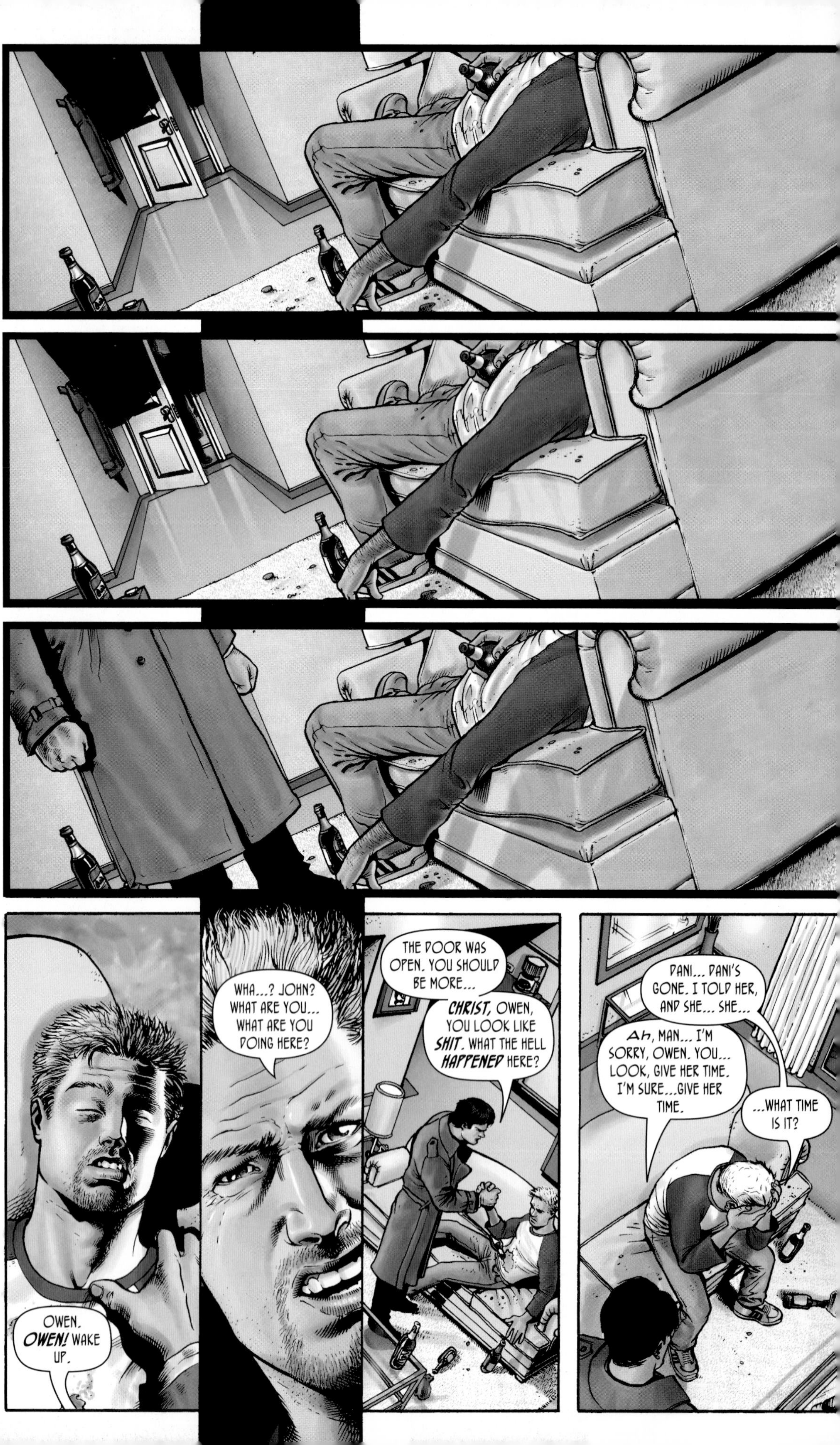
OWEN. OWEN! WAKE UP.
WHA...? JOHN? WHAT ARE YOU... WHAT ARE YOU DOING HERE?
THE DOOR WAS OPEN. YOU SHOULD BE MORE...
CHRIST, OWEN, YOU LOOK LIKE SHIT. WHAT THE HELL HAPPENED HERE?
DANI... DANI'S GONE. I TOLD HER, AND SHE... SHE...
AH, MAN... I'M SORRY, OWEN. YOU... LOOK, GIVE HER TIME. I'M SURE...GIVE HER TIME.
...WHAT TIME IS IT?

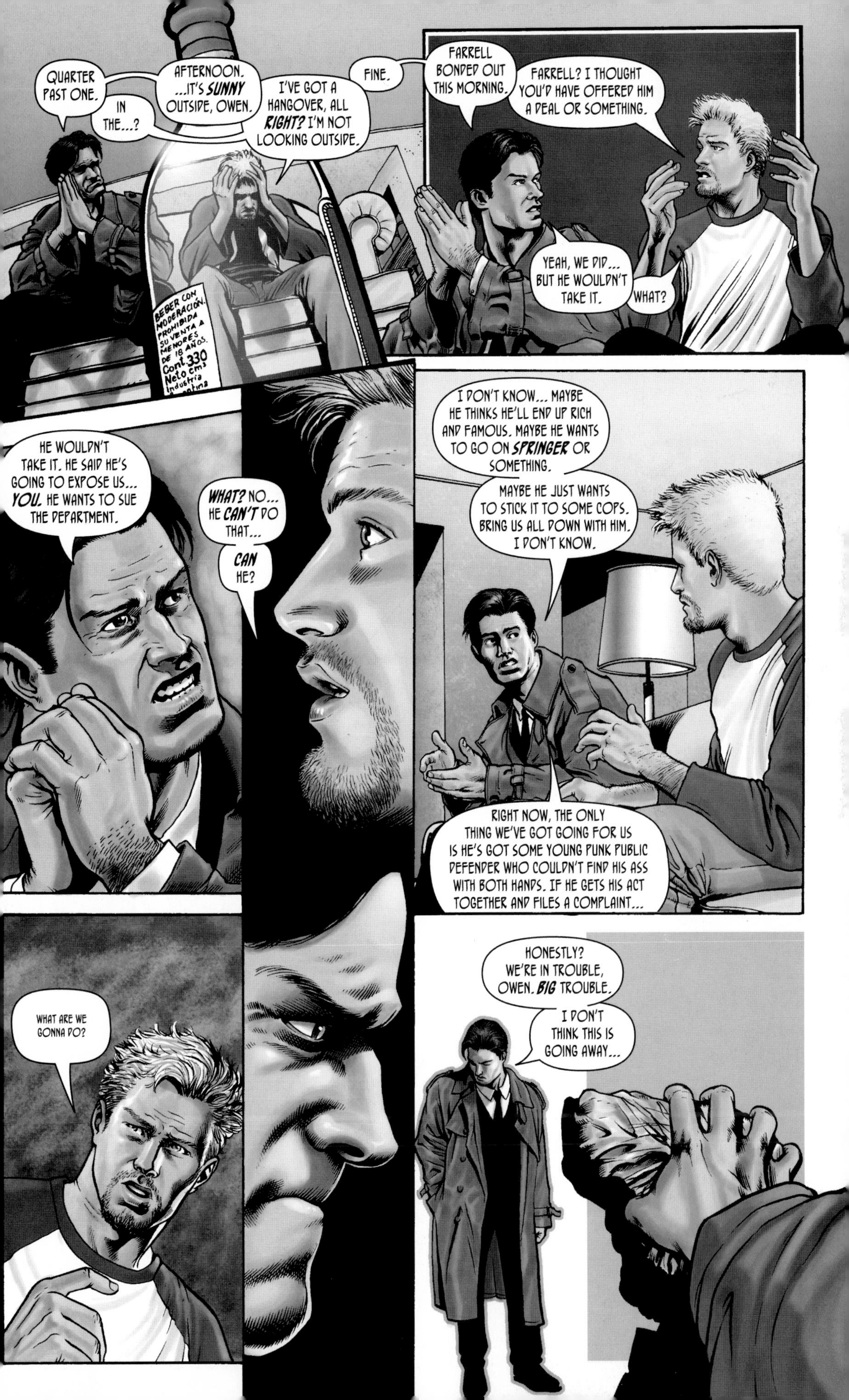
QUARTER PAST ONE.
IN THE...?
AFTERNOON. ...IT'S SUNNY OUTSIDE, OWEN.
I'VE GOT A HANGOVER, ALL RIGHT? I'M NOT LOOKING OUTSIDE.
FINE.
BEBER CON MODERACIÓN. PROHIBIDA SU VENTA A MENORES DE 18 AÑOS. Cont. 330 Neto cm3
FARRELL BONDED OUT THIS MORNING.
FARRELL? I THOUGHT YOU'D HAVE OFFERED HIM A DEAL OR SOMETHING.
YEAH, WE DID... BUT HE WOULDN'T TAKE IT.
WHAT?
HE WOULDN'T TAKE IT. HE SAID HE'S GOING TO EXPOSE US... YOU. HE WANTS TO SUE THE DEPARTMENT.
WHAT? NO... HE CAN'T DO THAT...
CAN HE?
I DON'T KNOW... MAYBE HE THINKS HE'LL END UP RICH AND FAMOUS. MAYBE HE WANTS TO GO ON SPRINGER OR SOMETHING.
MAYBE HE JUST WANTS TO STICK IT TO SOME COPS. BRING US ALL DOWN WITH HIM. I DON'T KNOW.
RIGHT NOW, THE ONLY THING WE'VE GOT GOING FOR US IS HE'S GOT SOME YOUNG PUNK PUBLIC DEFENDER WHO COULDN'T FIND HIS ASS WITH BOTH HANDS. IF HE GETS HIS ACT TOGETHER AND FILES A COMPLAINT...
WHAT ARE WE GONNA DO?
HONESTLY? WE'RE IN TROUBLE, OWEN. BIG TROUBLE.
I DON'T THINK THIS IS GOING AWAY...

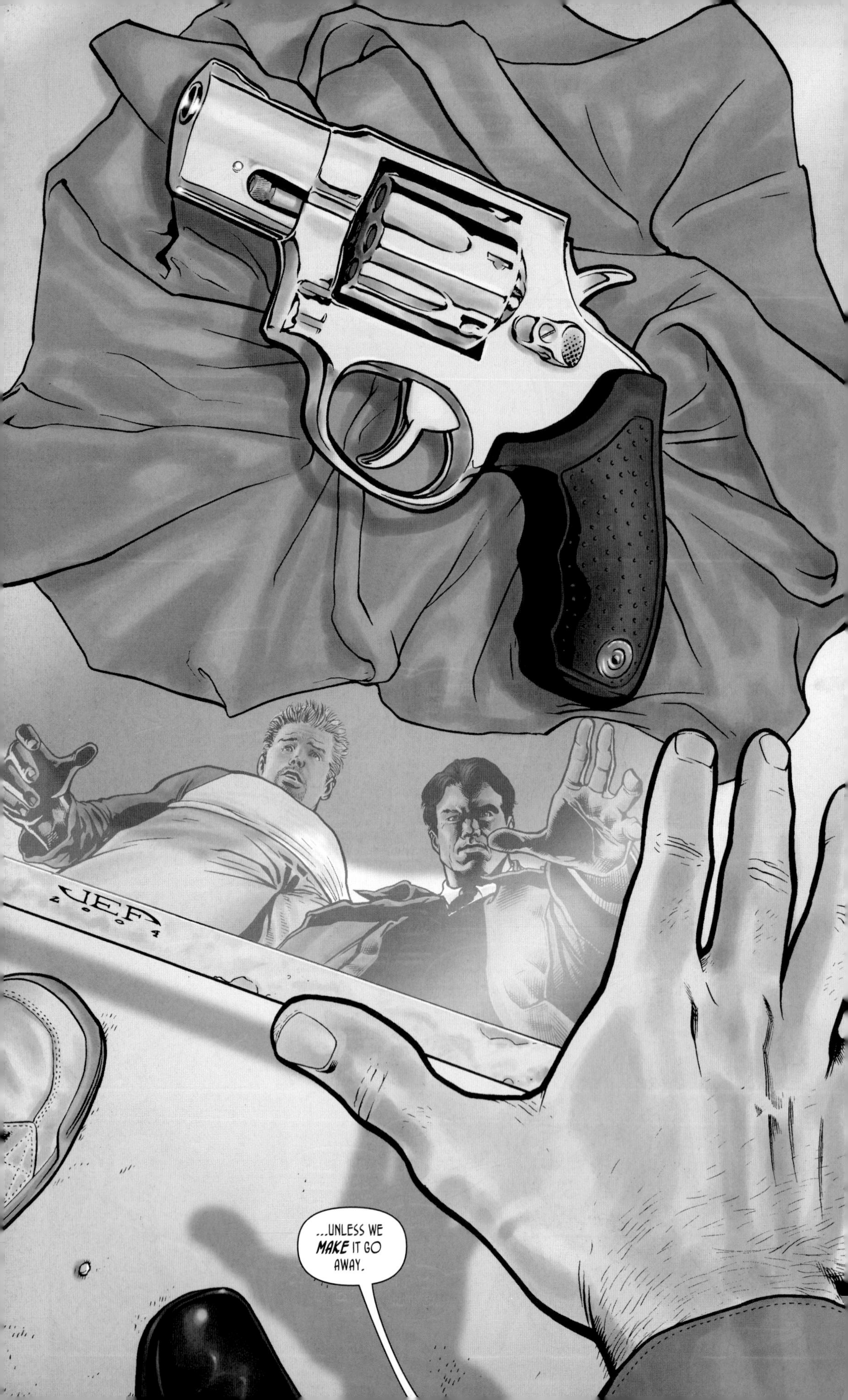
...UNLESS WE MAKE IT GO AWAY.

CHAPTER THREE

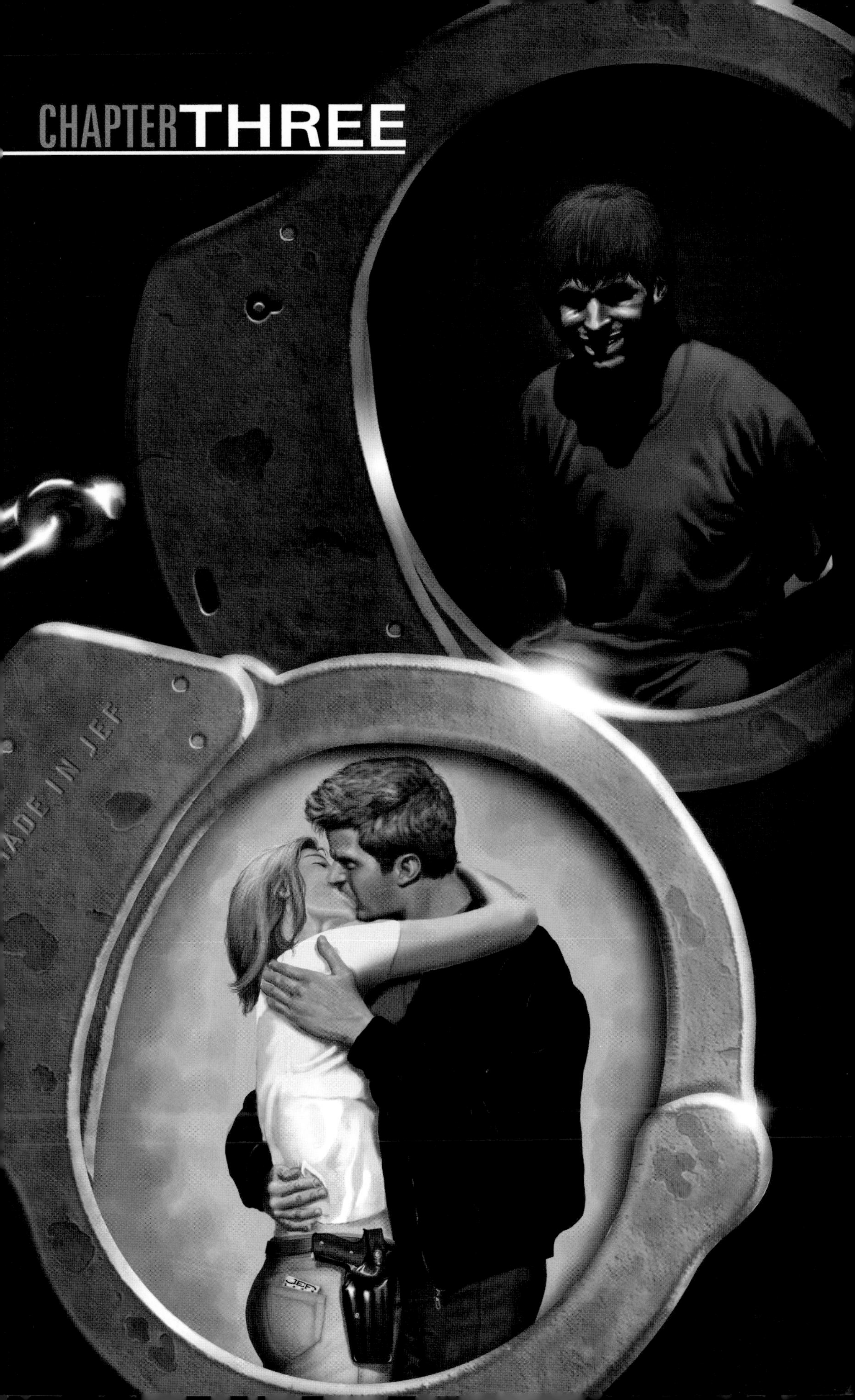
ADE IN JEF

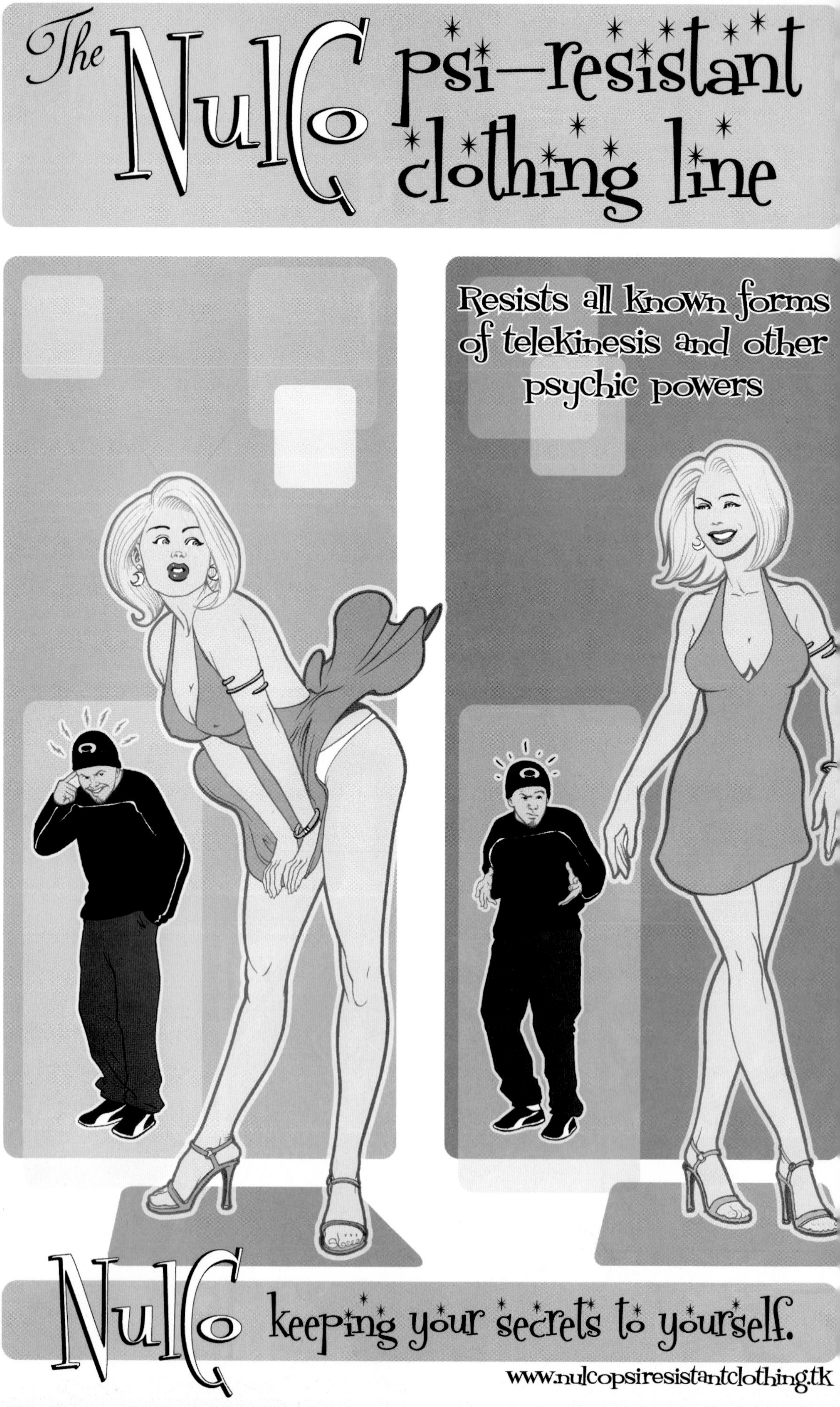

The NulCo psi-resistant clothing line
Resists all known forms of telekinesis and other psychic powers
NulCo keeping your secrets to yourself.
www.nulcopsiresistantclothing.tk

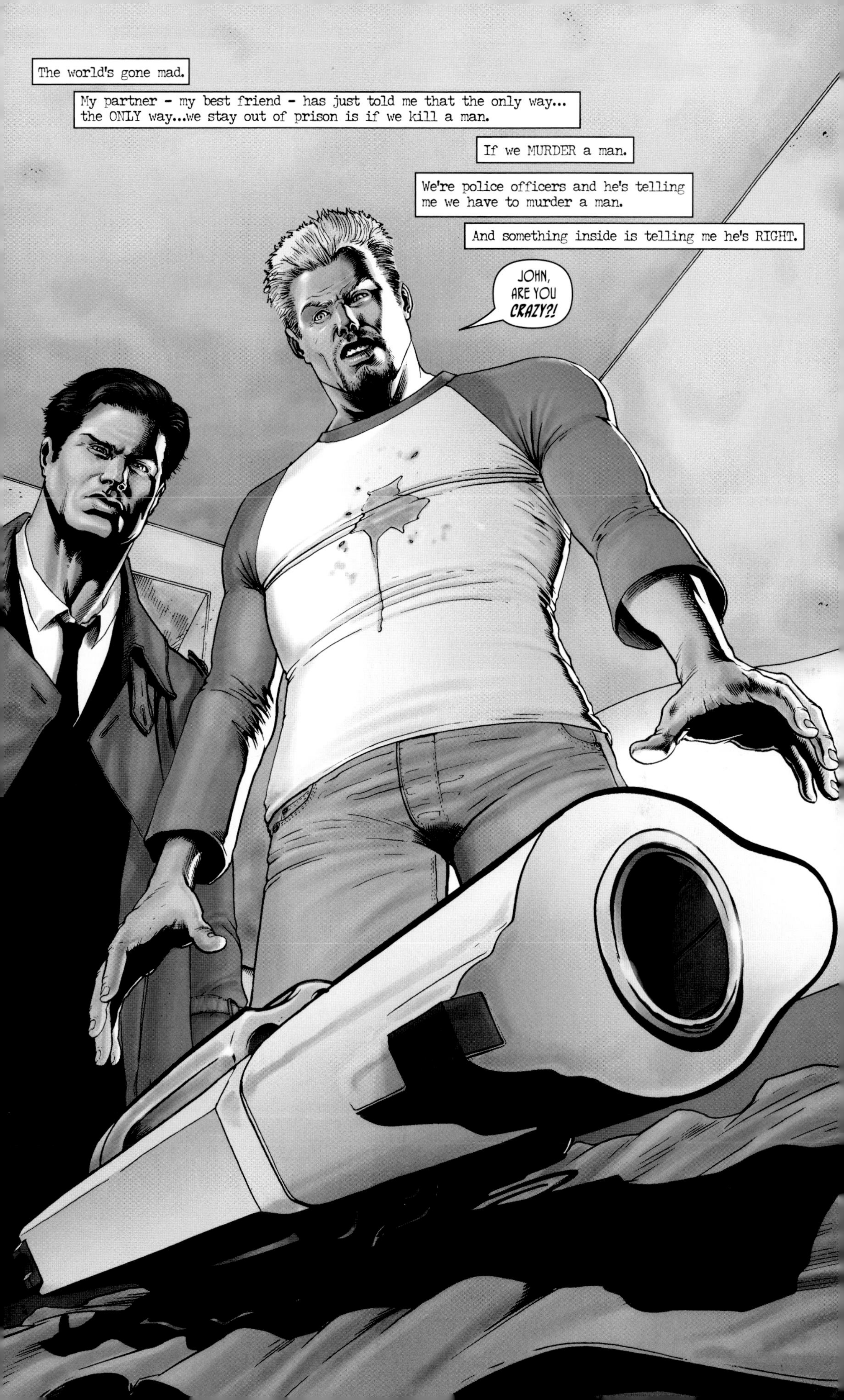
The world's gone mad.
My partner - my best friend - has just told me that the only way... the ONLY way...we stay out of prison is if we kill a man.
If we MURDER a man.
We're police officers and he's telling me we have to murder a man.
And something inside is telling me he's RIGHT.
JOHN, ARE YOU CRAZY?!

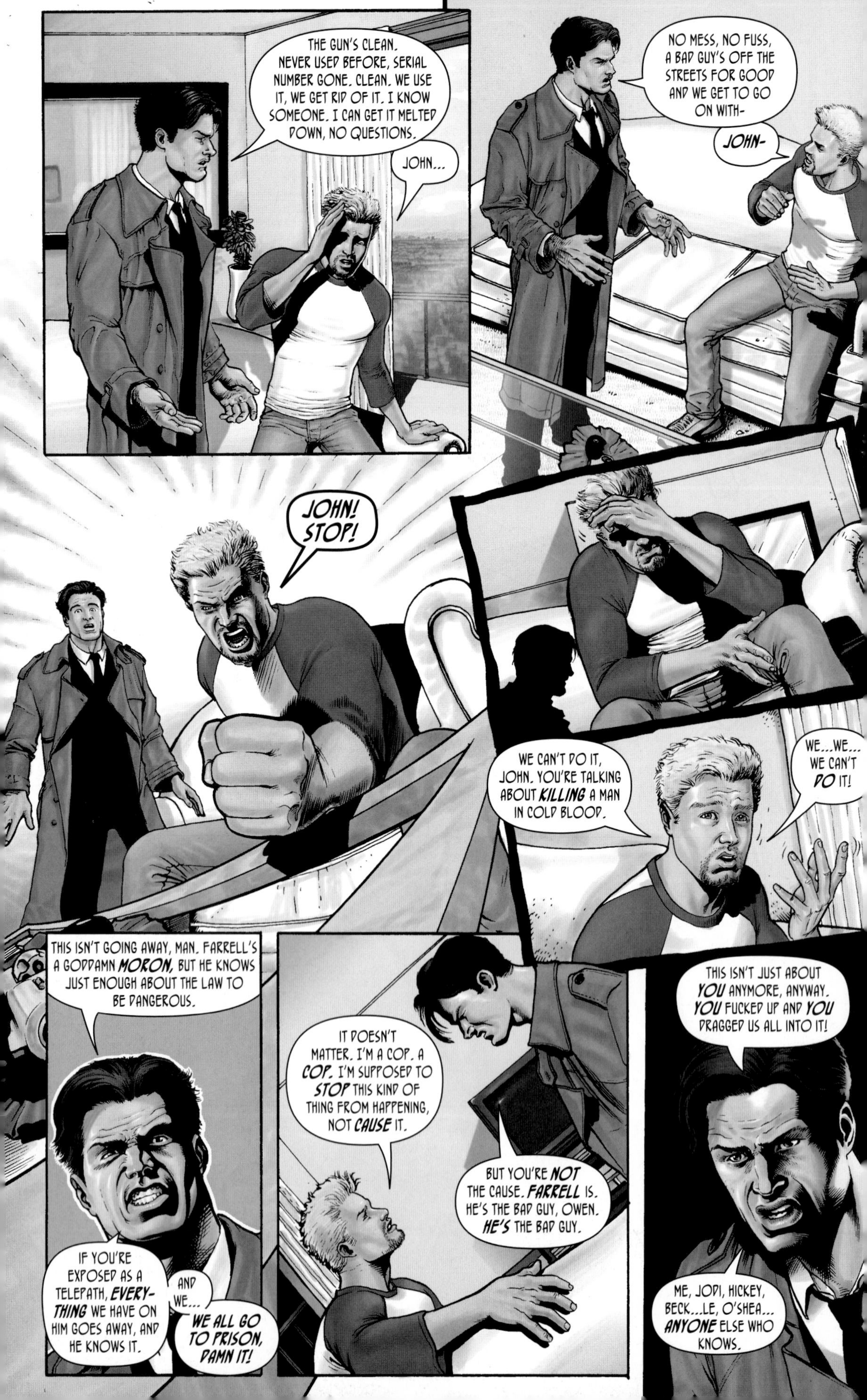
THE GUN'S CLEAN. NEVER USED BEFORE, SERIAL NUMBER GONE. CLEAN. WE USE IT, WE GET RID OF IT. I KNOW SOMEONE. I CAN GET IT MELTED DOWN, NO QUESTIONS.
JOHN...
NO MESS, NO FUSS, A BAD GUY'S OFF THE STREETS FOR GOOD AND WE GET TO GO ON WITH-
JOHN-
JOHN! STOP!
WE CAN'T DO IT, JOHN. YOU'RE TALKING ABOUT KILLING A MAN IN COLD BLOOD.
WE...WE... WE CAN'T DO IT!
THIS ISN'T GOING AWAY, MAN. FARRELL'S A GODDAMN MORON, BUT HE KNOWS JUST ENOUGH ABOUT THE LAW TO BE DANGEROUS.
IF YOU'RE EXPOSED AS A TELEPATH, EVERYTHING WE HAVE ON HIM GOES AWAY, AND HE KNOWS IT.
AND WE...
WE ALL GO TO PRISON, DAMN IT!
IT DOESN'T MATTER. I'M A COP. A COP. I'M SUPPOSED TO STOP THIS KIND OF THING FROM HAPPENING, NOT CAUSE IT.
BUT YOU'RE NOT THE CAUSE. FARRELL IS. HE'S THE BAD GUY, OWEN. HE'S THE BAD GUY.
THIS ISN'T JUST ABOUT YOU ANYMORE, ANYWAY. YOU FUCKED UP AND YOU DRAGGED US ALL INTO IT!
ME, JODI, HICKEY, BECK...LE, O'SHEA... ANYONE ELSE WHO KNOWS.

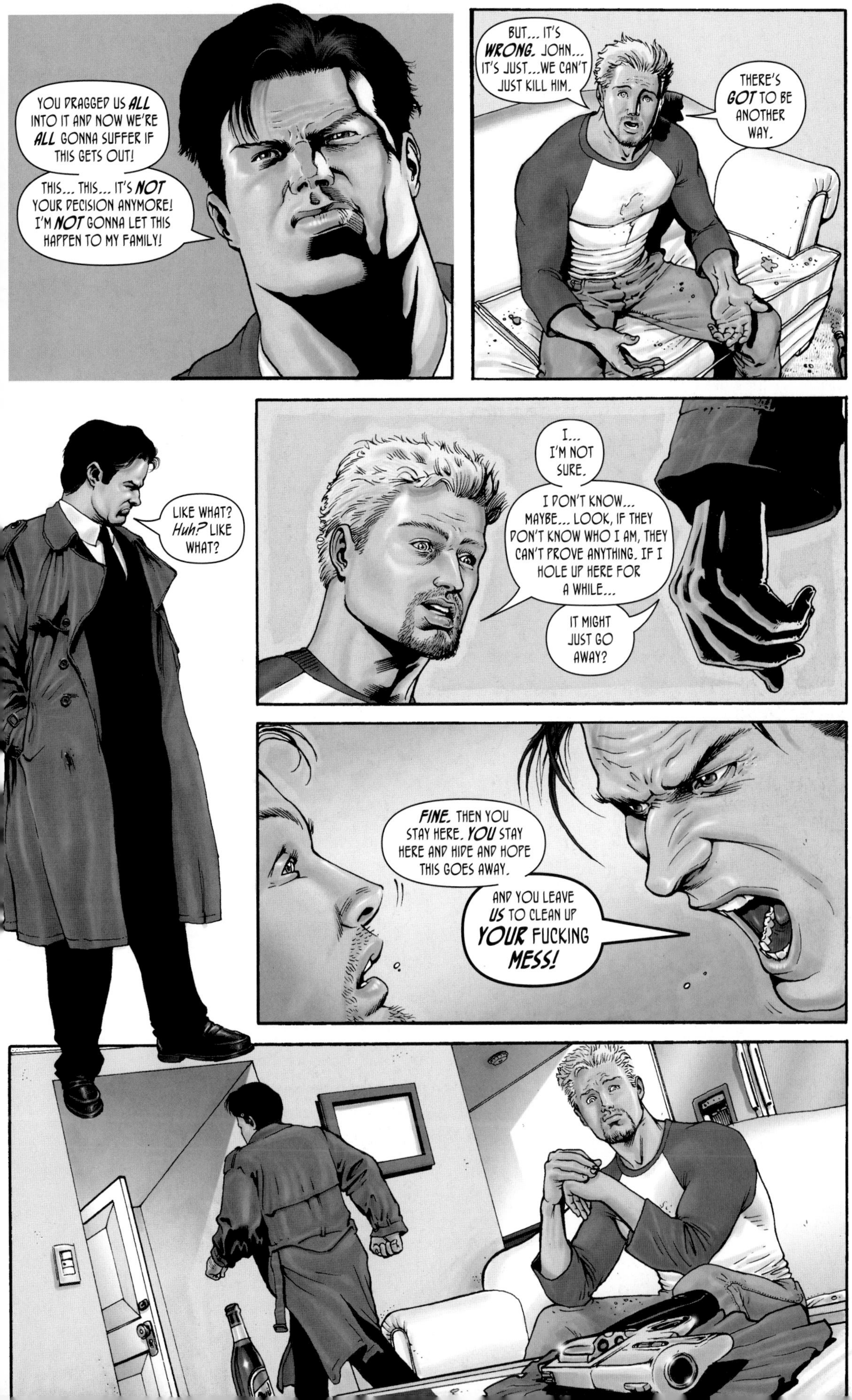
YOU DRAGGED US ALL INTO IT AND NOW WE'RE ALL GONNA SUFFER IF THIS GETS OUT!
THIS... THIS... IT'S NOT YOUR DECISION ANYMORE! I'M NOT GONNA LET THIS HAPPEN TO MY FAMILY!
BUT... IT'S WRONG. JOHN... IT'S JUST...WE CAN'T JUST KILL HIM.
THERE'S GOT TO BE ANOTHER WAY.
LIKE WHAT? Huh? LIKE WHAT?
I... I'M NOT SURE.
I DON'T KNOW... MAYBE... LOOK, IF THEY DON'T KNOW WHO I AM, THEY CAN'T PROVE ANYTHING. IF I HOLE UP HERE FOR A WHILE...
IT MIGHT JUST GO AWAY?
FINE. THEN YOU STAY HERE. YOU STAY HERE AND HIDE AND HOPE THIS GOES AWAY.
AND YOU LEAVE US TO CLEAN UP YOUR FUCKING MESS!

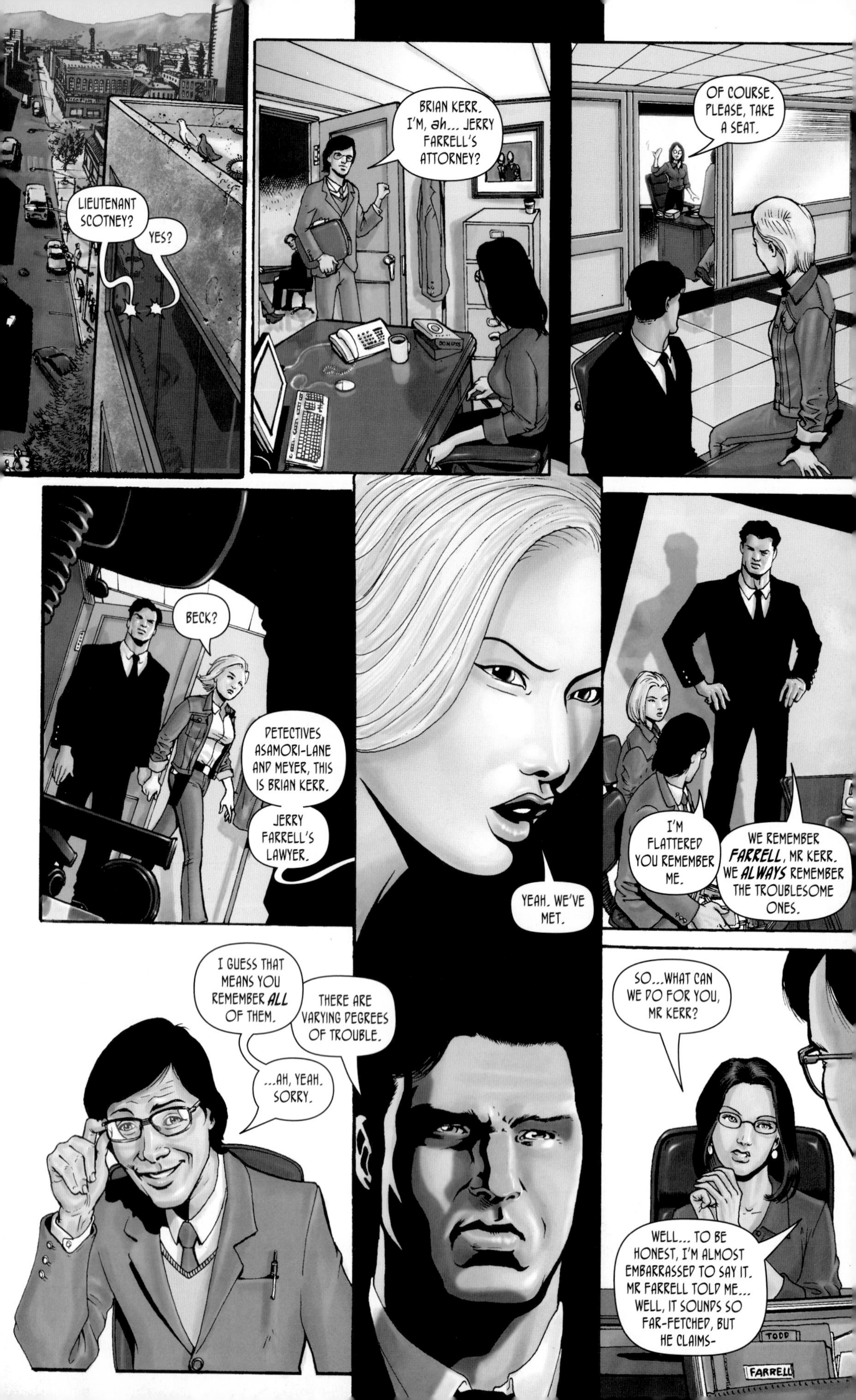
LIEUTENANT SCOTNEY?
YES?
BRIAN KERR. I'M, ah... JERRY FARRELL'S ATTORNEY?
OF COURSE. PLEASE, TAKE A SEAT.
BECK?
DETECTIVES ASAMORI-LANE AND MEYER, THIS IS BRIAN KERR.
JERRY FARRELL'S LAWYER.
YEAH. WE'VE MET.
I'M FLATTERED YOU REMEMBER ME.
WE REMEMBER FARRELL, MR KERR. WE ALWAYS REMEMBER THE TROUBLESOME ONES.
I GUESS THAT MEANS YOU REMEMBER ALL OF THEM.
THERE ARE VARYING DEGREES OF TROUBLE.
...AH, YEAH. SORRY.
SO...WHAT CAN WE DO FOR YOU, MR KERR?
WELL... TO BE HONEST, I'M ALMOST EMBARRASSED TO SAY IT. MR FARRELL TOLD ME... WELL, IT SOUNDS SO FAR-FETCHED, BUT HE CLAIMS-
DONUTS
TODD
FARRELL

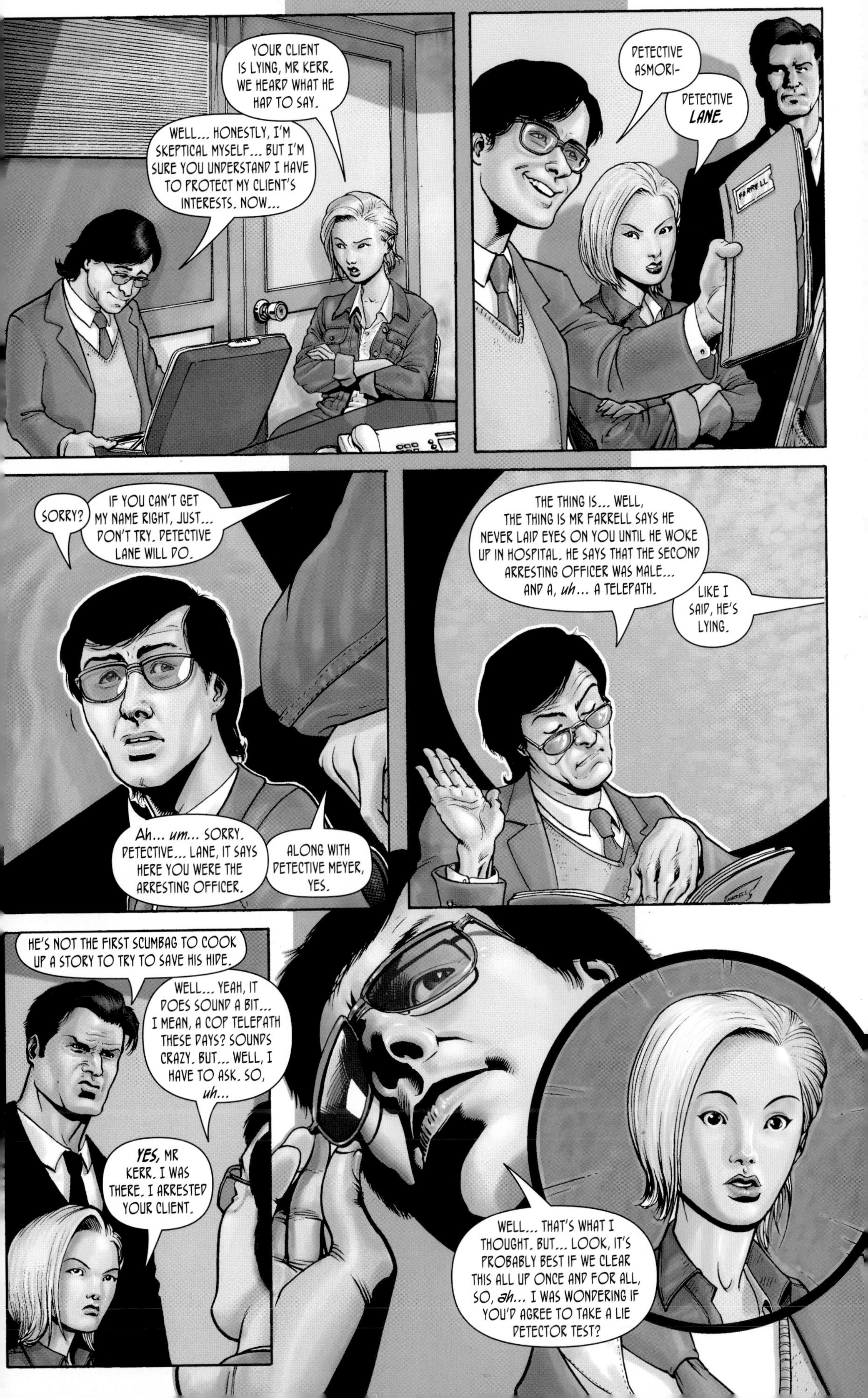
YOUR CLIENT IS LYING, MR KERR. WE HEARD WHAT HE HAD TO SAY.
WELL... HONESTLY, I'M SKEPTICAL MYSELF... BUT I'M SURE YOU UNDERSTAND I HAVE TO PROTECT MY CLIENT'S INTERESTS. NOW...
DETECTIVE ASMORI-
DETECTIVE LANE.
FARRELL
SORRY?
IF YOU CAN'T GET MY NAME RIGHT, JUST... DON'T TRY. DETECTIVE LANE WILL DO.
Ah... um... SORRY. DETECTIVE... LANE, IT SAYS HERE YOU WERE THE ARRESTING OFFICER.
ALONG WITH DETECTIVE MEYER, YES.
THE THING IS... WELL, THE THING IS MR FARRELL SAYS HE NEVER LAID EYES ON YOU UNTIL HE WOKE UP IN HOSPITAL. HE SAYS THAT THE SECOND ARRESTING OFFICER WAS MALE... AND A, uh... A TELEPATH.
LIKE I SAID, HE'S LYING.
HE'S NOT THE FIRST SCUMBAG TO COOK UP A STORY TO TRY TO SAVE HIS HIDE.
WELL... YEAH, IT DOES SOUND A BIT... I MEAN, A COP TELEPATH THESE DAYS? SOUNDS CRAZY. BUT... WELL, I HAVE TO ASK. SO, uh...
YES, MR KERR. I WAS THERE. I ARRESTED YOUR CLIENT.
WELL... THAT'S WHAT I THOUGHT. BUT... LOOK, IT'S PROBABLY BEST IF WE CLEAR THIS ALL UP ONCE AND FOR ALL, SO, ah... I WAS WONDERING IF YOU'D AGREE TO TAKE A LIE DETECTOR TEST?

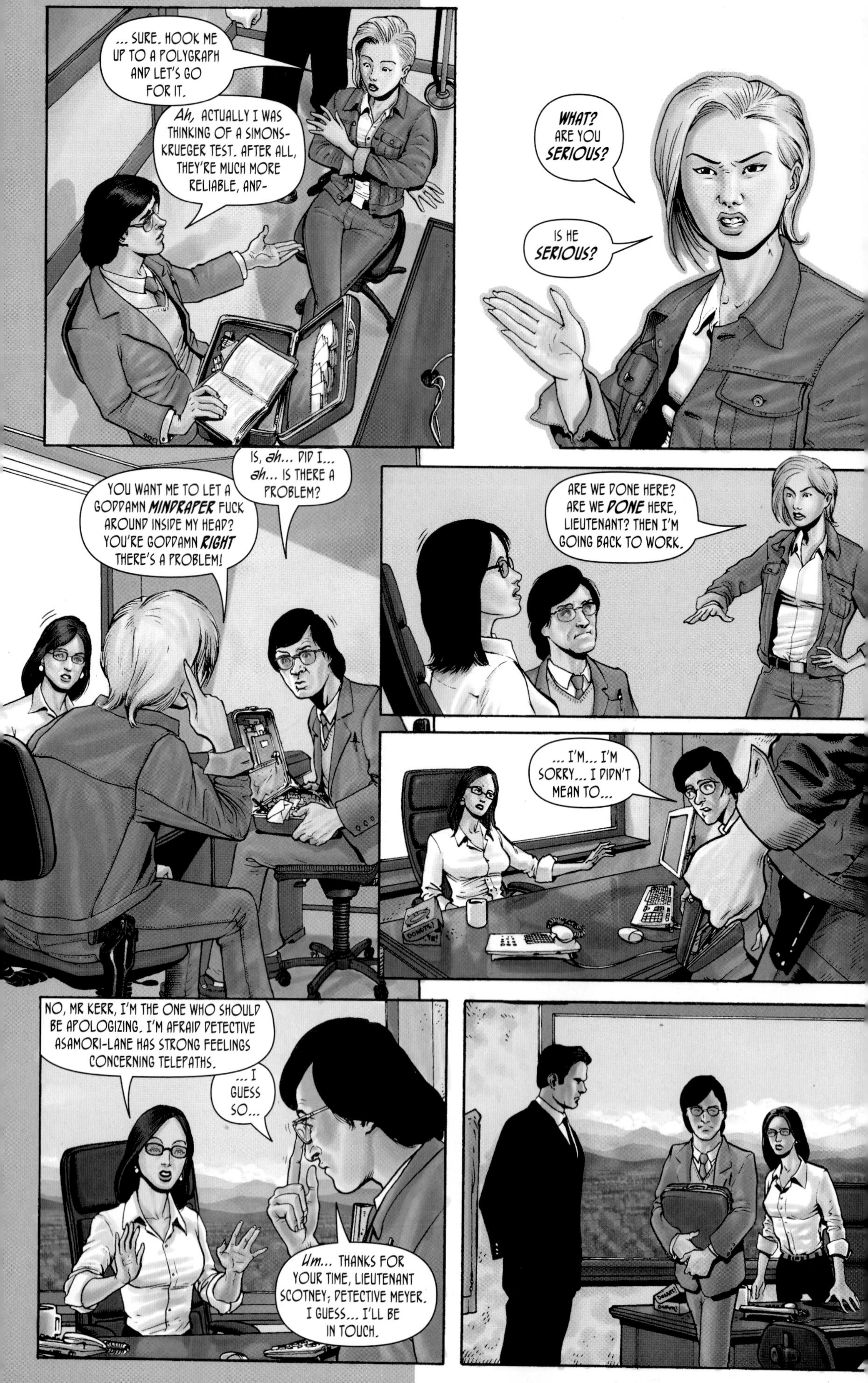
... SURE. HOOK ME UP TO A POLYGRAPH AND LET'S GO FOR IT.
Ah, ACTUALLY I WAS THINKING OF A SIMONS-KRUEGER TEST. AFTER ALL, THEY'RE MUCH MORE RELIABLE, AND-
WHAT? ARE YOU SERIOUS?
IS HE SERIOUS?
YOU WANT ME TO LET A GODDAMN MINDRAPER FUCK AROUND INSIDE MY HEAD? YOU'RE GODDAMN RIGHT THERE'S A PROBLEM!
IS, ah... DID I... ah... IS THERE A PROBLEM?
ARE WE DONE HERE? ARE WE DONE HERE, LIEUTENANT? THEN I'M GOING BACK TO WORK.
... I'M... I'M SORRY... I DIDN'T MEAN TO...
NO, MR KERR, I'M THE ONE WHO SHOULD BE APOLOGIZING. I'M AFRAID DETECTIVE ASAMORI-LANE HAS STRONG FEELINGS CONCERNING TELEPATHS.
... I GUESS SO...
Um... THANKS FOR YOUR TIME, LIEUTENANT SCOTNEY; DETECTIVE MEYER. I GUESS... I'LL BE IN TOUCH.

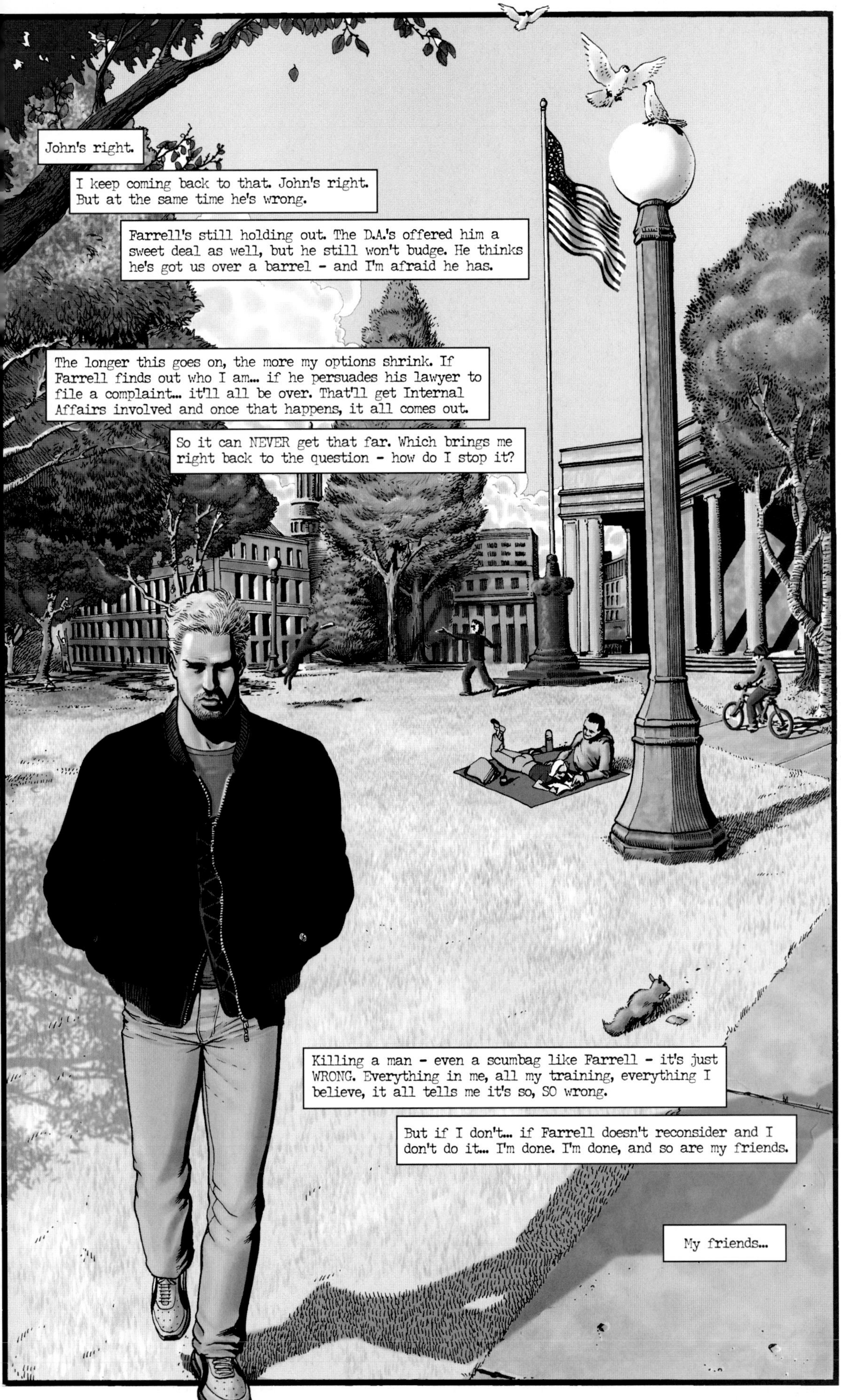
John's right.
I keep coming back to that. John's right. But at the same time he's wrong.
Farrell's still holding out. The D.A.'s offered him a sweet deal as well, but he still won't budge. He thinks he's got us over a barrel - and I'm afraid he has.
The longer this goes on, the more my options shrink. If Farrell finds out who I am... if he persuades his lawyer to file a complaint... it'll all be over. That'll get Internal Affairs involved and once that happens, it all comes out.
So it can NEVER get that far. Which brings me right back to the question - how do I stop it?
Killing a man - even a scumbag like Farrell - it's just WRONG. Everything in me, all my training, everything I believe, it all tells me it's so, SO wrong.
But if I don't... if Farrell doesn't reconsider and I don't do it... I'm done. I'm done, and so are my friends.
My friends...

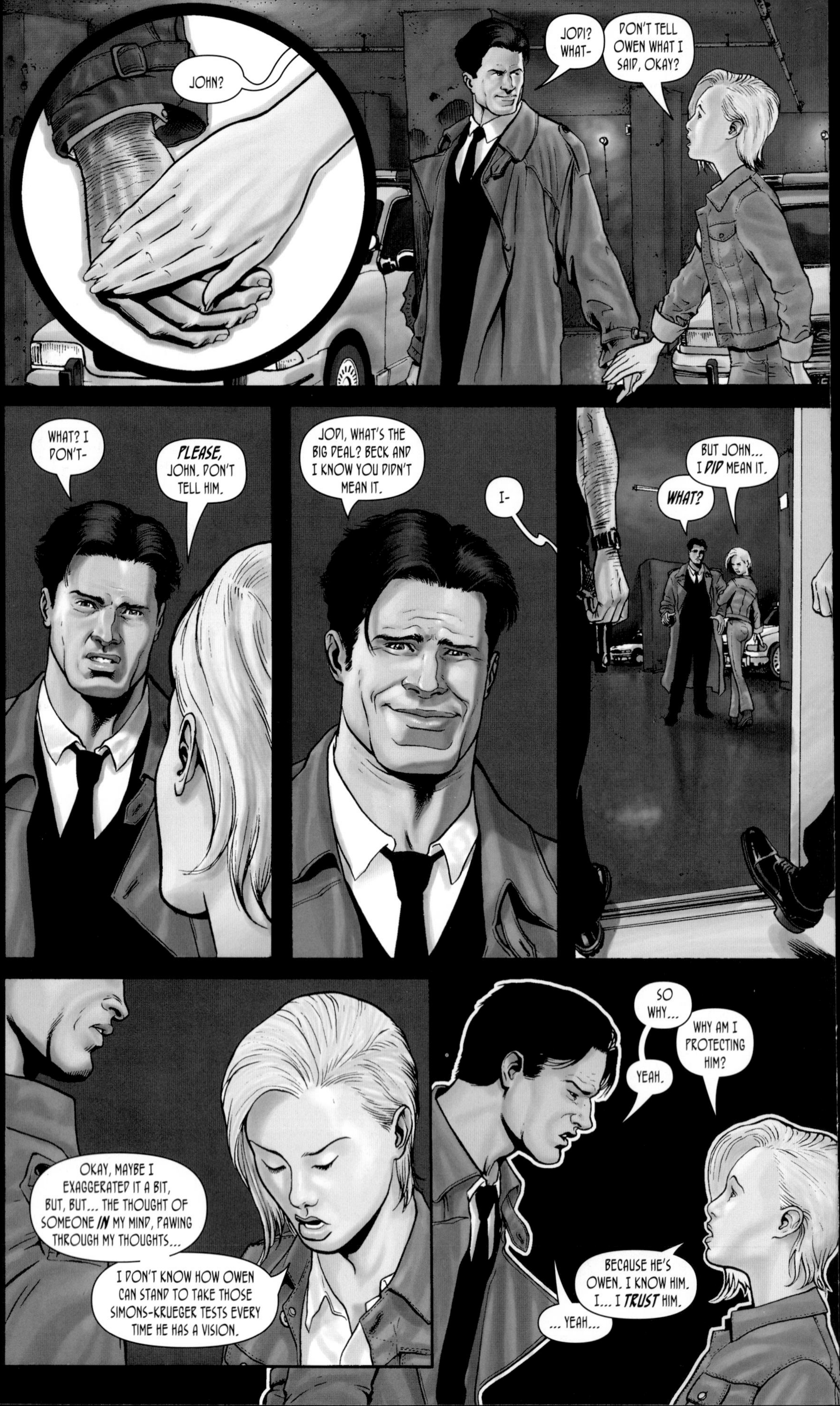
JOHN?
JODI? WHAT-
DON'T TELL OWEN WHAT I SAID, OKAY?
WHAT? I DON'T-
PLEASE, JOHN. DON'T TELL HIM.
JODI, WHAT'S THE BIG DEAL? BECK AND I KNOW YOU DIDN'T MEAN IT.
I-
BUT JOHN... I DID MEAN IT.
WHAT?
OKAY, MAYBE I EXAGGERATED IT A BIT, BUT, BUT... THE THOUGHT OF SOMEONE IN MY MIND, PAWING THROUGH MY THOUGHTS...
I DON'T KNOW HOW OWEN CAN STAND TO TAKE THOSE SIMONS-KRUEGER TESTS EVERY TIME HE HAS A VISION.
SO WHY...
WHY AM I PROTECTING HIM?
YEAH.
BECAUSE HE'S OWEN. I KNOW HIM. I... I TRUST HIM.
... YEAH...

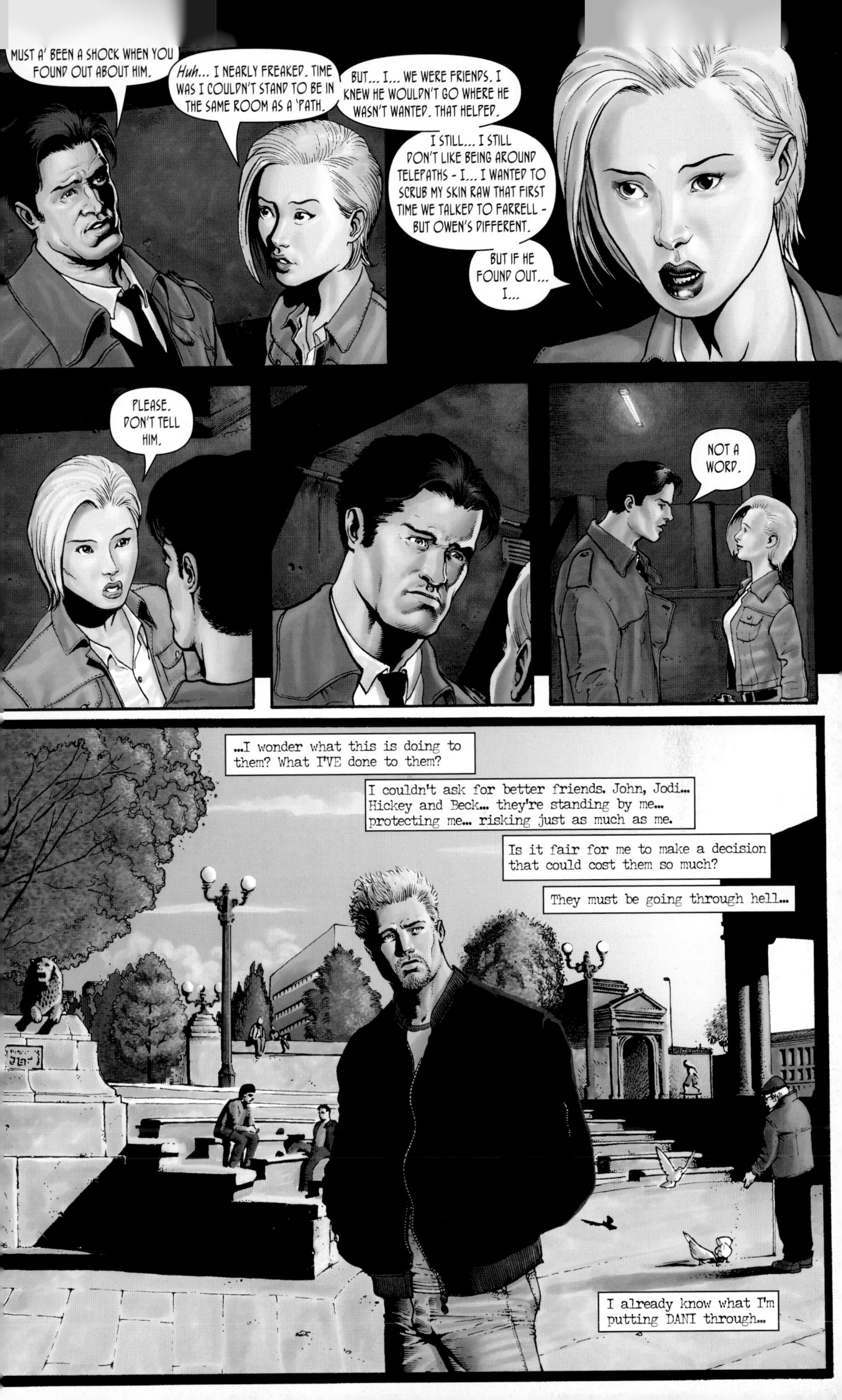
MUST A' BEEN A SHOCK WHEN YOU FOUND OUT ABOUT HIM.
Huh... I NEARLY FREAKED. TIME WAS I COULDN'T STAND TO BE IN THE SAME ROOM AS A 'PATH.
BUT... I... WE WERE FRIENDS. I KNEW HE WOULDN'T GO WHERE HE WASN'T WANTED. THAT HELPED.
I STILL... I STILL DON'T LIKE BEING AROUND TELEPATHS - I... I WANTED TO SCRUB MY SKIN RAW THAT FIRST TIME WE TALKED TO FARRELL - BUT OWEN'S DIFFERENT.
BUT IF HE FOUND OUT... I...
PLEASE. DON'T TELL HIM.
NOT A WORD.
...I wonder what this is doing to them? What I'VE done to them?
I couldn't ask for better friends. John, Jodi... Hickey and Beck... they're standing by me... protecting me... risking just as much as me.
Is it fair for me to make a decision that could cost them so much?
They must be going through hell...
I already know what I'm putting DANI through...

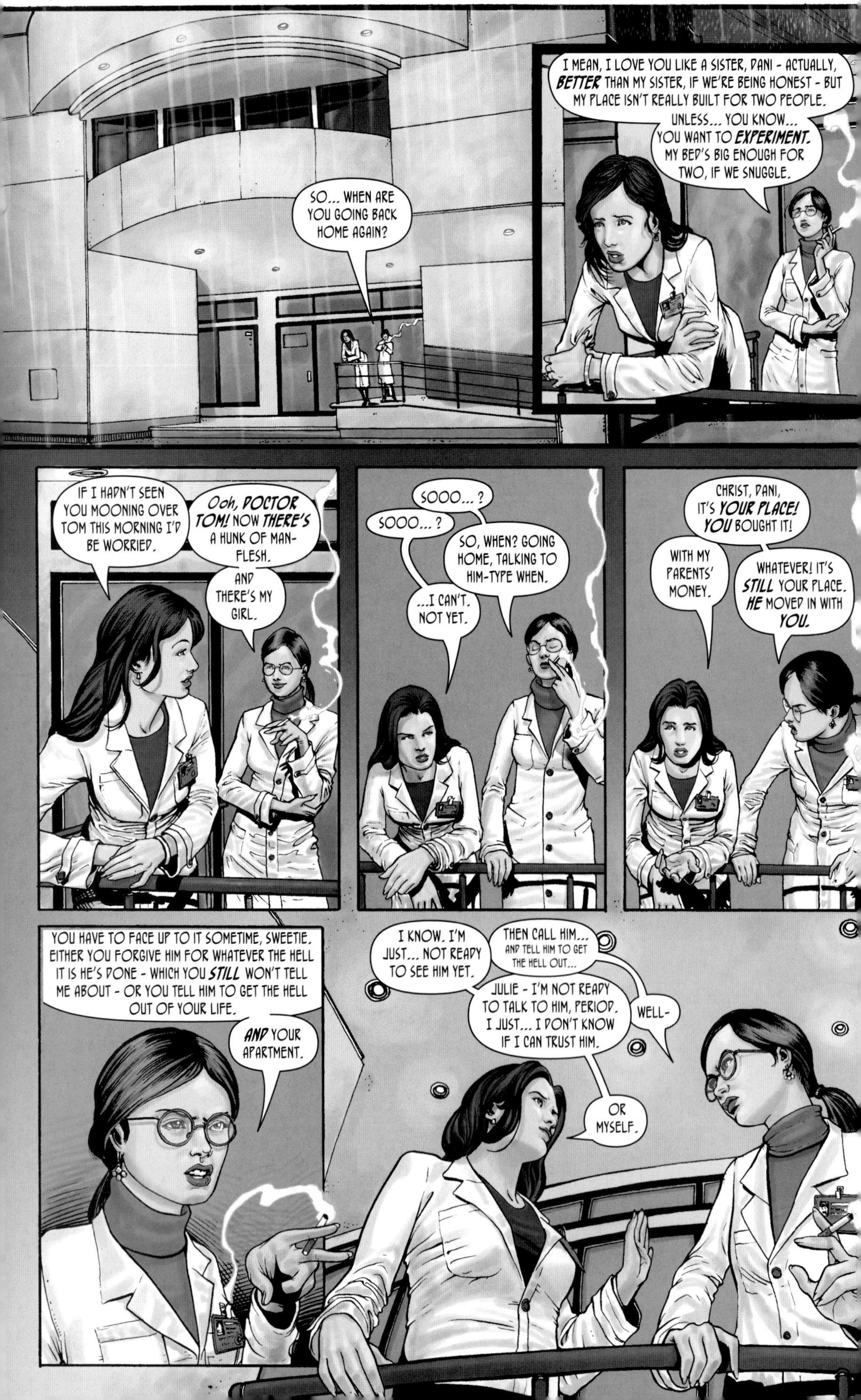
SO... WHEN ARE YOU GOING BACK HOME AGAIN?
I MEAN, I LOVE YOU LIKE A SISTER, DANI - ACTUALLY, BETTER THAN MY SISTER, IF WE'RE BEING HONEST - BUT MY PLACE ISN'T REALLY BUILT FOR TWO PEOPLE.
UNLESS... YOU KNOW... YOU WANT TO EXPERIMENT. MY BED'S BIG ENOUGH FOR TWO, IF WE SNUGGLE.
IF I HADN'T SEEN YOU MOONING OVER TOM THIS MORNING I'D BE WORRIED.
Ooh, DOCTOR TOM! NOW THERE'S A HUNK OF MAN-FLESH.
AND THERE'S MY GIRL.
SOOO...?
SOOO...?
SO, WHEN? GOING HOME, TALKING TO HIM-TYPE WHEN.
...I CAN'T. NOT YET.
CHRIST, DANI, IT'S YOUR PLACE! YOU BOUGHT IT!
WITH MY PARENTS' MONEY.
WHATEVER! IT'S STILL YOUR PLACE. HE MOVED IN WITH YOU.
YOU HAVE TO FACE UP TO IT SOMETIME, SWEETIE. EITHER YOU FORGIVE HIM FOR WHATEVER THE HELL IT IS HE'S DONE - WHICH YOU STILL WON'T TELL ME ABOUT - OR YOU TELL HIM TO GET THE HELL OUT OF YOUR LIFE.
AND YOUR APARTMENT.
I KNOW. I'M JUST... NOT READY TO SEE HIM YET.
THEN CALL HIM... AND TELL HIM TO GET THE HELL OUT...
JULIE - I'M NOT READY TO TALK TO HIM, PERIOD. I JUST... I DON'T KNOW IF I CAN TRUST HIM.
WELL-
OR MYSELF.

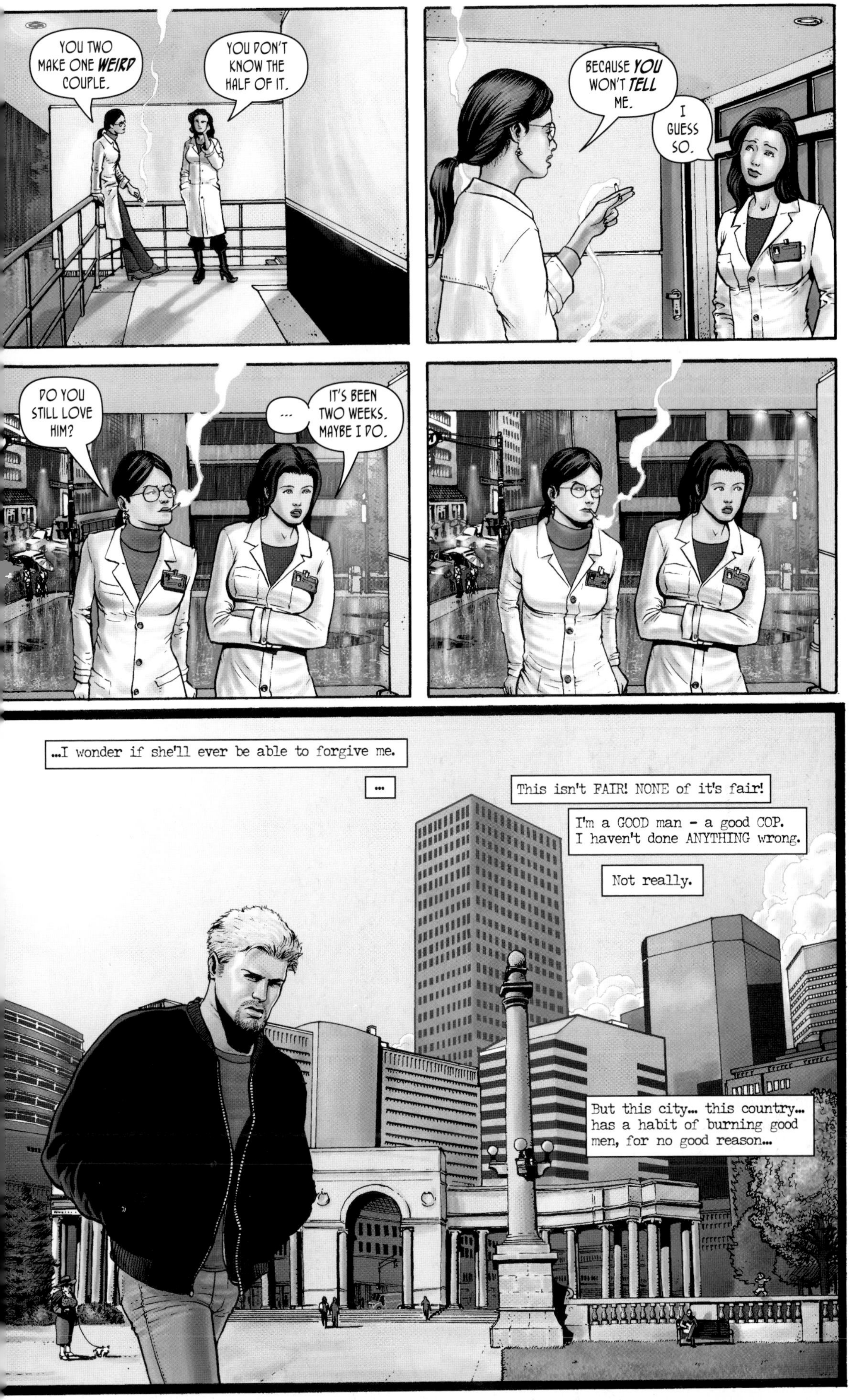

YOU TWO MAKE ONE WEIRD COUPLE.
YOU DON'T KNOW THE HALF OF IT.
BECAUSE YOU WON'T TELL ME.
I GUESS SO.
DO YOU STILL LOVE HIM?
...
IT'S BEEN TWO WEEKS. MAYBE I DO.
...I wonder if she'll ever be able to forgive me.
...
This isn't FAIR! NONE of it's fair!
I'm a GOOD man - a good COP. I haven't done ANYTHING wrong.
Not really.
But this city... this country... has a habit of burning good men, for no good reason...

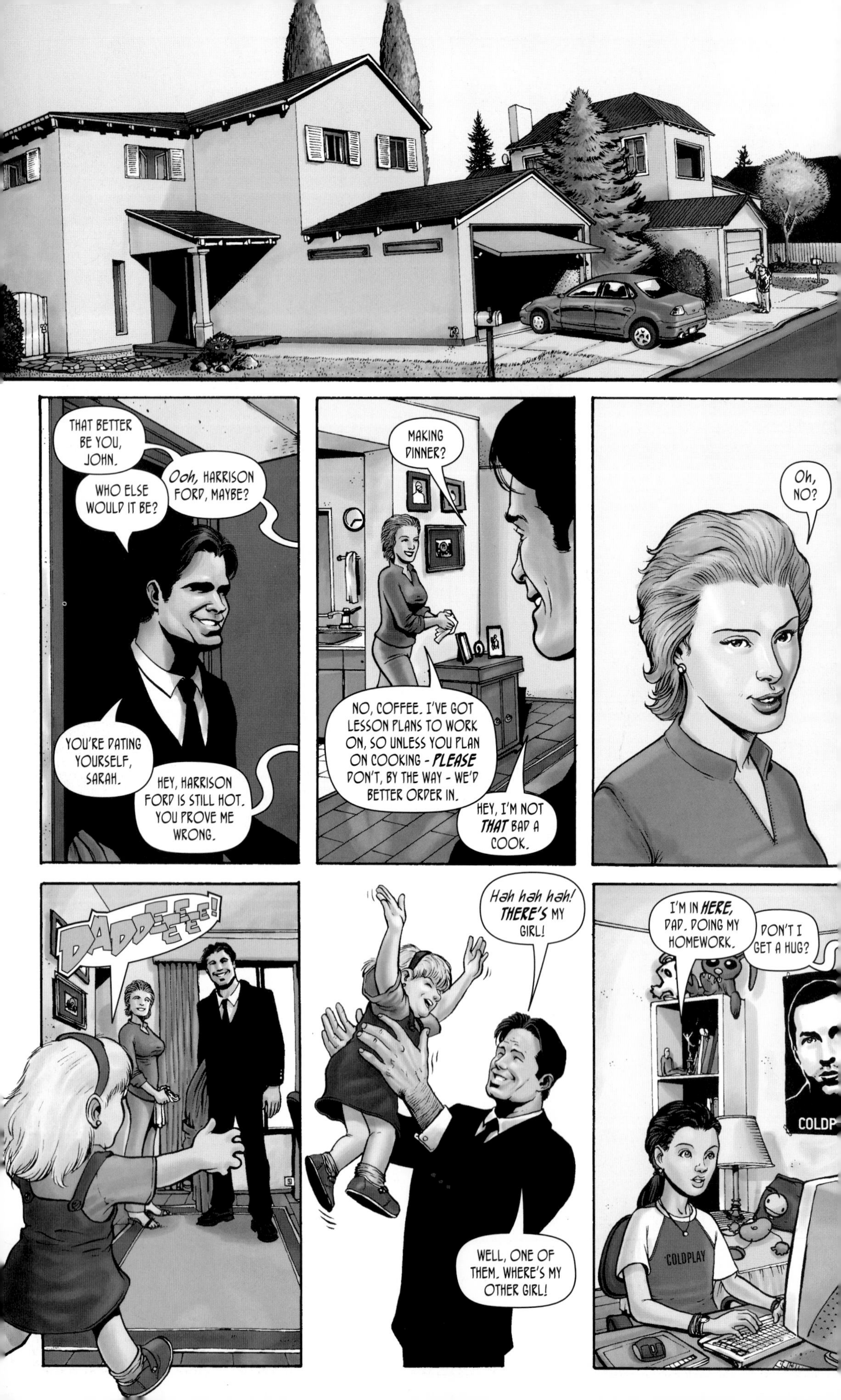
THAT BETTER BE YOU, JOHN.
WHO ELSE WOULD IT BE?
Ooh, HARRISON FORD, MAYBE?
YOU'RE DATING YOURSELF, SARAH.
HEY, HARRISON FORD IS STILL HOT. YOU PROVE ME WRONG.
MAKING DINNER?
NO, COFFEE. I'VE GOT LESSON PLANS TO WORK ON, SO UNLESS YOU PLAN ON COOKING - PLEASE DON'T, BY THE WAY - WE'D BETTER ORDER IN.
HEY, I'M NOT THAT BAD A COOK.
Oh, NO?
DADDEEEEE!
Hah hah hah! THERE'S MY GIRL!
WELL, ONE OF THEM. WHERE'S MY OTHER GIRL!
I'M IN HERE, DAD. DOING MY HOMEWORK.
DON'T I GET A HUG?
COLDP
COLDPLAY

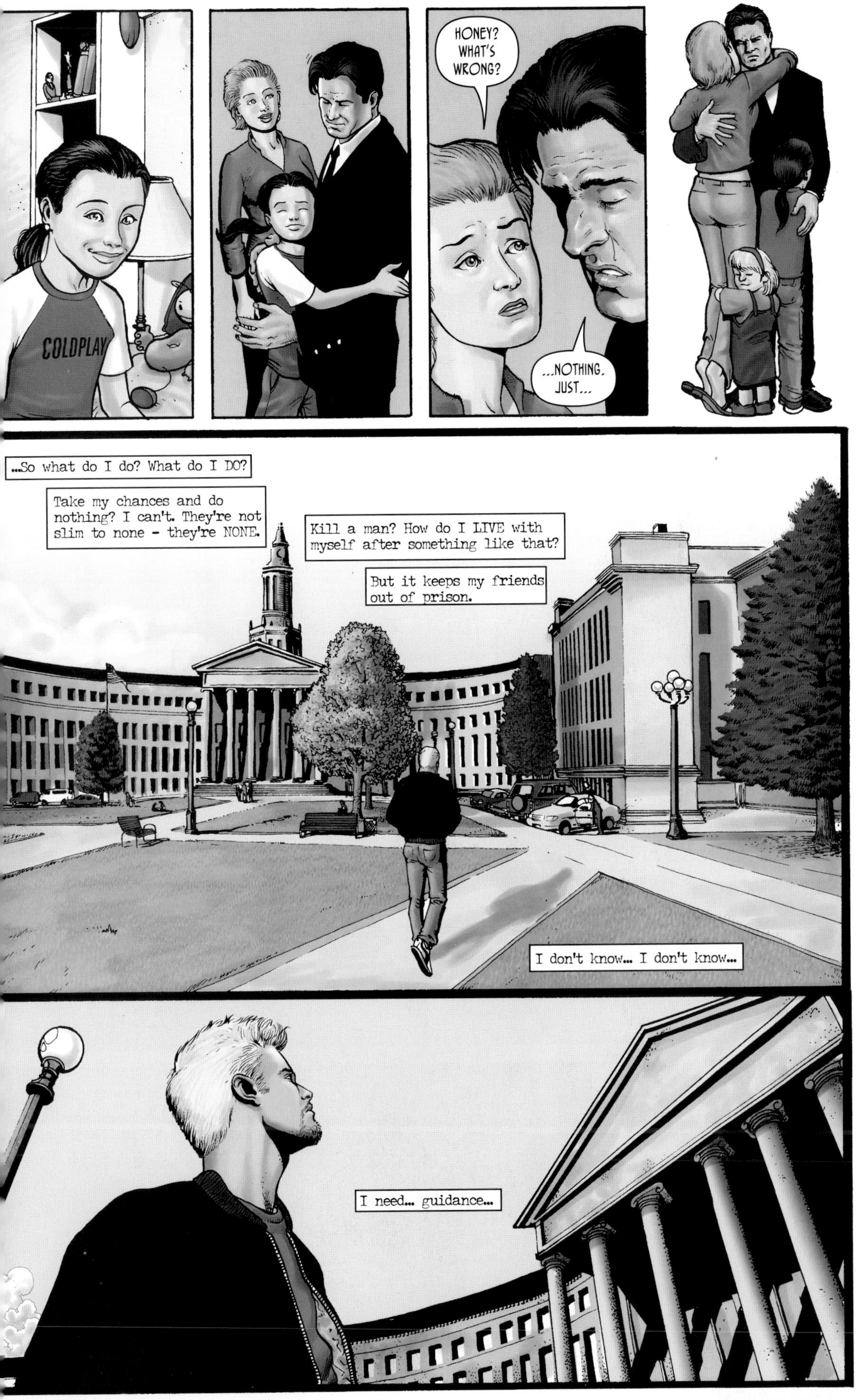
COLDPLAY
HONEY? WHAT'S WRONG?
...NOTHING. JUST...
...So what do I do? What do I DO?
Take my chances and do nothing? I can't. They're not slim to none - they're NONE.
Kill a man? How do I LIVE with myself after something like that?
But it keeps my friends out of prison.
I don't know... I don't know...
I need... guidance...

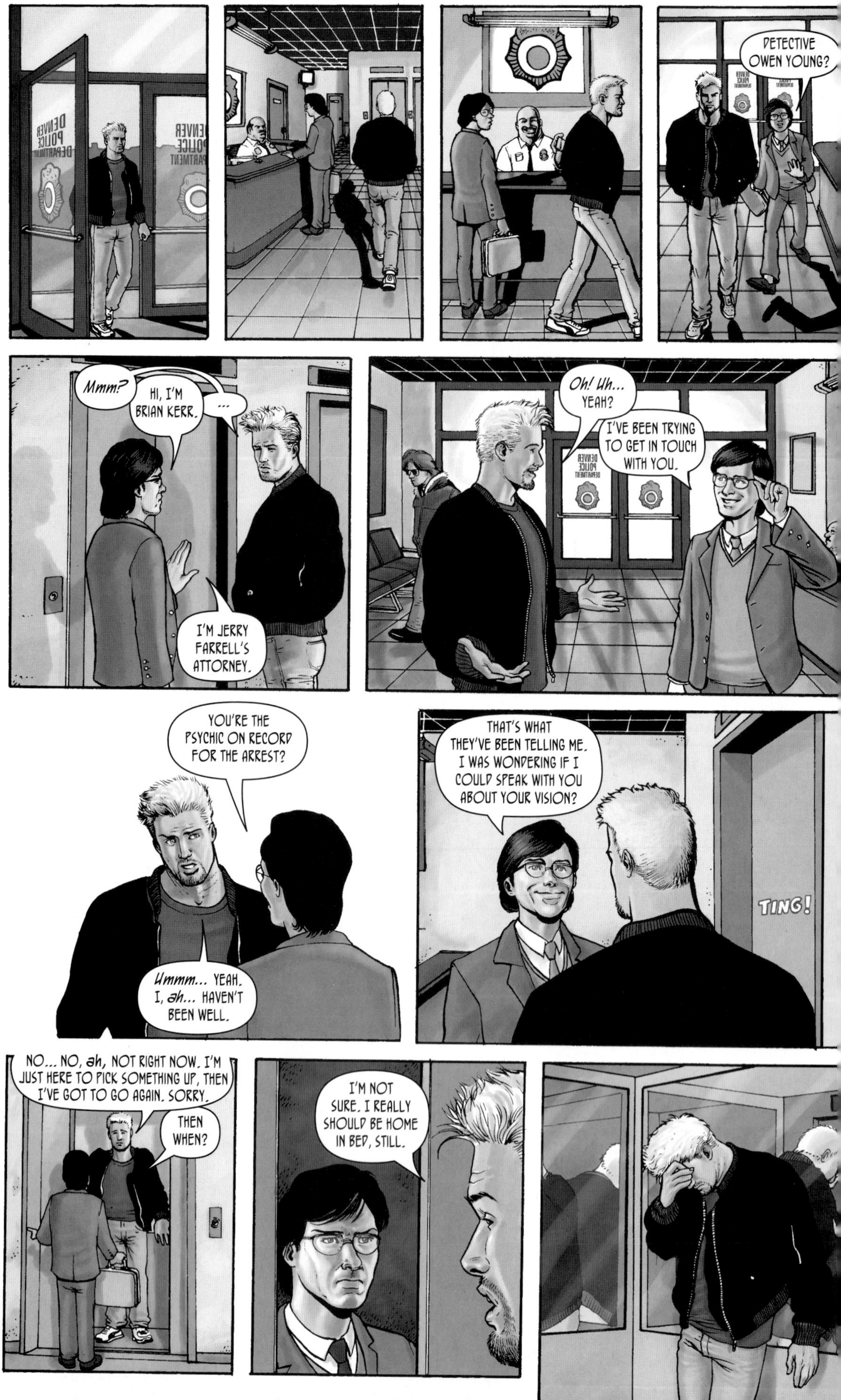
DETECTIVE OWEN YOUNG?
Mmm?
HI, I'M BRIAN KERR.
...
I'M JERRY FARRELL'S ATTORNEY.
Oh! Uh... YEAH?
I'VE BEEN TRYING TO GET IN TOUCH WITH YOU.
YOU'RE THE PSYCHIC ON RECORD FOR THE ARREST?
Ummm... YEAH. I, ah... HAVEN'T BEEN WELL.
THAT'S WHAT THEY'VE BEEN TELLING ME. I WAS WONDERING IF I COULD SPEAK WITH YOU ABOUT YOUR VISION?
TING!
NO... NO, ah, NOT RIGHT NOW. I'M JUST HERE TO PICK SOMETHING UP, THEN I'VE GOT TO GO AGAIN. SORRY.
THEN WHEN?
I'M NOT SURE. I REALLY SHOULD BE HOME IN BED, STILL.

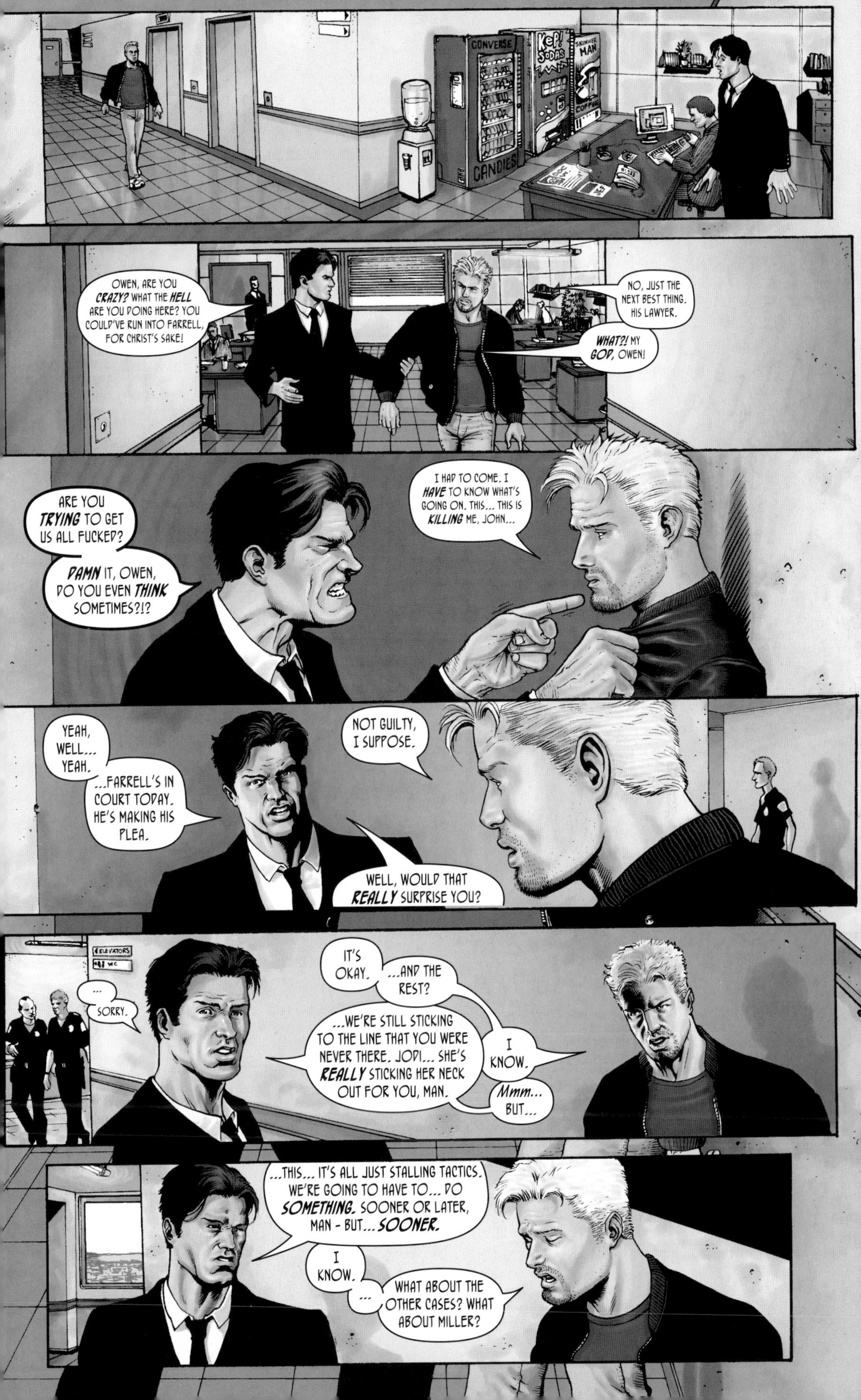
CONVERSE
CANDIES
KEP! SODAS
SKINNER MAN COFFEE
OWEN, ARE YOU CRAZY? WHAT THE HELL ARE YOU DOING HERE? YOU COULD'VE RUN INTO FARRELL, FOR CHRIST'S SAKE!
NO, JUST THE NEXT BEST THING. HIS LAWYER.
WHAT?! MY GOD, OWEN!
ARE YOU TRYING TO GET US ALL FUCKED?
DAMN IT, OWEN, DO YOU EVEN THINK SOMETIMES?!?
I HAD TO COME. I HAVE TO KNOW WHAT'S GOING ON. THIS... THIS IS KILLING ME, JOHN...
YEAH, WELL... YEAH.
...FARRELL'S IN COURT TODAY. HE'S MAKING HIS PLEA.
NOT GUILTY, I SUPPOSE.
WELL, WOULD THAT REALLY SURPRISE YOU?
ELEVATORS
WC
...
SORRY.
IT'S OKAY.
...AND THE REST?
...WE'RE STILL STICKING TO THE LINE THAT YOU WERE NEVER THERE. JODI... SHE'S REALLY STICKING HER NECK OUT FOR YOU, MAN.
I KNOW.
Mmm... BUT...
...THIS... IT'S ALL JUST STALLING TACTICS. WE'RE GOING TO HAVE TO... DO SOMETHING. SOONER OR LATER, MAN - BUT... SOONER.
I KNOW.
...
WHAT ABOUT THE OTHER CASES? WHAT ABOUT MILLER?

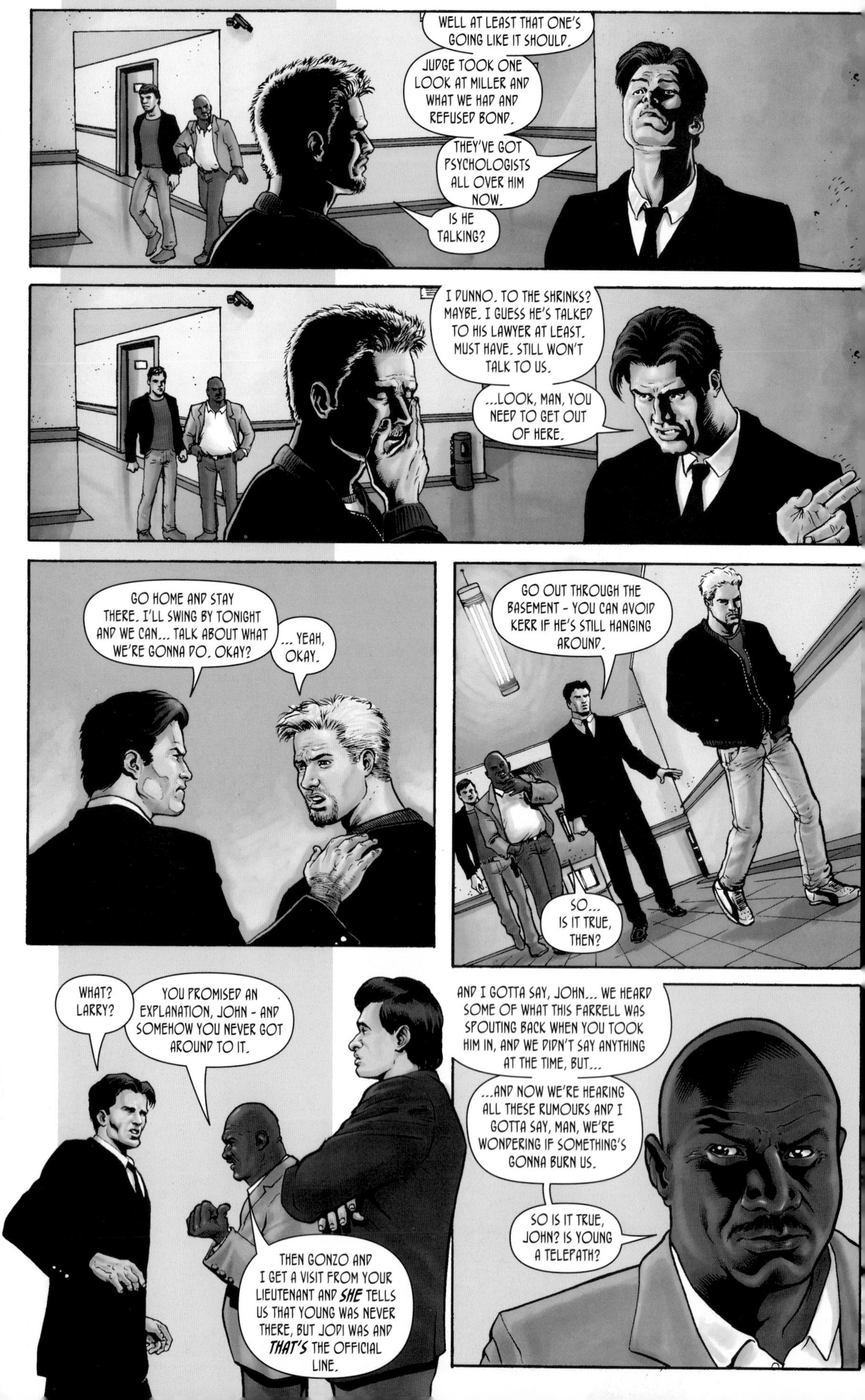
WELL AT LEAST THAT ONE'S GOING LIKE IT SHOULD.
JUDGE TOOK ONE LOOK AT MILLER AND WHAT WE HAD AND REFUSED BOND.
THEY'VE GOT PSYCHOLOGISTS ALL OVER HIM NOW.
IS HE TALKING?
I DUNNO. TO THE SHRINKS? MAYBE. I GUESS HE'S TALKED TO HIS LAWYER AT LEAST. MUST HAVE. STILL WON'T TALK TO US.
...LOOK, MAN, YOU NEED TO GET OUT OF HERE.
GO HOME AND STAY THERE. I'LL SWING BY TONIGHT AND WE CAN... TALK ABOUT WHAT WE'RE GONNA DO. OKAY?
... YEAH, OKAY.
GO OUT THROUGH THE BASEMENT - YOU CAN AVOID KERR IF HE'S STILL HANGING AROUND.
SO... IS IT TRUE, THEN?
WHAT? LARRY?
YOU PROMISED AN EXPLANATION, JOHN - AND SOMEHOW YOU NEVER GOT AROUND TO IT.
THEN GONZO AND I GET A VISIT FROM YOUR LIEUTENANT AND *SHE* TELLS US THAT YOUNG WAS NEVER THERE, BUT JODI WAS AND *THAT'S* THE OFFICIAL LINE.
AND I GOTTA SAY, JOHN... WE HEARD SOME OF WHAT THIS FARRELL WAS SPOUTING BACK WHEN YOU TOOK HIM IN, AND WE DIDN'T SAY ANYTHING AT THE TIME, BUT...
...AND NOW WE'RE HEARING ALL THESE RUMOURS AND I GOTTA SAY, MAN, WE'RE WONDERING IF SOMETHING'S GONNA BURN US.
SO IS IT TRUE, JOHN? IS YOUNG A TELEPATH?

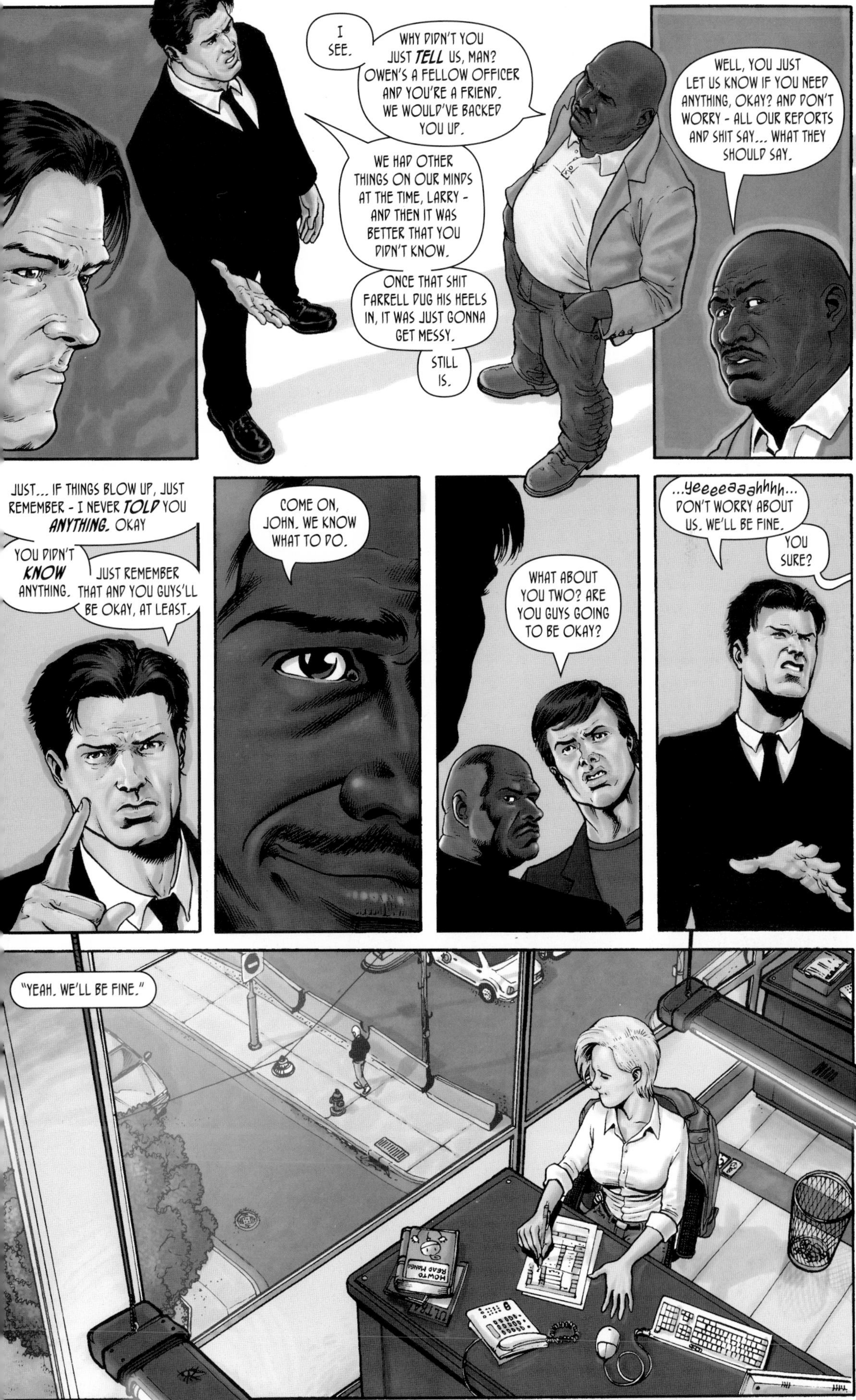

I SEE.
WHY DIDN'T YOU JUST TELL US, MAN? OWEN'S A FELLOW OFFICER AND YOU'RE A FRIEND. WE WOULD'VE BACKED YOU UP.
WE HAD OTHER THINGS ON OUR MINDS AT THE TIME, LARRY - AND THEN IT WAS BETTER THAT YOU DIDN'T KNOW.
ONCE THAT SHIT FARRELL DUG HIS HEELS IN, IT WAS JUST GONNA GET MESSY.
STILL IS.
WELL, YOU JUST LET US KNOW IF YOU NEED ANYTHING, OKAY? AND DON'T WORRY - ALL OUR REPORTS AND SHIT SAY... WHAT THEY SHOULD SAY.
JUST... IF THINGS BLOW UP, JUST REMEMBER - I NEVER TOLD YOU ANYTHING. OKAY
YOU DIDN'T KNOW ANYTHING.
JUST REMEMBER THAT AND YOU GUYS'LL BE OKAY, AT LEAST.
COME ON, JOHN. WE KNOW WHAT TO DO.
WHAT ABOUT YOU TWO? ARE YOU GUYS GOING TO BE OKAY?
...yeeeeaaahhhh... DON'T WORRY ABOUT US. WE'LL BE FINE.
YOU SURE?
"YEAH. WE'LL BE FINE."

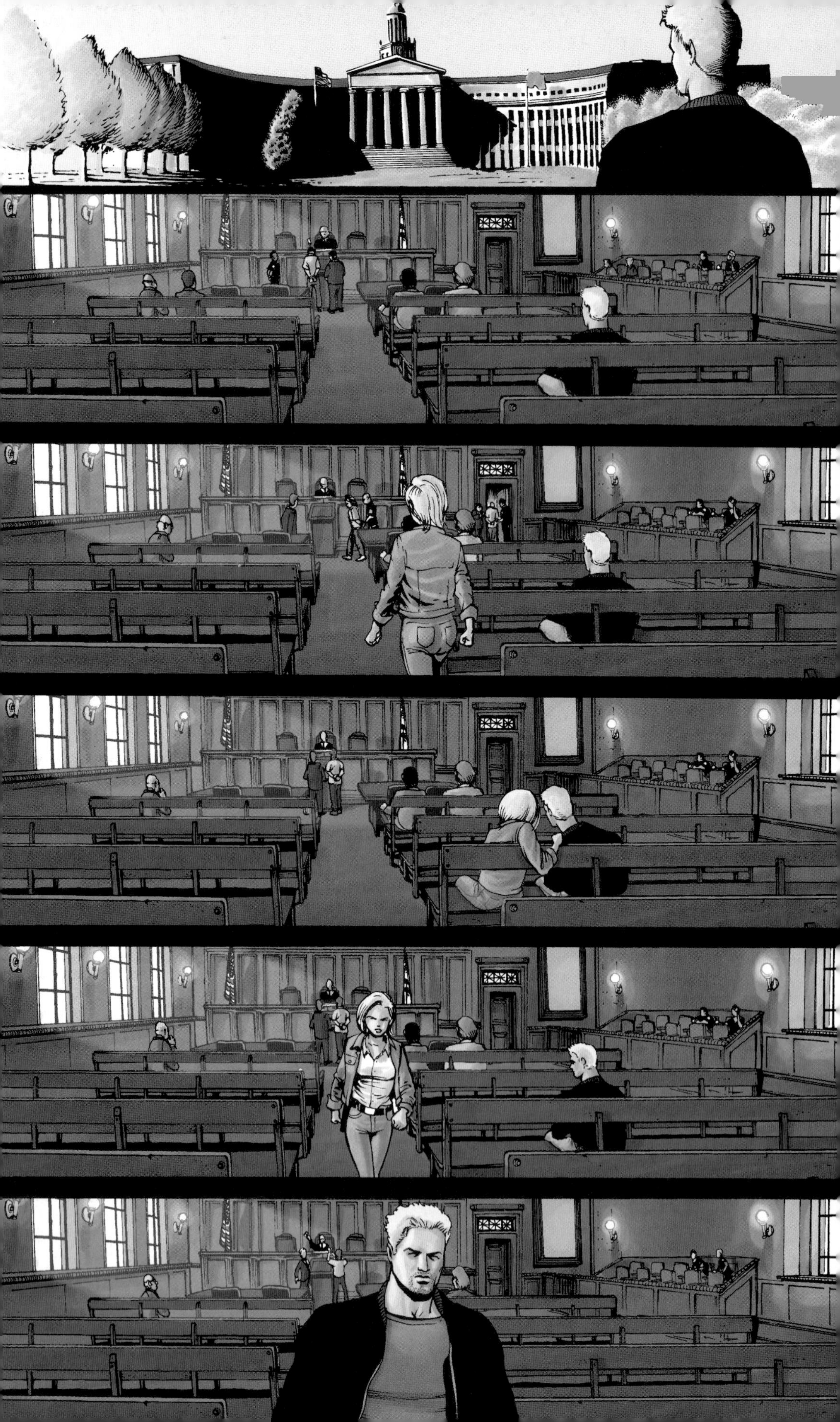

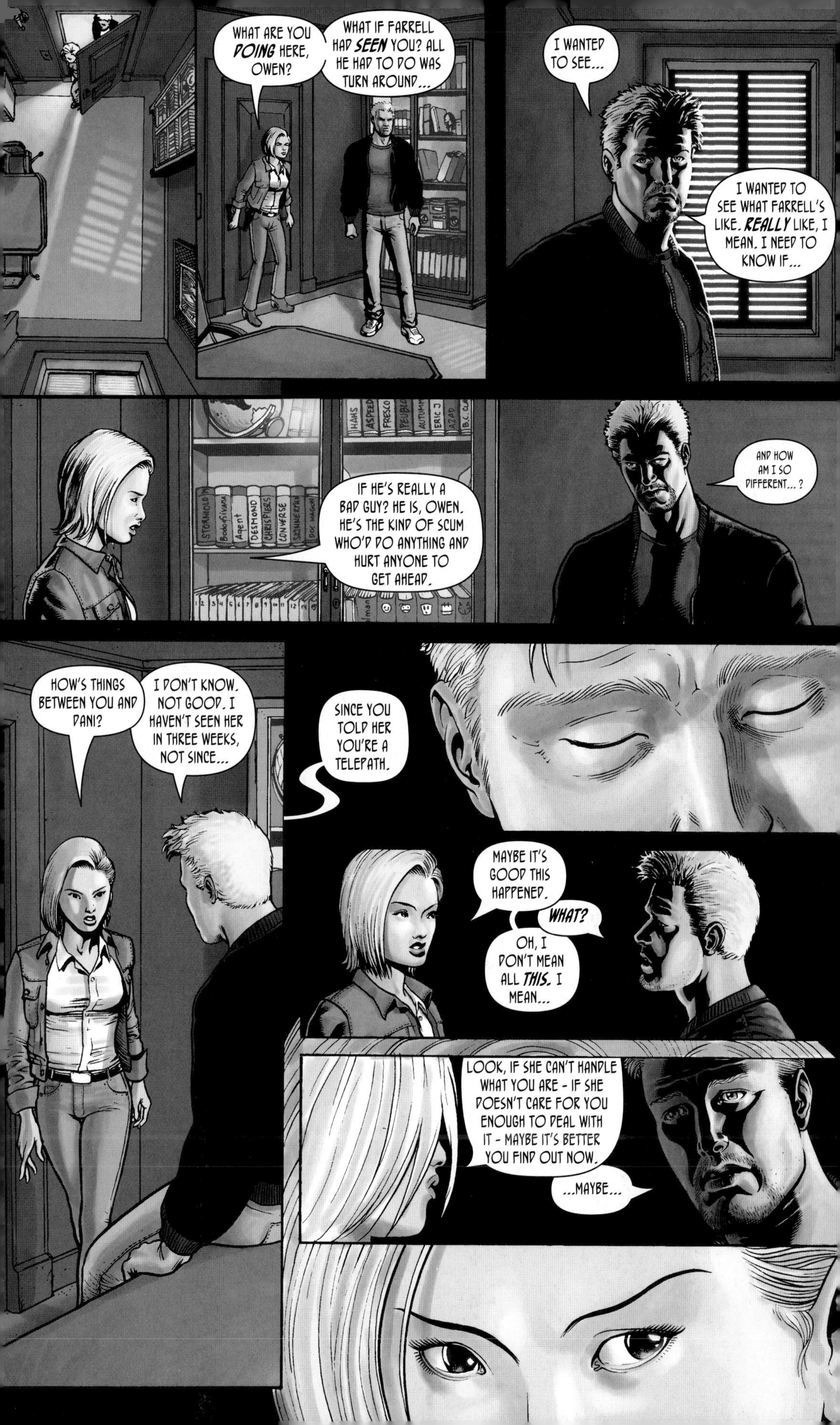

WHAT ARE YOU DOING HERE, OWEN?
WHAT IF FARRELL HAD SEEN YOU? ALL HE HAD TO DO WAS TURN AROUND...
I WANTED TO SEE...
I WANTED TO SEE WHAT FARRELL'S LIKE. REALLY LIKE, I MEAN. I NEED TO KNOW IF...
IF HE'S REALLY A BAD GUY? HE IS, OWEN. HE'S THE KIND OF SCUM WHO'D DO ANYTHING AND HURT ANYONE TO GET AHEAD.
AND HOW AM I SO DIFFERENT... ?
HOW'S THINGS BETWEEN YOU AND DANI?
I DON'T KNOW. NOT GOOD. I HAVEN'T SEEN HER IN THREE WEEKS, NOT SINCE...
SINCE YOU TOLD HER YOU'RE A TELEPATH.
MAYBE IT'S GOOD THIS HAPPENED.
WHAT?
OH, I DON'T MEAN ALL THIS. I MEAN...
LOOK, IF SHE CAN'T HANDLE WHAT YOU ARE - IF SHE DOESN'T CARE FOR YOU ENOUGH TO DEAL WITH IT - MAYBE IT'S BETTER YOU FIND OUT NOW.
...MAYBE...

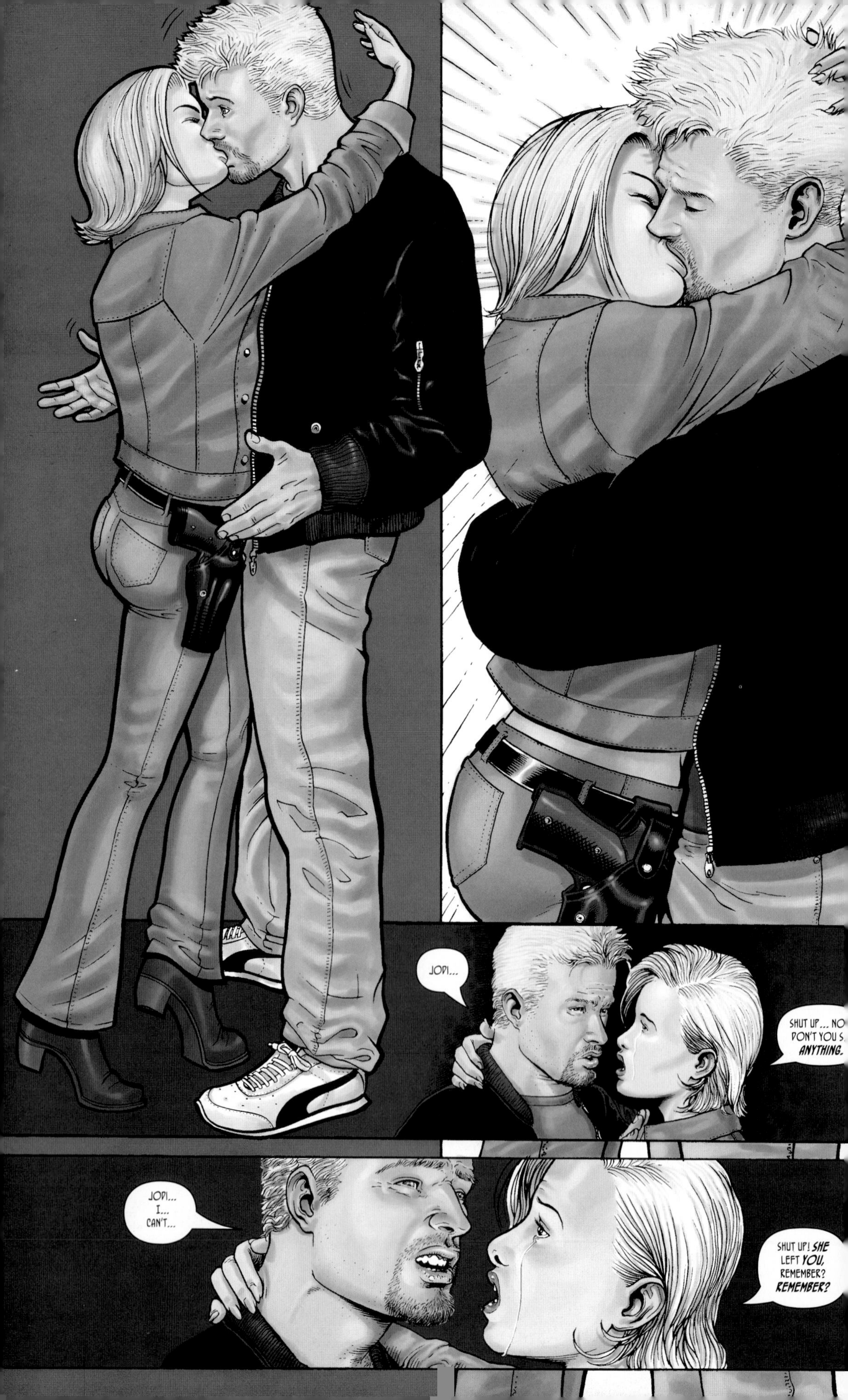
JODI...
SHUT UP... NO
DON'T YOU S
ANYTHING.
JODI... I... CAN'T...
SHUT UP! SHE LEFT YOU, REMEMBER? REMEMBER?

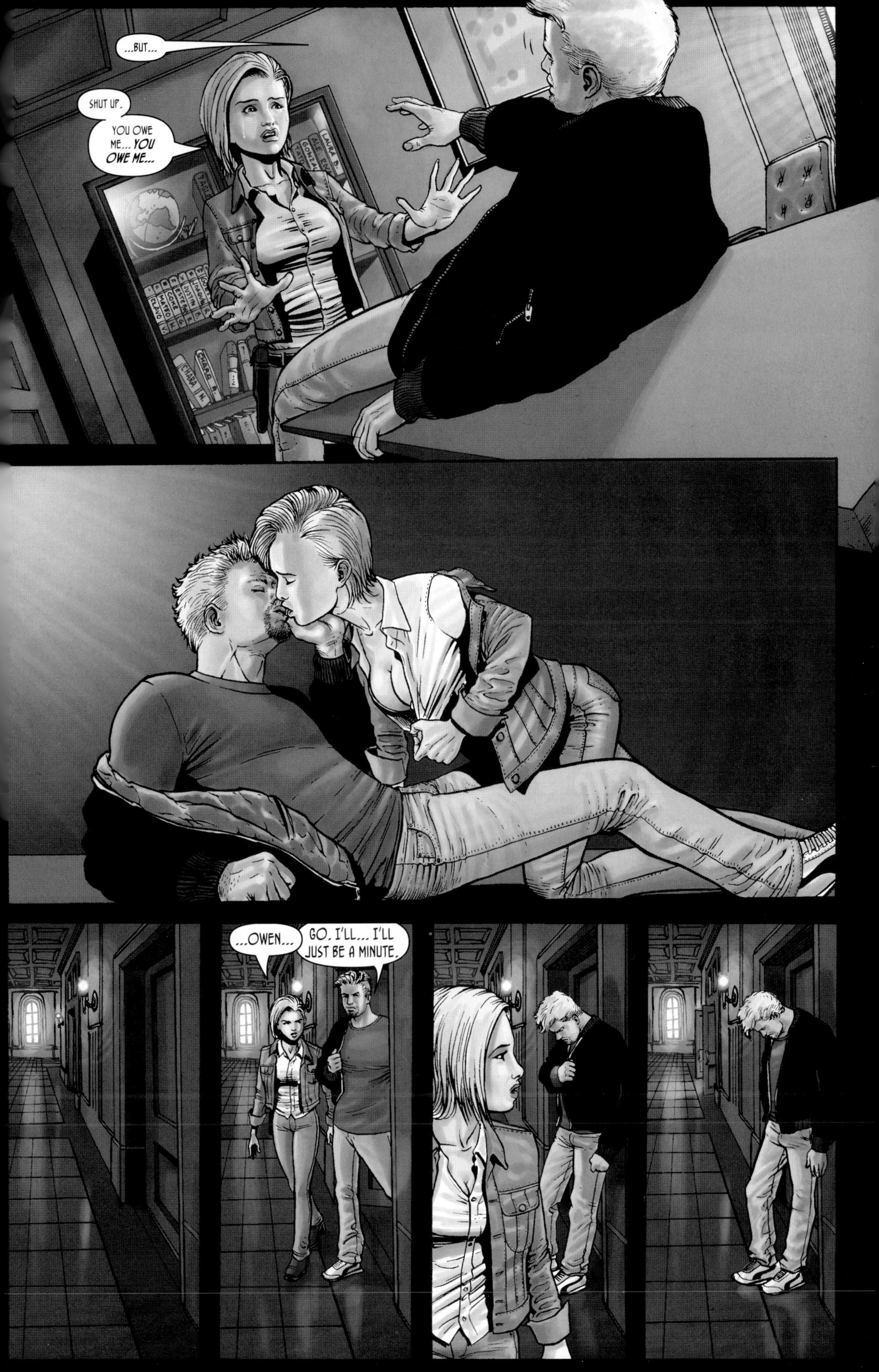
...BUT...
SHUT UP.
YOU OWE ME... YOU OWE ME...
...OWEN...
GO. I'LL... I'LL JUST BE A MINUTE.

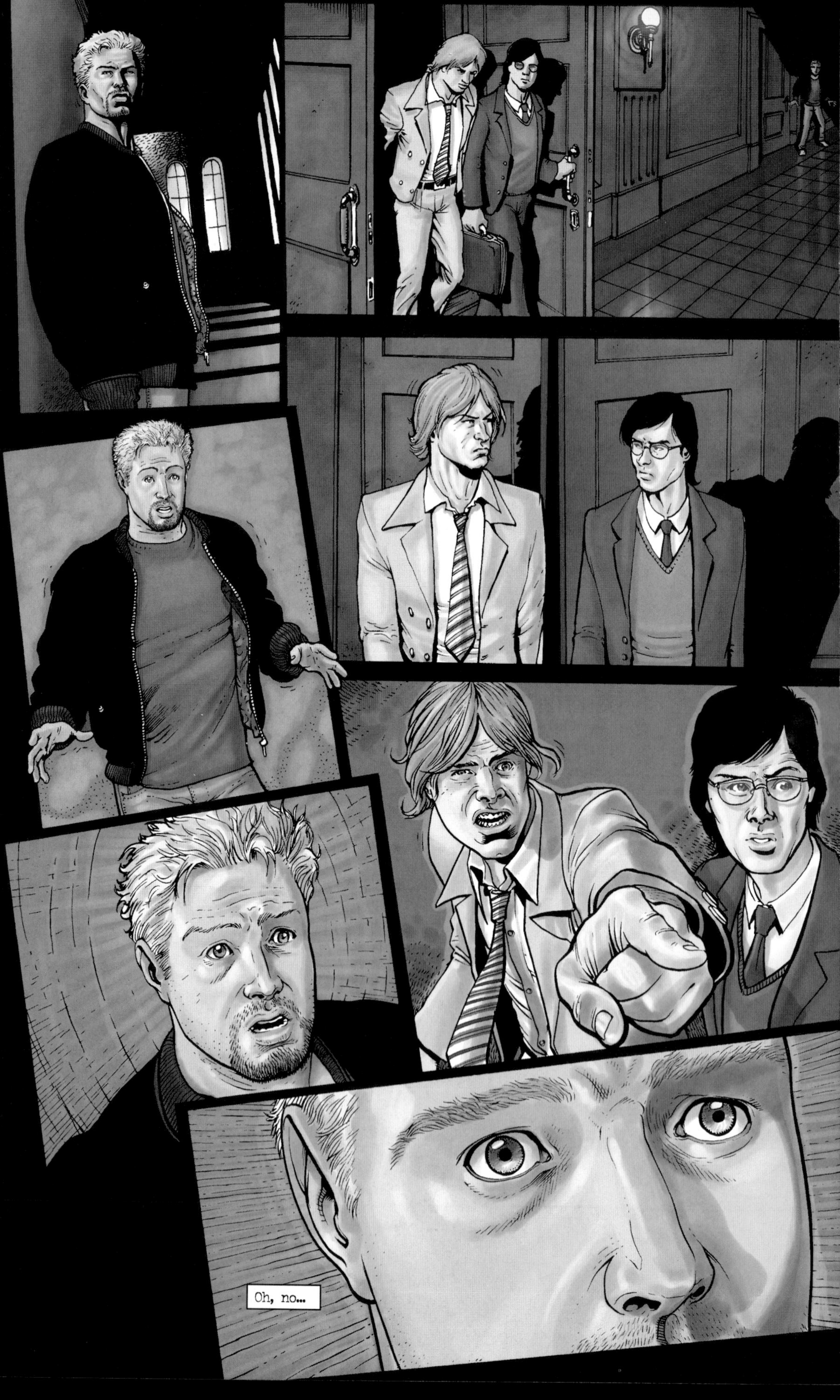
Oh, no...

CHAPTER FOUR

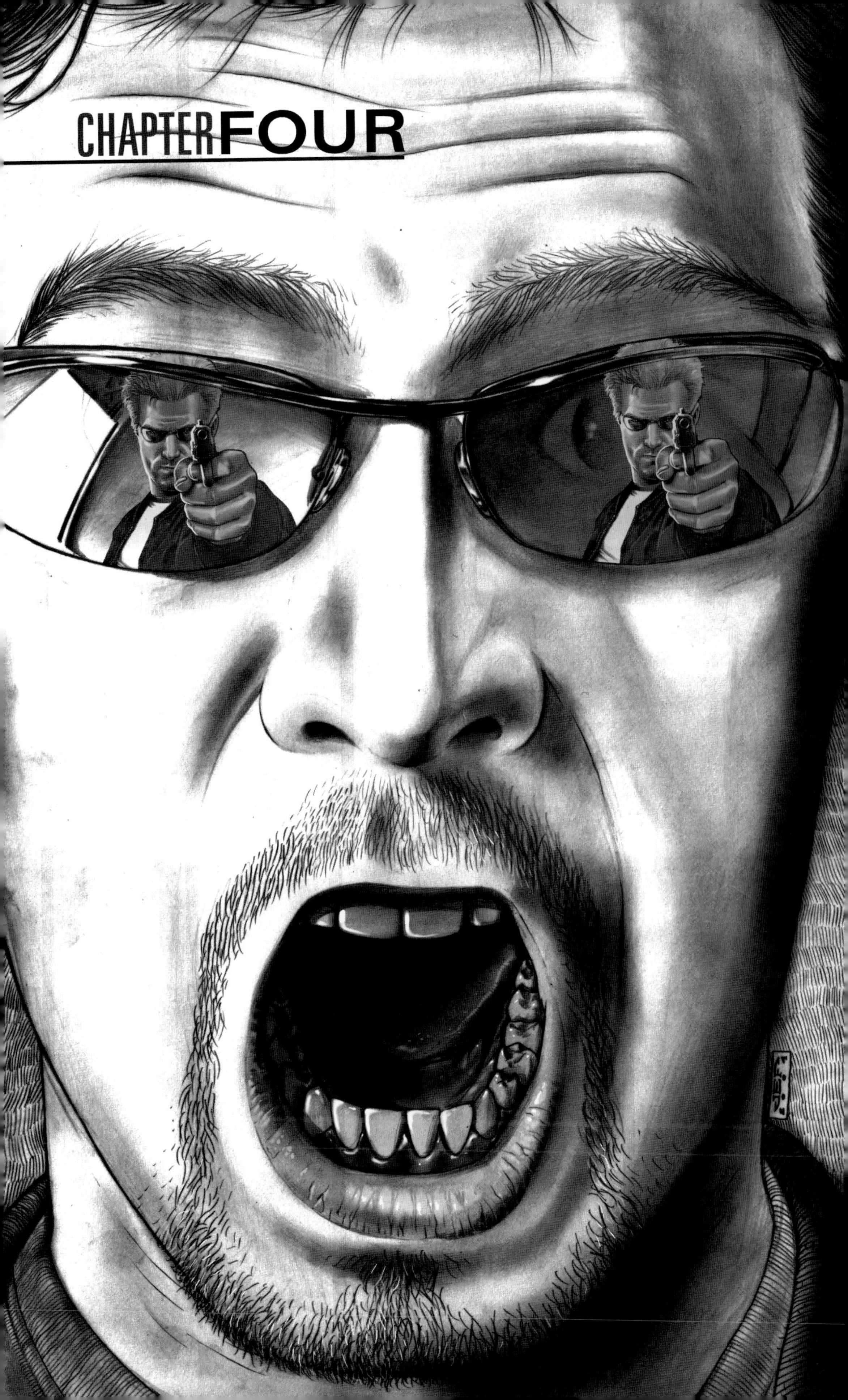

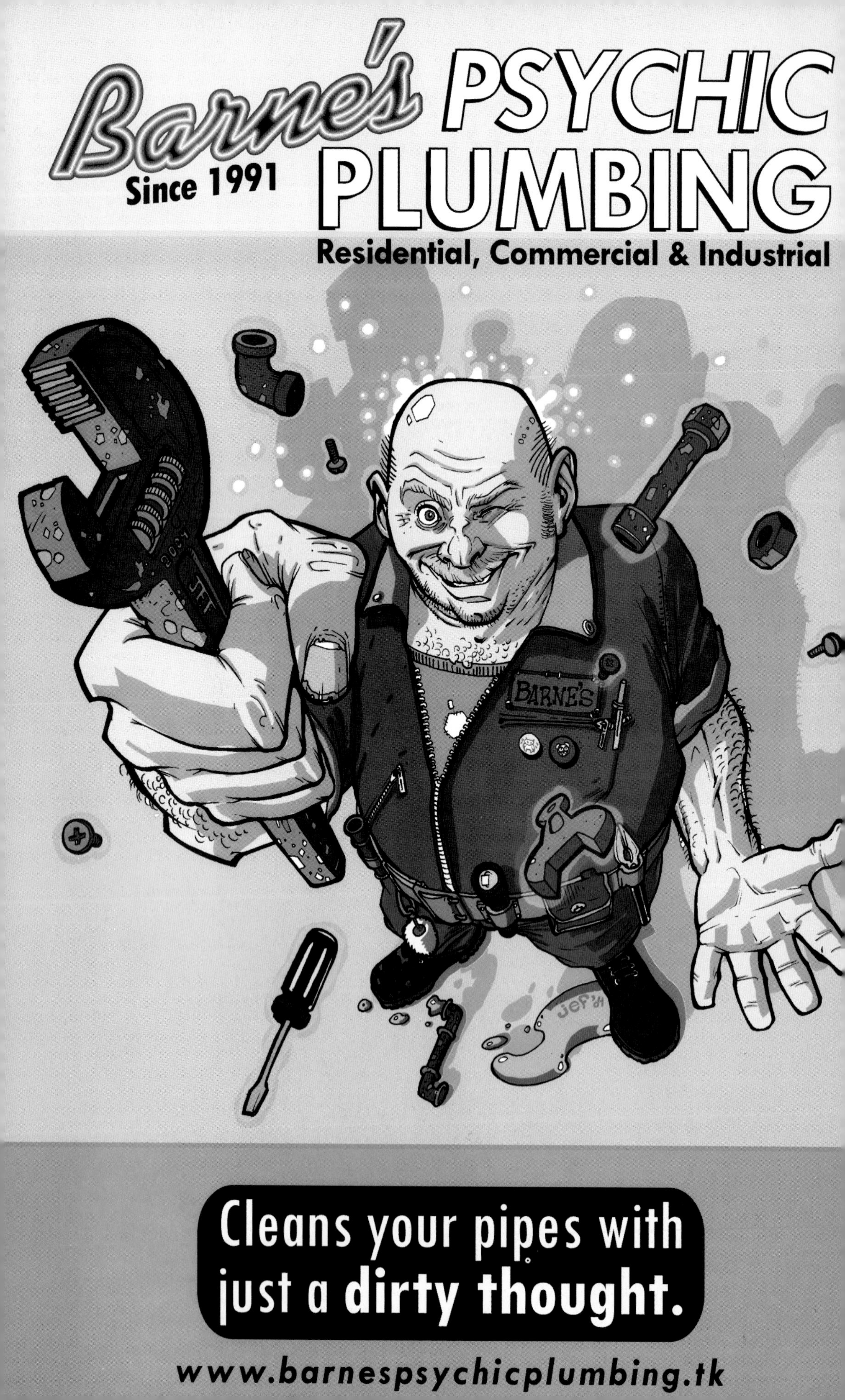
Barne's PSYCHIC PLUMBING
Since 1991
Residential, Commercial & Industrial
BARNE'S
Cleans your pipes with just a dirty thought.
www.barnespsychicplumbing.tk

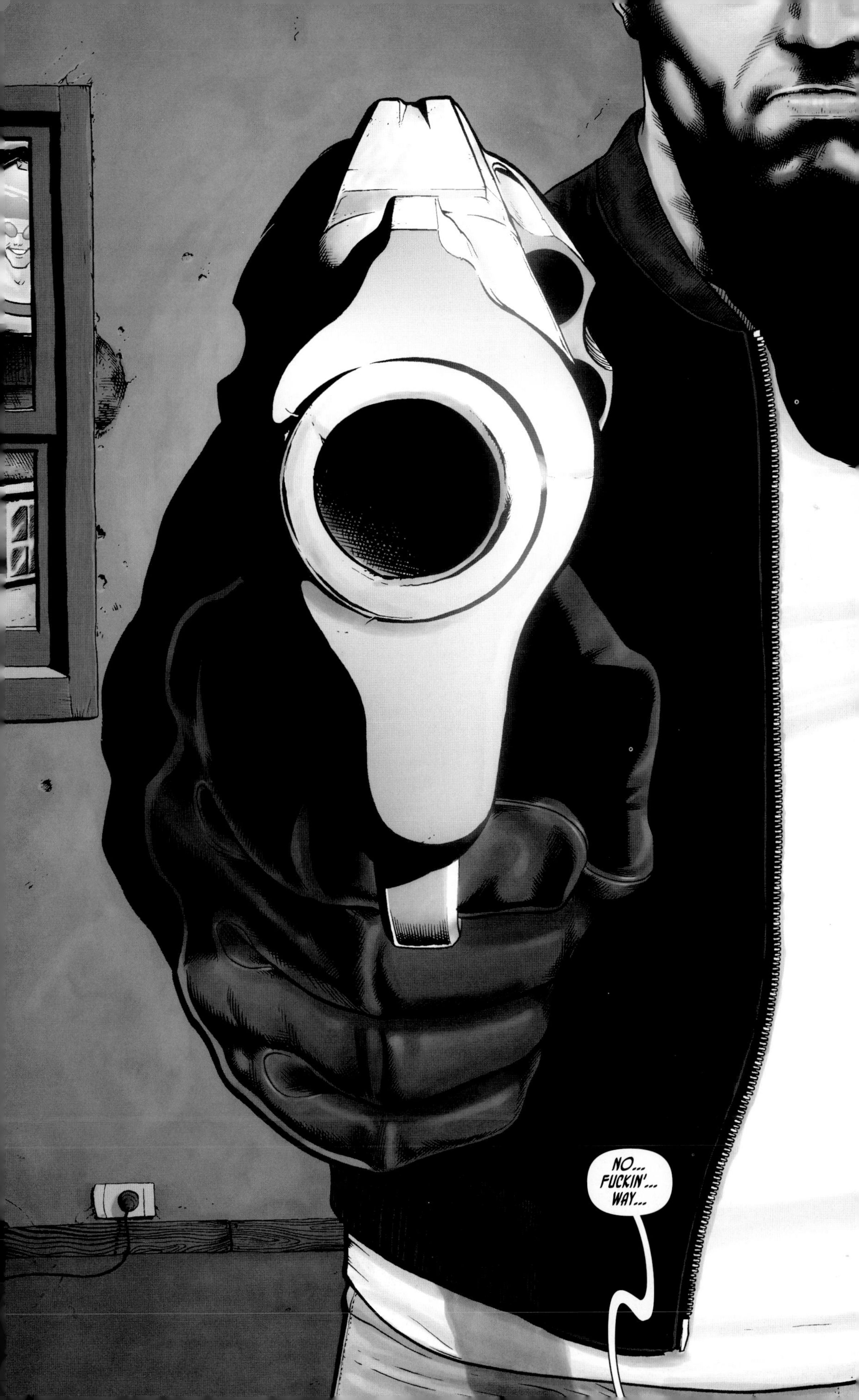
NO... FUCKIN'... WAY...

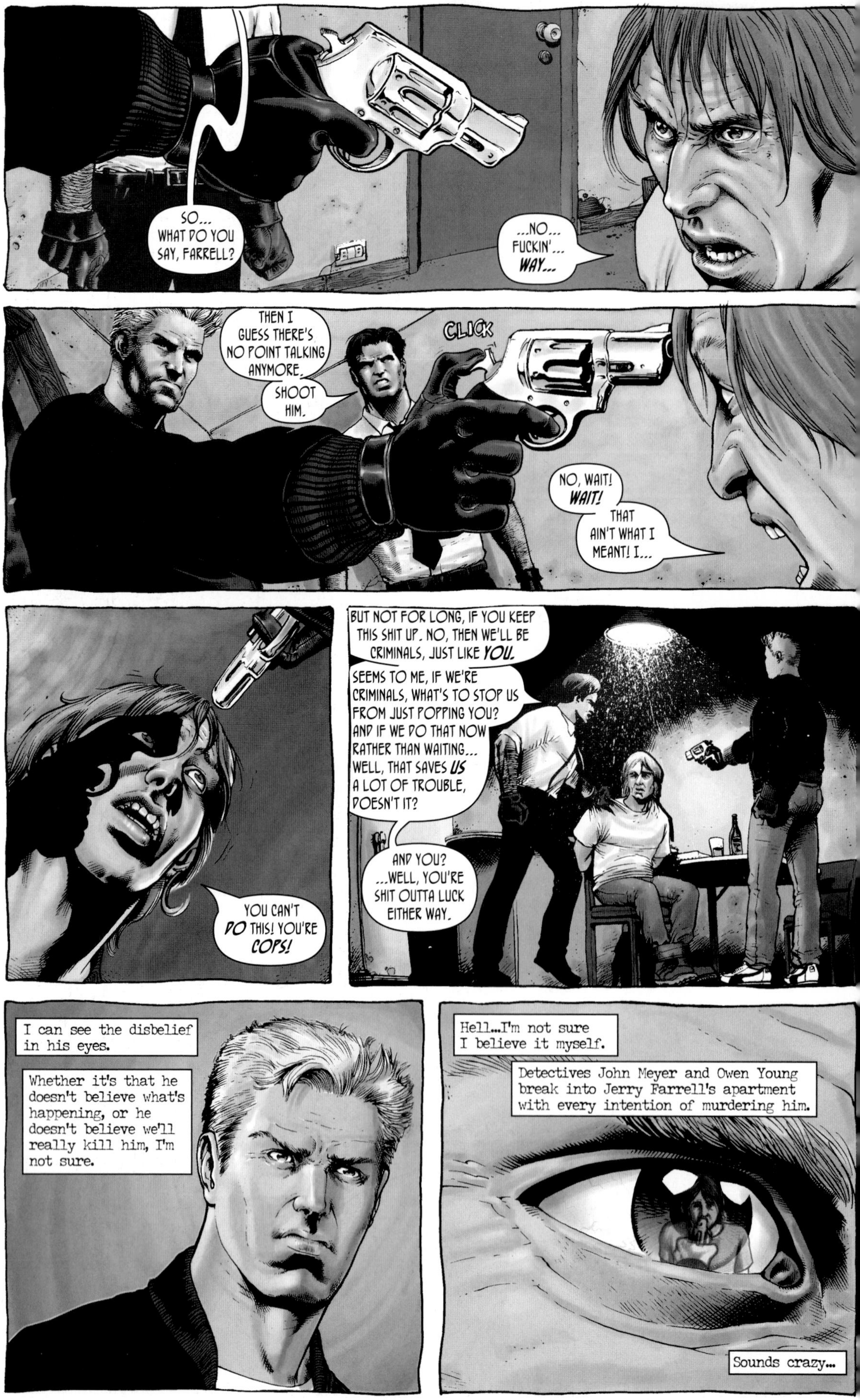
SO... WHAT DO YOU SAY, FARRELL?
...NO... FUCKIN'... WAY...
THEN I GUESS THERE'S NO POINT TALKING ANYMORE.
SHOOT HIM.
CLICK
NO, WAIT! WAIT! THAT AIN'T WHAT I MEANT! I...
YOU CAN'T DO THIS! YOU'RE COPS!
BUT NOT FOR LONG, IF YOU KEEP THIS SHIT UP. NO, THEN WE'LL BE CRIMINALS, JUST LIKE YOU.
SEEMS TO ME, IF WE'RE CRIMINALS, WHAT'S TO STOP US FROM JUST POPPING YOU? AND IF WE DO THAT NOW RATHER THAN WAITING... WELL, THAT SAVES US A LOT OF TROUBLE, DOESN'T IT?
AND YOU? ...WELL, YOU'RE SHIT OUTTA LUCK EITHER WAY.
I can see the disbelief in his eyes.
Whether it's that he doesn't believe what's happening, or he doesn't believe we'll really kill him, I'm not sure.
Hell...I'm not sure I believe it myself.
Detectives John Meyer and Owen Young break into Jerry Farrell's apartment with every intention of murdering him.
Sounds crazy...

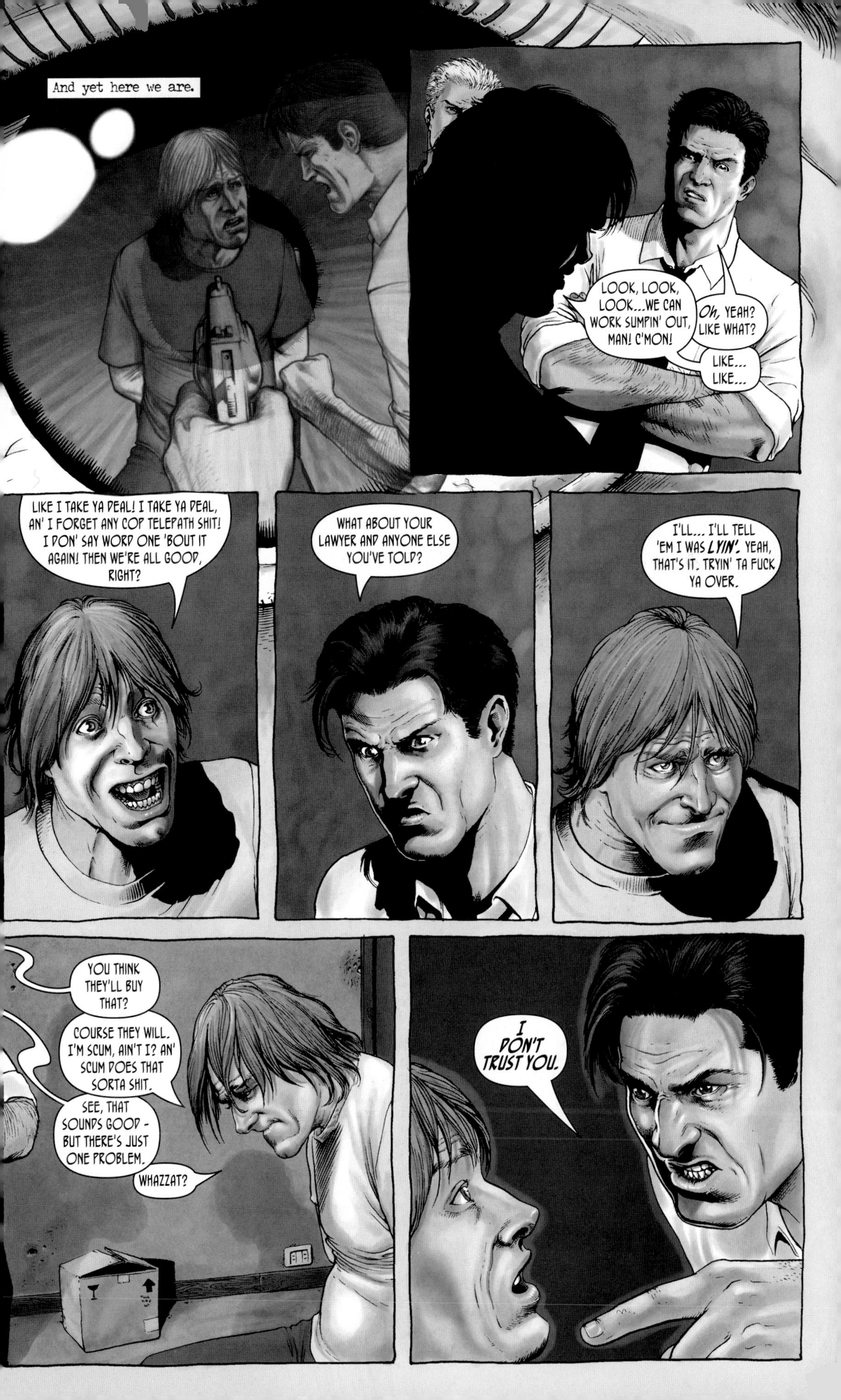
And yet here we are.
LOOK, LOOK, LOOK...WE CAN WORK SUMPIN' OUT, MAN! C'MON!
Oh, YEAH? LIKE WHAT?
LIKE... LIKE...
LIKE I TAKE YA DEAL! I TAKE YA DEAL, AN' I FORGET ANY COP TELEPATH SHIT! I DON' SAY WORD ONE 'BOUT IT AGAIN! THEN WE'RE ALL GOOD, RIGHT?
WHAT ABOUT YOUR LAWYER AND ANYONE ELSE YOU'VE TOLD?
I'LL... I'LL TELL 'EM I WAS LYIN'. YEAH, THAT'S IT. TRYIN' TA FUCK YA OVER.
YOU THINK THEY'LL BUY THAT?
COURSE THEY WILL. I'M SCUM, AIN'T I? AN' SCUM DOES THAT SORTA SHIT.
SEE, THAT SOUNDS GOOD - BUT THERE'S JUST ONE PROBLEM.
WHAZZAT?
I DON'T TRUST YOU.

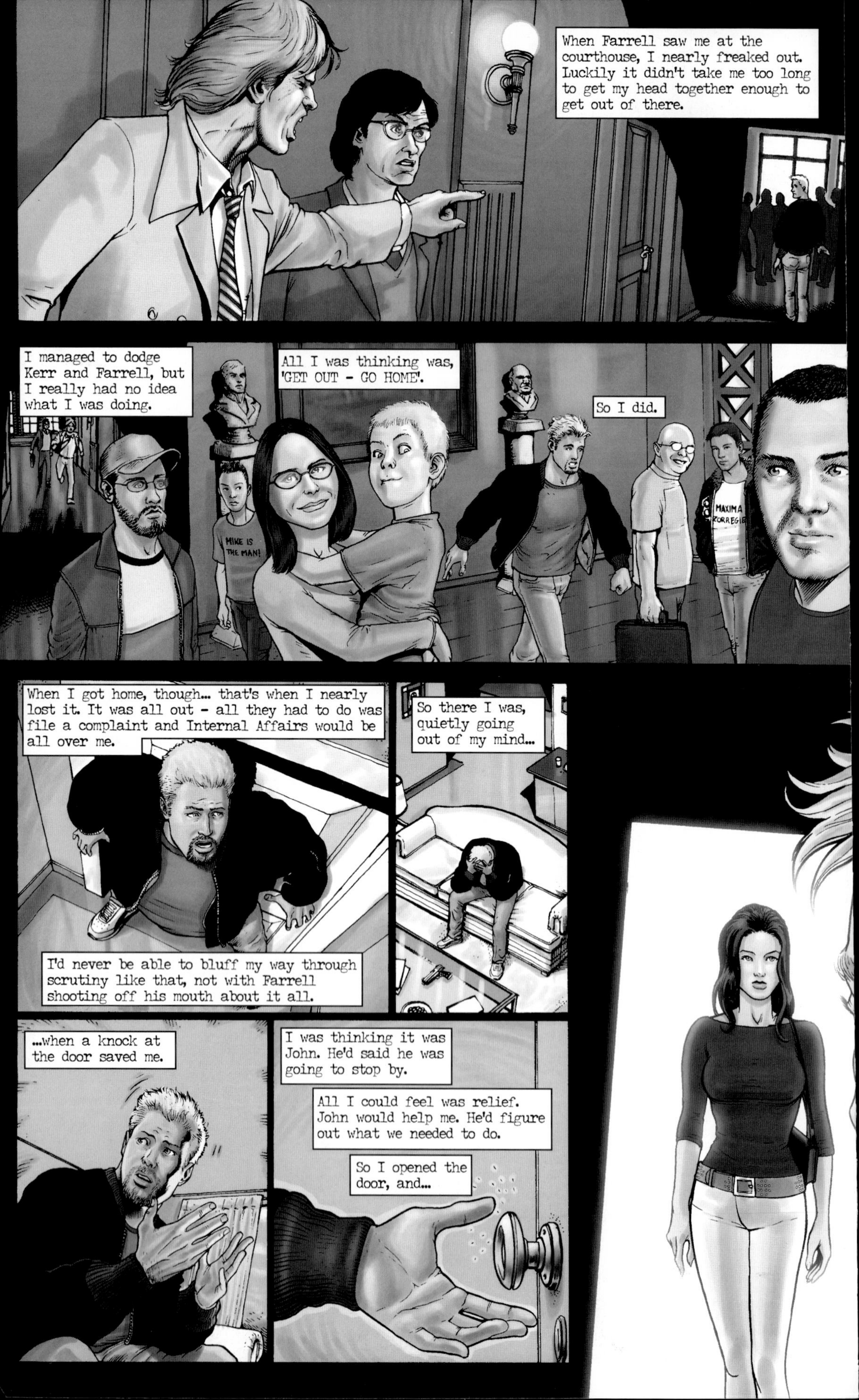
When Farrell saw me at the courthouse, I nearly freaked out. Luckily it didn't take me too long to get my head together enough to get out of there.
I managed to dodge Kerr and Farrell, but I really had no idea what I was doing.
All I was thinking was, 'GET OUT - GO HOME'.
So I did.
MIKE IS THE MAN!
When I got home, though... that's when I nearly lost it. It was all out - all they had to do was file a complaint and Internal Affairs would be all over me.
I'd never be able to bluff my way through scrutiny like that, not with Farrell shooting off his mouth about it all.
So there I was, quietly going out of my mind...
...when a knock at the door saved me.
I was thinking it was John. He'd said he was going to stop by.
All I could feel was relief. John would help me. He'd figure out what we needed to do.
So I opened the door, and...

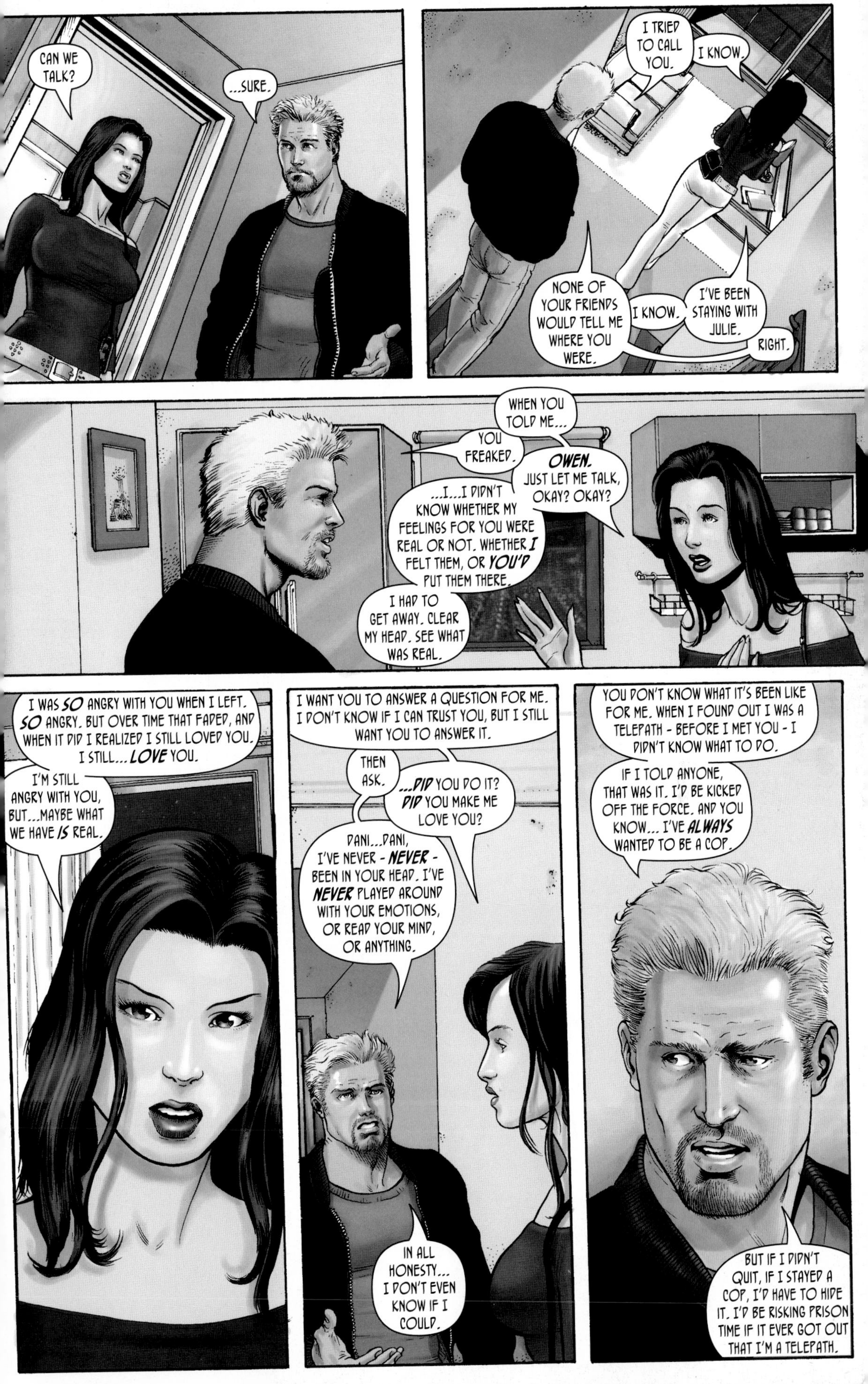

CAN WE TALK?
...SURE.
I TRIED TO CALL YOU.
I KNOW.
NONE OF YOUR FRIENDS WOULD TELL ME WHERE YOU WERE.
I KNOW.
I'VE BEEN STAYING WITH JULIE.
RIGHT.
WHEN YOU TOLD ME...
YOU FREAKED.
OWEN. JUST LET ME TALK, OKAY? OKAY?
...I...I DIDN'T KNOW WHETHER MY FEELINGS FOR YOU WERE REAL OR NOT. WHETHER I FELT THEM, OR YOU'D PUT THEM THERE.
I HAD TO GET AWAY. CLEAR MY HEAD. SEE WHAT WAS REAL.
I WAS SO ANGRY WITH YOU WHEN I LEFT. SO ANGRY. BUT OVER TIME THAT FADED, AND WHEN IT DID I REALIZED I STILL LOVED YOU. I STILL... LOVE YOU.
I'M STILL ANGRY WITH YOU, BUT...MAYBE WHAT WE HAVE IS REAL.
I WANT YOU TO ANSWER A QUESTION FOR ME. I DON'T KNOW IF I CAN TRUST YOU, BUT I STILL WANT YOU TO ANSWER IT.
THEN ASK.
...DID YOU DO IT? DID YOU MAKE ME LOVE YOU?
DANI...DANI, I'VE NEVER - NEVER - BEEN IN YOUR HEAD. I'VE NEVER PLAYED AROUND WITH YOUR EMOTIONS, OR READ YOUR MIND, OR ANYTHING.
IN ALL HONESTY... I DON'T EVEN KNOW IF I COULD.
YOU DON'T KNOW WHAT IT'S BEEN LIKE FOR ME. WHEN I FOUND OUT I WAS A TELEPATH - BEFORE I MET YOU - I DIDN'T KNOW WHAT TO DO.
IF I TOLD ANYONE, THAT WAS IT. I'D BE KICKED OFF THE FORCE. AND YOU KNOW... I'VE ALWAYS WANTED TO BE A COP.
BUT IF I DIDN'T QUIT, IF I STAYED A COP, I'D HAVE TO HIDE IT. I'D BE RISKING PRISON TIME IF IT EVER GOT OUT THAT I'M A TELEPATH.

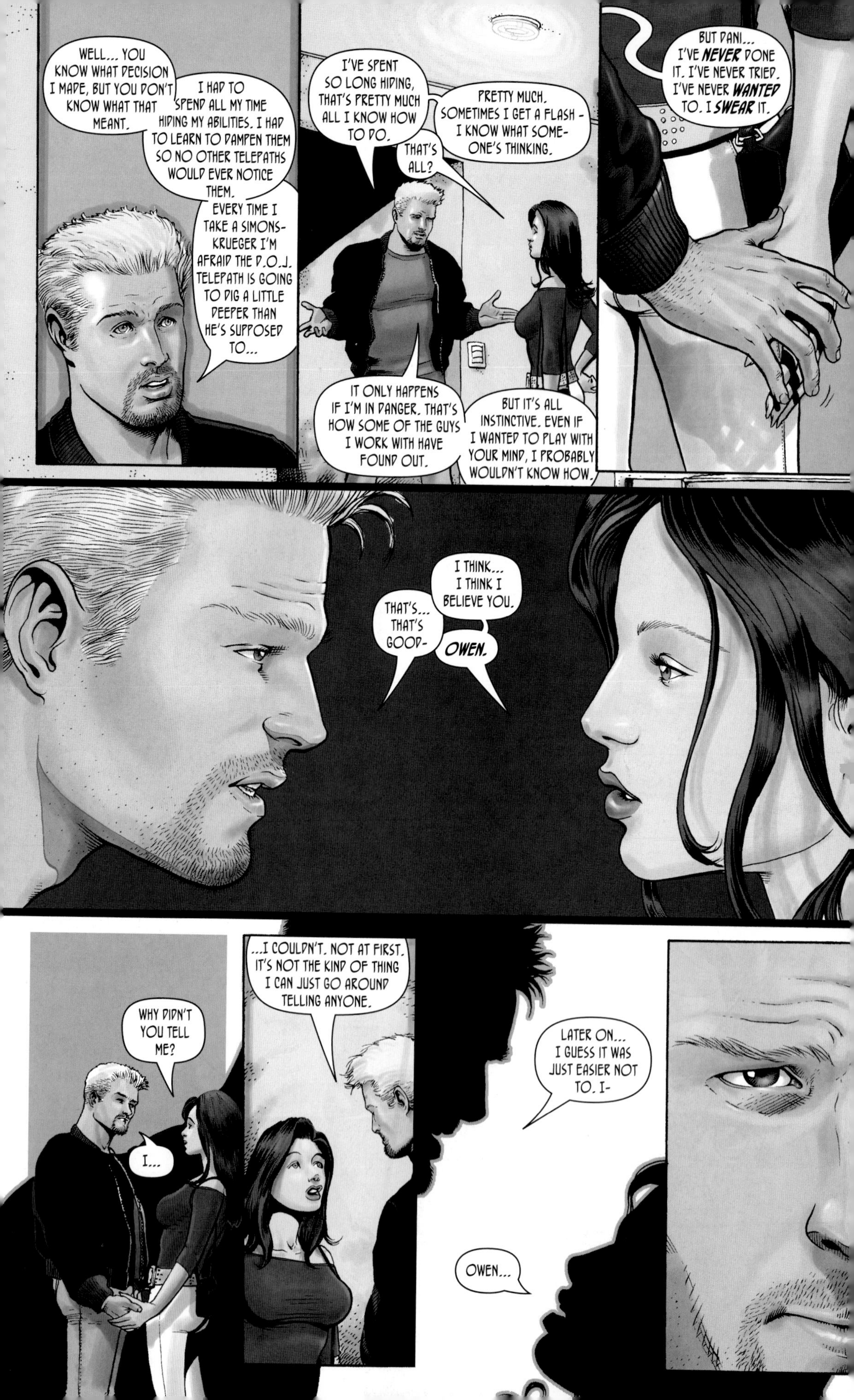

WELL... YOU KNOW WHAT DECISION I MADE, BUT YOU DON'T KNOW WHAT THAT MEANT.
I HAD TO SPEND ALL MY TIME HIDING MY ABILITIES. I HAD TO LEARN TO DAMPEN THEM SO NO OTHER TELEPATHS WOULD EVER NOTICE THEM.
EVERY TIME I TAKE A SIMONS-KRUEGER I'M AFRAID THE D.O.J. TELEPATH IS GOING TO DIG A LITTLE DEEPER THAN HE'S SUPPOSED TO...
I'VE SPENT SO LONG HIDING, THAT'S PRETTY MUCH ALL I KNOW HOW TO DO.
THAT'S ALL?
PRETTY MUCH. SOMETIMES I GET A FLASH - I KNOW WHAT SOME-ONE'S THINKING.
IT ONLY HAPPENS IF I'M IN DANGER. THAT'S HOW SOME OF THE GUYS I WORK WITH HAVE FOUND OUT.
BUT IT'S ALL INSTINCTIVE. EVEN IF I WANTED TO PLAY WITH YOUR MIND, I PROBABLY WOULDN'T KNOW HOW.
BUT DANI... I'VE NEVER DONE IT. I'VE NEVER TRIED. I'VE NEVER WANTED TO. I SWEAR IT.
I THINK... I THINK I BELIEVE YOU.
THAT'S... THAT'S GOOD-
OWEN.
WHY DIDN'T YOU TELL ME?
I...
...I COULDN'T. NOT AT FIRST. IT'S NOT THE KIND OF THING I CAN JUST GO AROUND TELLING ANYONE.
LATER ON... I GUESS IT WAS JUST EASIER NOT TO. I-
OWEN...

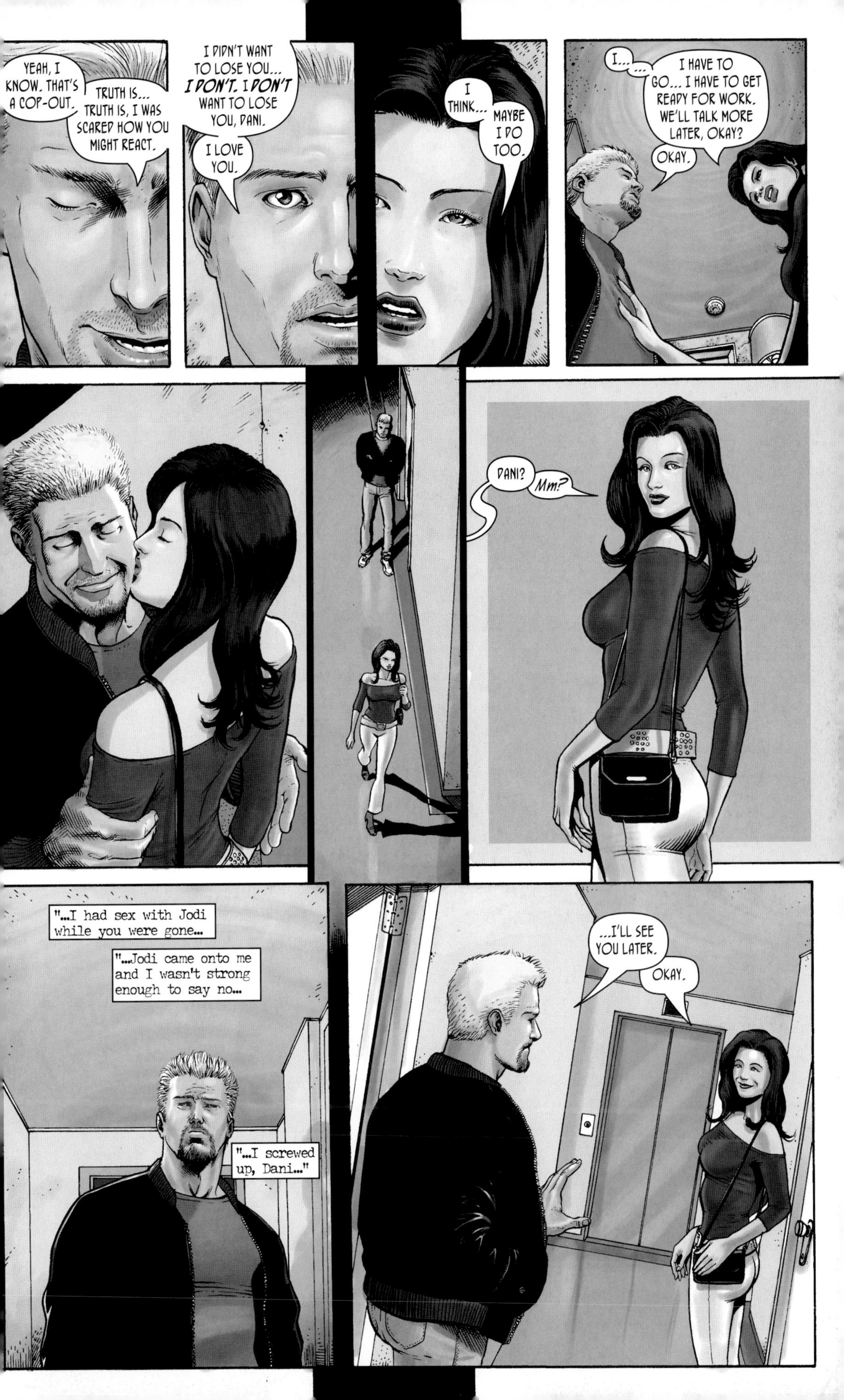
YEAH, I KNOW. THAT'S A COP-OUT.
TRUTH IS... TRUTH IS, I WAS SCARED HOW YOU MIGHT REACT.
I DIDN'T WANT TO LOSE YOU... I DON'T. I DON'T WANT TO LOSE YOU, DANI.
I LOVE YOU.
I THINK...
MAYBE I DO TOO.
I...
...
I HAVE TO GO... I HAVE TO GET READY FOR WORK. WE'LL TALK MORE LATER, OKAY?
OKAY.
DANI?
Mm?
"...I had sex with Jodi while you were gone...
"...Jodi came onto me and I wasn't strong enough to say no...
"...I screwed up, Dani..."
...I'LL SEE YOU LATER.
OKAY.

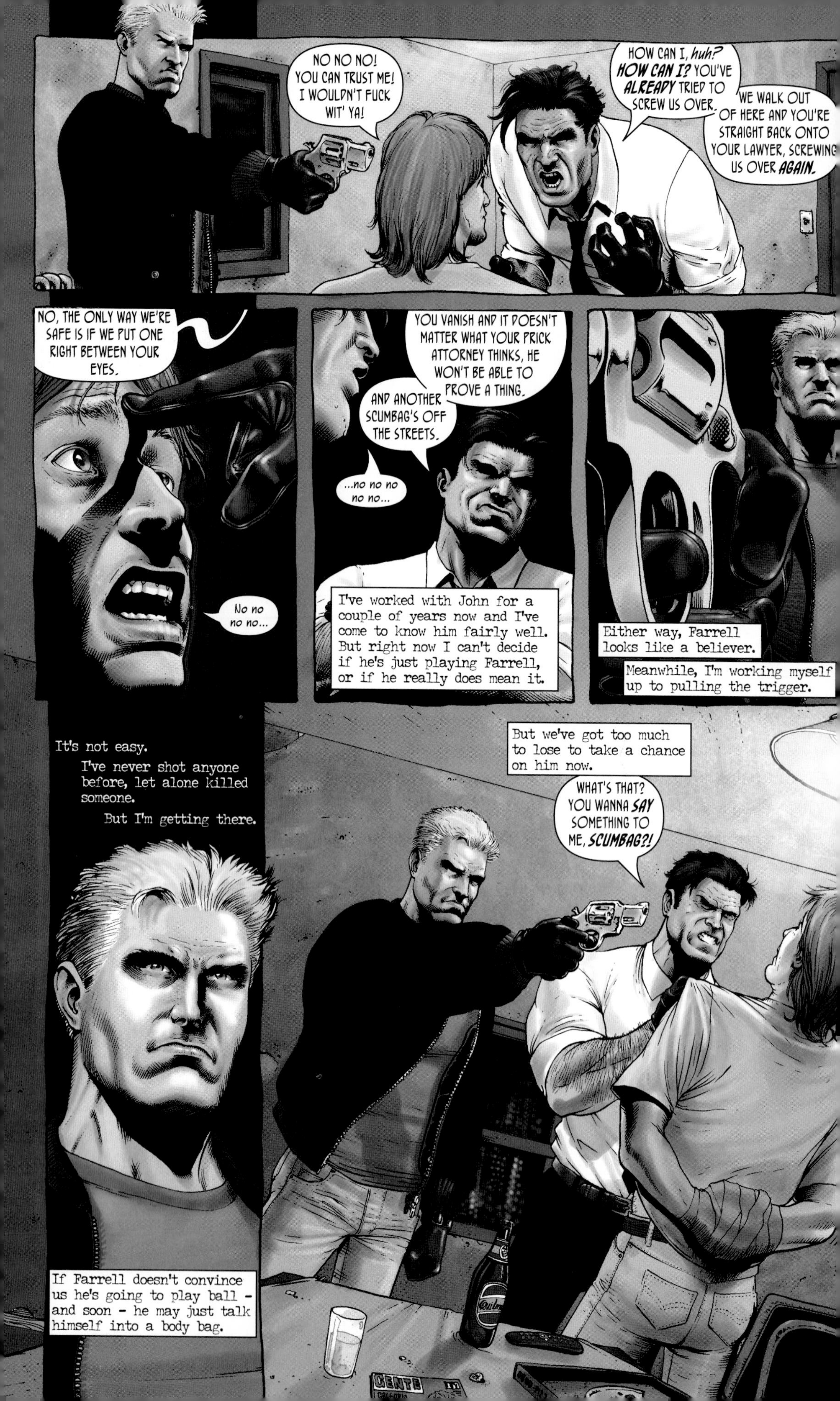
NO NO NO! YOU CAN TRUST ME! I WOULDN'T FUCK WIT' YA!
HOW CAN I, huh? HOW CAN I? YOU'VE ALREADY TRIED TO SCREW US OVER.
WE WALK OUT OF HERE AND YOU'RE STRAIGHT BACK ONTO YOUR LAWYER, SCREWING US OVER AGAIN.
NO, THE ONLY WAY WE'RE SAFE IS IF WE PUT ONE RIGHT BETWEEN YOUR EYES.
No no no no...
YOU VANISH AND IT DOESN'T MATTER WHAT YOUR PRICK ATTORNEY THINKS, HE WON'T BE ABLE TO PROVE A THING.
AND ANOTHER SCUMBAG'S OFF THE STREETS.
...no no no no no...
I've worked with John for a couple of years now and I've come to know him fairly well. But right now I can't decide if he's just playing Farrell, or if he really does mean it.
Either way, Farrell looks like a believer.
Meanwhile, I'm working myself up to pulling the trigger.
It's not easy.
I've never shot anyone before, let alone killed someone.
But I'm getting there.
But we've got too much to lose to take a chance on him now.
WHAT'S THAT? YOU WANNA SAY SOMETHING TO ME, SCUMBAG?!
If Farrell doesn't convince us he's going to play ball - and soon - he may just talk himself into a body bag.

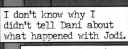

I don't know why I didn't tell Dani about what happened with Jodi.

I do know I didn't want to shake things up more, when they're already so fragile.

But I am going to tell her. I am. Maybe tomorrow, when we can really sit down and talk.

Maybe later, once we're past the whole telepath thing.

Maybe never.

One thing's for sure — I'm never telling her about Farrell. No... there's already too much...

I can't. I just can't.

But when I think about it... when I really stop and think about it...I realise I meant it. Every word I said to her.

I love her. I want to be with her. I want it to be like it was.

And that means I have to do something. I have to stop Farrell from screwing everything up.

No matter what it takes.

I don't like the face I see in the mirror.

I wanted to be better than this.

I thought I was.

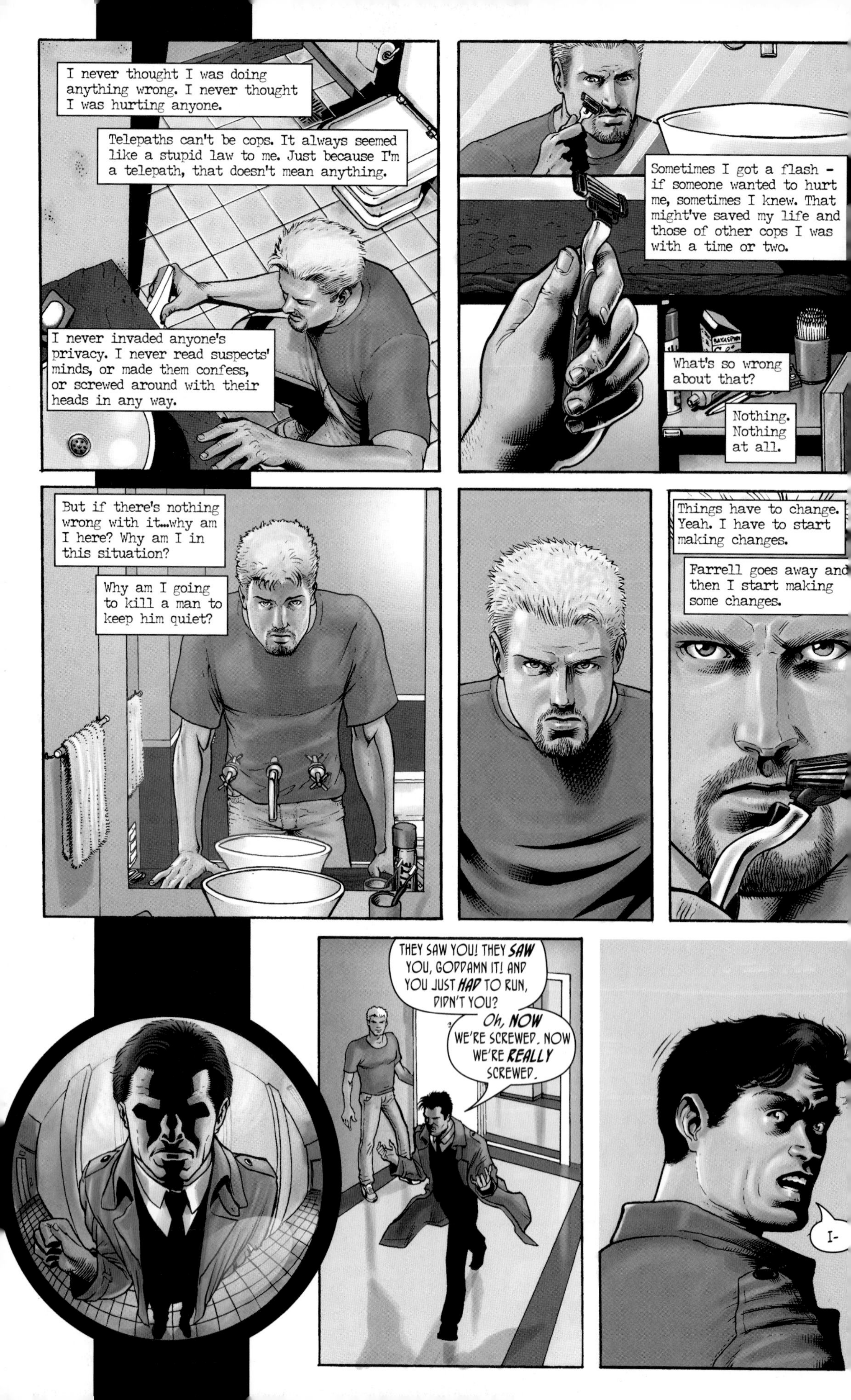

I never thought I was doing anything wrong. I never thought I was hurting anyone.
Telepaths can't be cops. It always seemed like a stupid law to me. Just because I'm a telepath, that doesn't mean anything.
I never invaded anyone's privacy. I never read suspects' minds, or made them confess, or screwed around with their heads in any way.
Sometimes I got a flash - if someone wanted to hurt me, sometimes I knew. That might've saved my life and those of other cops I was with a time or two.
What's so wrong about that?
Nothing. Nothing at all.
But if there's nothing wrong with it...why am I here? Why am I in this situation?
Why am I going to kill a man to keep him quiet?
Things have to change. Yeah. I have to start making changes.
Farrell goes away and then I start making some changes.
THEY SAW YOU! THEY SAW YOU, GODDAMN IT! AND YOU JUST HAD TO RUN, DIDN'T YOU?
Oh, NOW WE'RE SCREWED. NOW WE'RE REALLY SCREWED.
I-

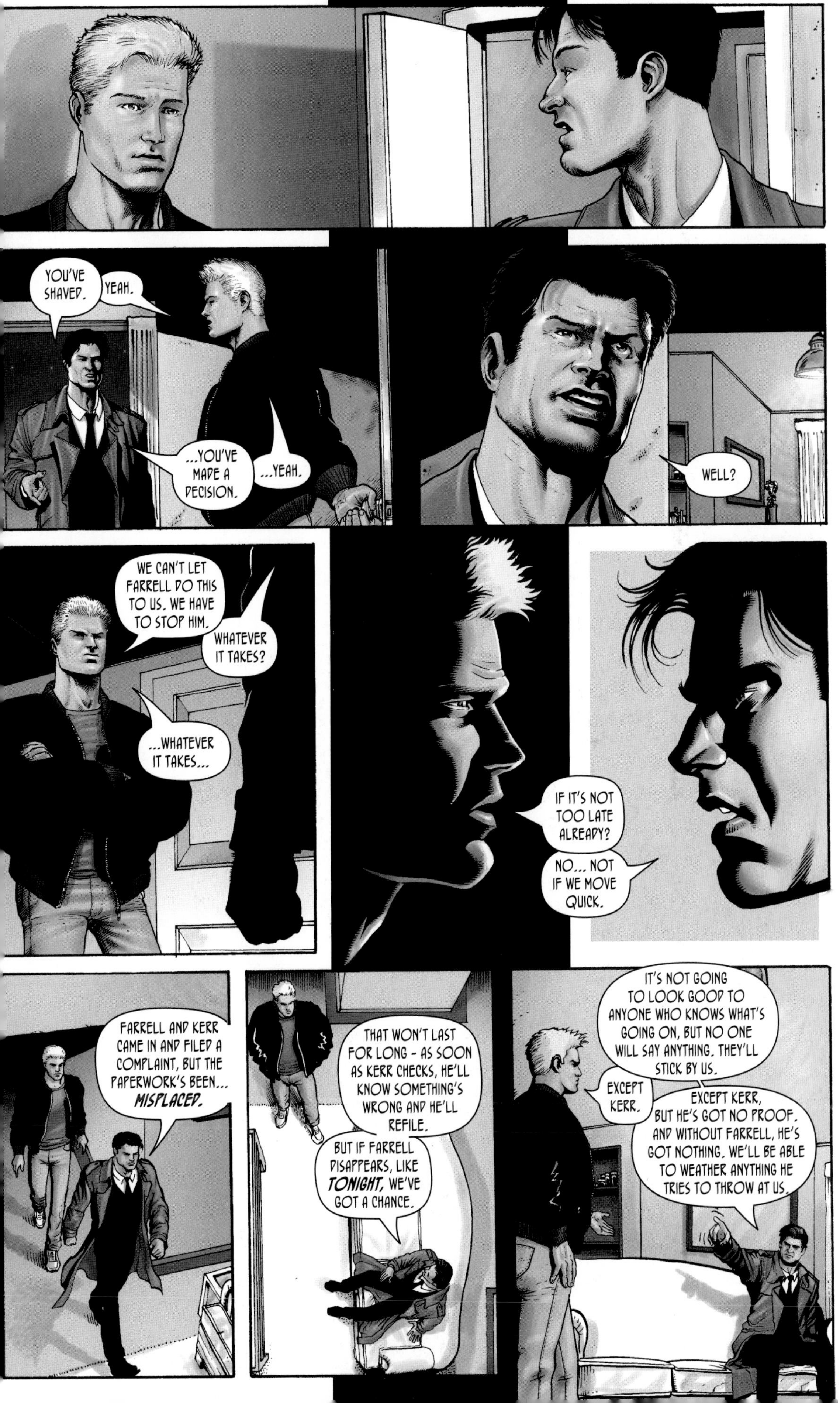
YOU'VE SHAVED.
YEAH.
...YOU'VE MADE A DECISION.
...YEAH.
WELL?
WE CAN'T LET FARRELL DO THIS TO US. WE HAVE TO STOP HIM.
WHATEVER IT TAKES?
...WHATEVER IT TAKES...
IF IT'S NOT TOO LATE ALREADY?
NO... NOT IF WE MOVE QUICK.
FARRELL AND KERR CAME IN AND FILED A COMPLAINT, BUT THE PAPERWORK'S BEEN... *MISPLACED.*
THAT WON'T LAST FOR LONG - AS SOON AS KERR CHECKS, HE'LL KNOW SOMETHING'S WRONG AND HE'LL REFILE.
BUT IF FARRELL DISAPPEARS, LIKE *TONIGHT,* WE'VE GOT A CHANCE.
IT'S NOT GOING TO LOOK GOOD TO ANYONE WHO KNOWS WHAT'S GOING ON, BUT NO ONE WILL SAY ANYTHING. THEY'LL STICK BY US.
EXCEPT KERR.
EXCEPT KERR, BUT HE'S GOT NO PROOF. AND WITHOUT FARRELL, HE'S GOT NOTHING. WE'LL BE ABLE TO WEATHER ANYTHING HE TRIES TO THROW AT US.

IF FARRELL'S GONE.

IF FARRELL'S GONE.

JOHN...

... DOESN'T THIS *GET* TO YOU?

YEAH, IT DOES. A BIT.

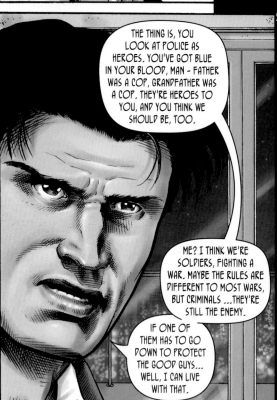

THE THING IS, YOU LOOK AT POLICE AS HEROES. YOU'VE GOT BLUE IN YOUR BLOOD, MAN - FATHER WAS A COP, GRANDFATHER WAS A COP. THEY'RE HEROES TO YOU, AND YOU THINK WE SHOULD BE, TOO.

ME? I THINK WE'RE SOLDIERS, FIGHTING A WAR. MAYBE THE RULES ARE DIFFERENT TO MOST WARS, BUT CRIMINALS ...THEY'RE STILL THE ENEMY.

IF ONE OF THEM HAS TO GO DOWN TO PROTECT THE GOOD GUYS... WELL, I CAN LIVE WITH THAT.

WHAT'S THE OTHER SIDE, ANYWAY? IF WE DON'T DO ANYTHING, FARRELL LIVES. A BAD GUY WHO ROBS BANKS AND ASSOCIATES WITH KILLERS. MIGHT EVEN BE ONE HIMSELF.

HE GETS OFF. MAYBE EVEN MAKES MONEY SUING US AND THE DEPARTMENT.

YOU, ME AND JODI, WE ALL GO TO PRISON. BECK AND HICKEY AND THE OTHERS - WELL, IF THEY'RE LUCKY, THEY JUST LOSE THEIR JOBS. IF THEY'RE NOT, THEY GET TO JOIN US.

ALL OF US... OR ONE OF HIM. YOU LOOK AT IT THAT WAY... AND YEAH.

I CAN LIVE WITH THAT.

SO...

...STILL GOT THAT GUN?

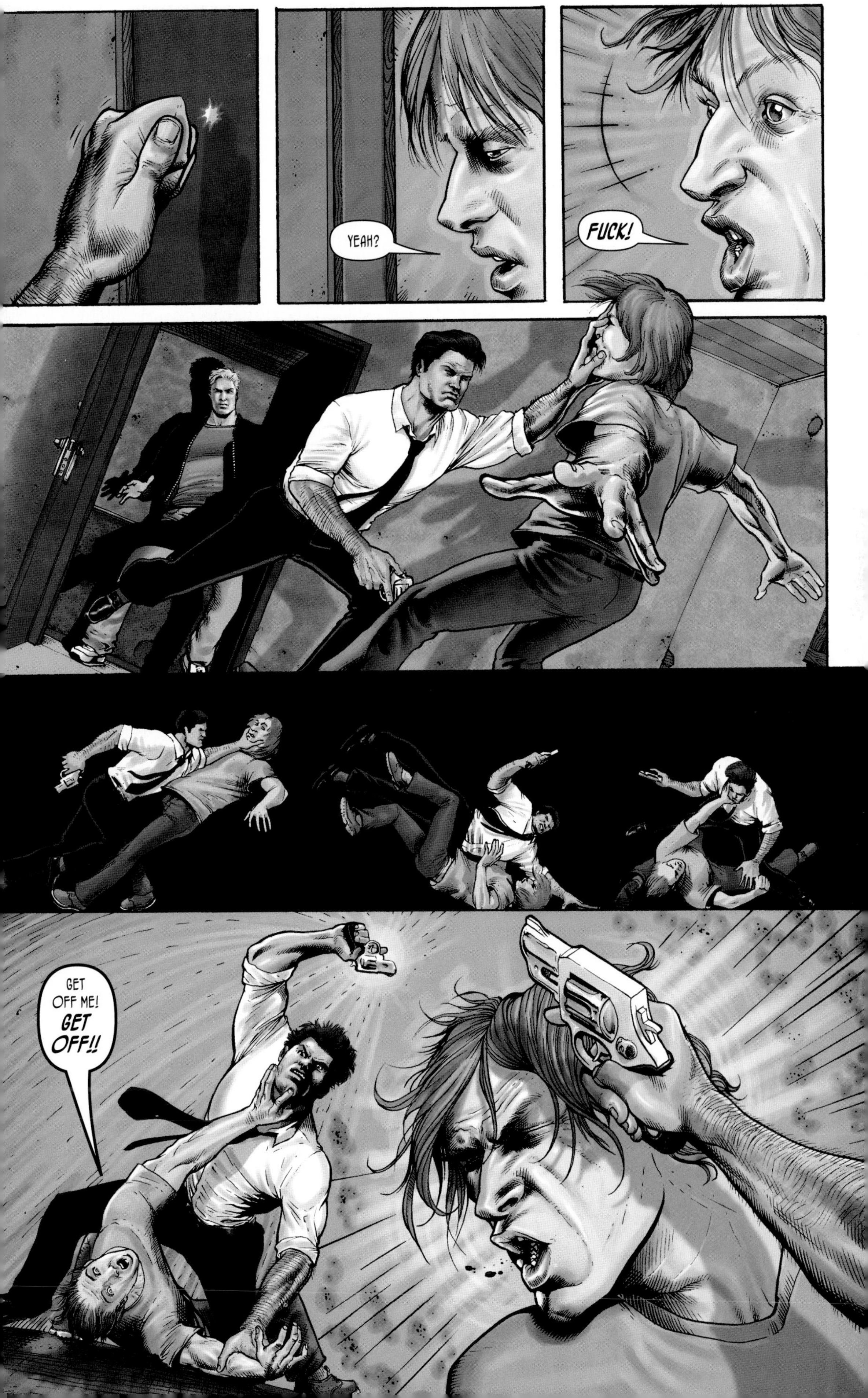
YEAH?
FUCK!
GET OFF ME! GET OFF!!

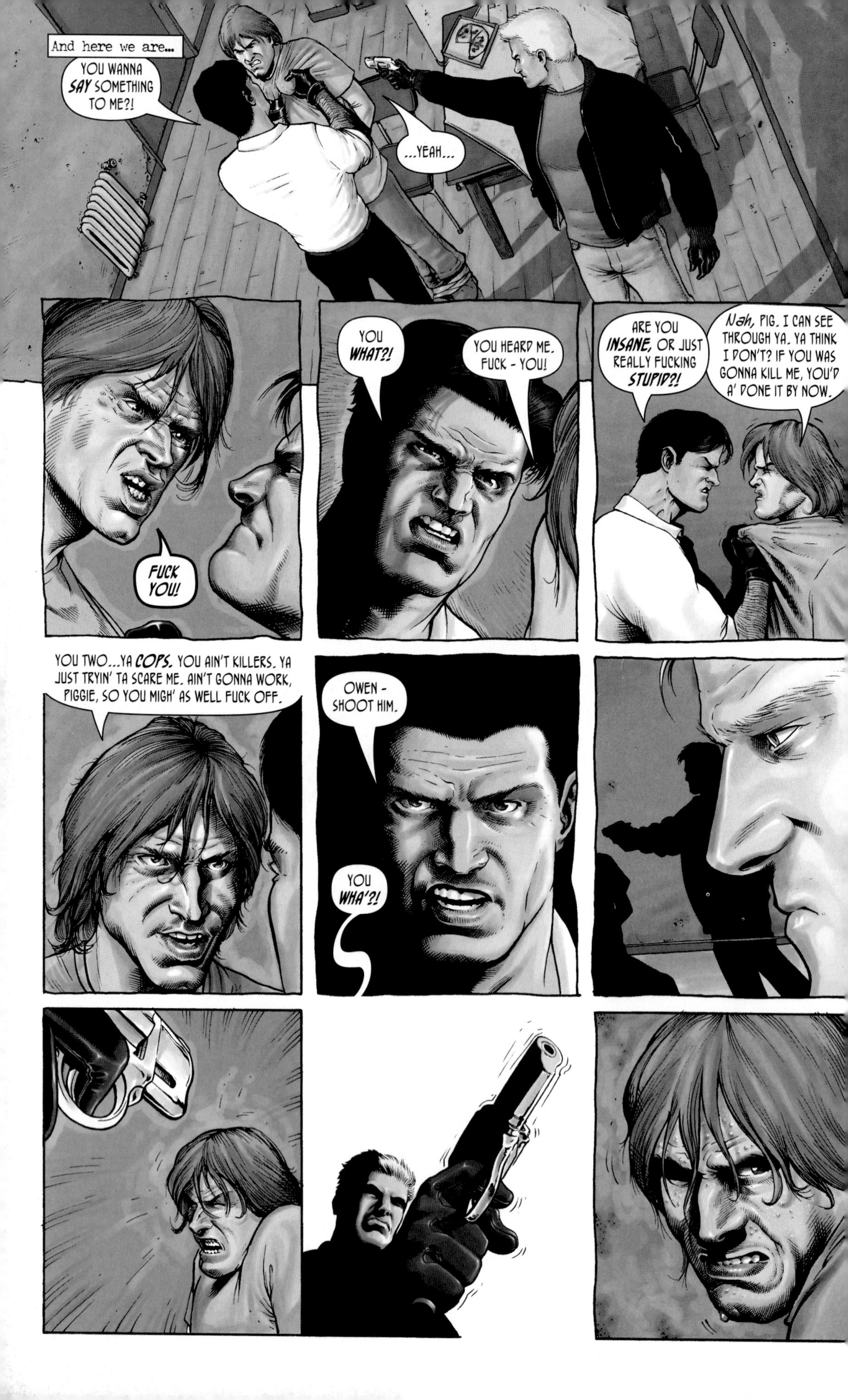

And here we are...
YOU WANNA SAY SOMETHING TO ME?!
...YEAH...
FUCK YOU!
YOU WHAT?!
YOU HEARD ME. FUCK - YOU!
ARE YOU INSANE, OR JUST REALLY FUCKING STUPID?!
Nah, PIG. I CAN SEE THROUGH YA. YA THINK I DON'T? IF YOU WAS GONNA KILL ME, YOU'D A' DONE IT BY NOW.
YOU TWO...YA COPS. YOU AIN'T KILLERS. YA JUST TRYIN' TA SCARE ME. AIN'T GONNA WORK, PIGGIE, SO YOU MIGH' AS WELL FUCK OFF.
OWEN - SHOOT HIM.
YOU WHA'?!

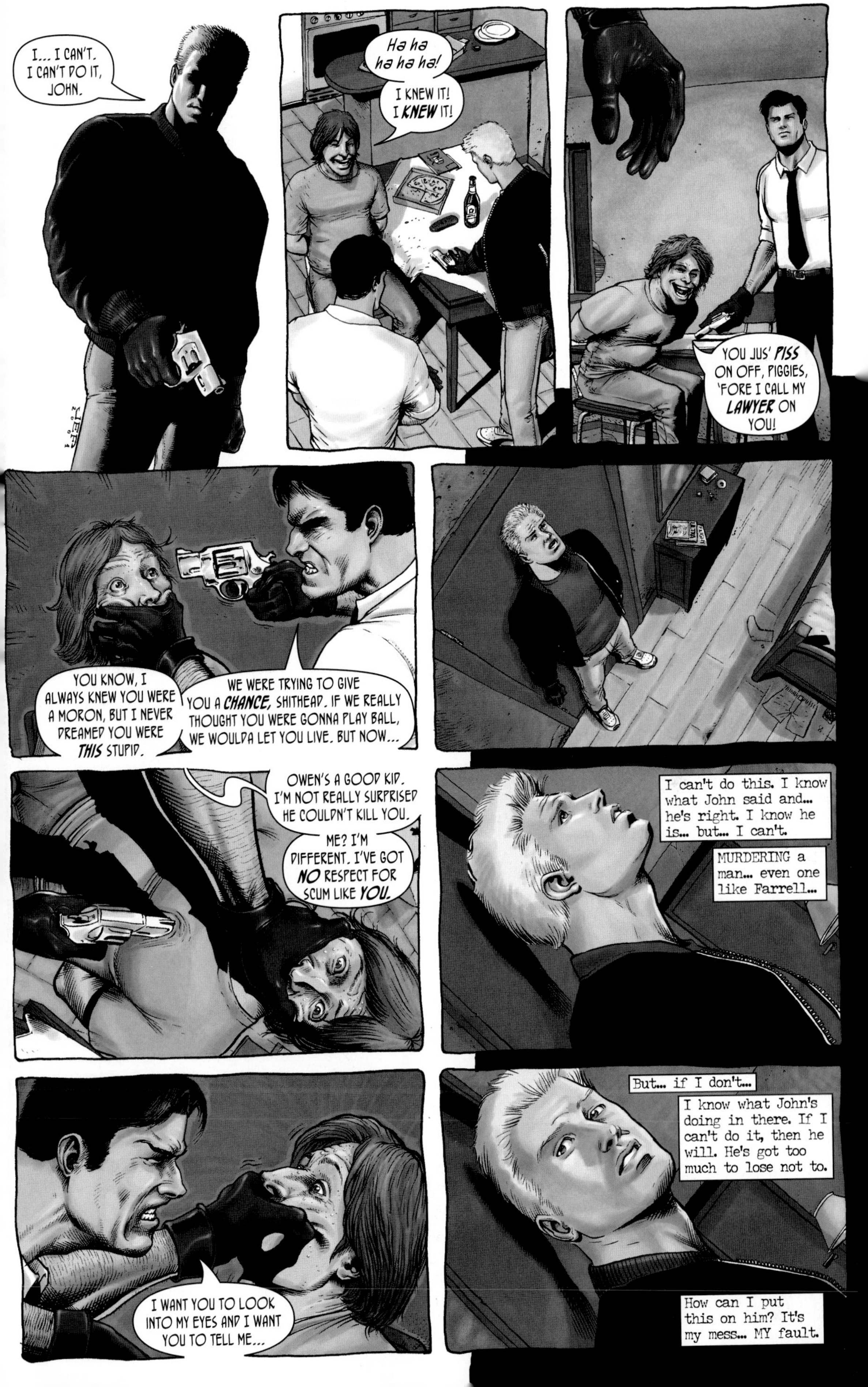
I... I CAN'T. I CAN'T DO IT, JOHN.
Ha ha ha ha ha!
I KNEW IT! I KNEW IT!
YOU JUS' PISS ON OFF, PIGGIES, 'FORE I CALL MY LAWYER ON YOU!
YOU KNOW, I ALWAYS KNEW YOU WERE A MORON, BUT I NEVER DREAMED YOU WERE THIS STUPID.
WE WERE TRYING TO GIVE YOU A CHANCE, SHITHEAD. IF WE REALLY THOUGHT YOU WERE GONNA PLAY BALL, WE WOULDA LET YOU LIVE. BUT NOW...
OWEN'S A GOOD KID. I'M NOT REALLY SURPRISED HE COULDN'T KILL YOU.
ME? I'M DIFFERENT. I'VE GOT NO RESPECT FOR SCUM LIKE YOU.
I can't do this. I know what John said and... he's right. I know he is... but... I can't.
MURDERING a man... even one like Farrell...
I WANT YOU TO LOOK INTO MY EYES AND I WANT YOU TO TELL ME...
But... if I don't...
I know what John's doing in there. If I can't do it, then he will. He's got too much to lose not to.
How can I put this on him? It's my mess... MY fault.

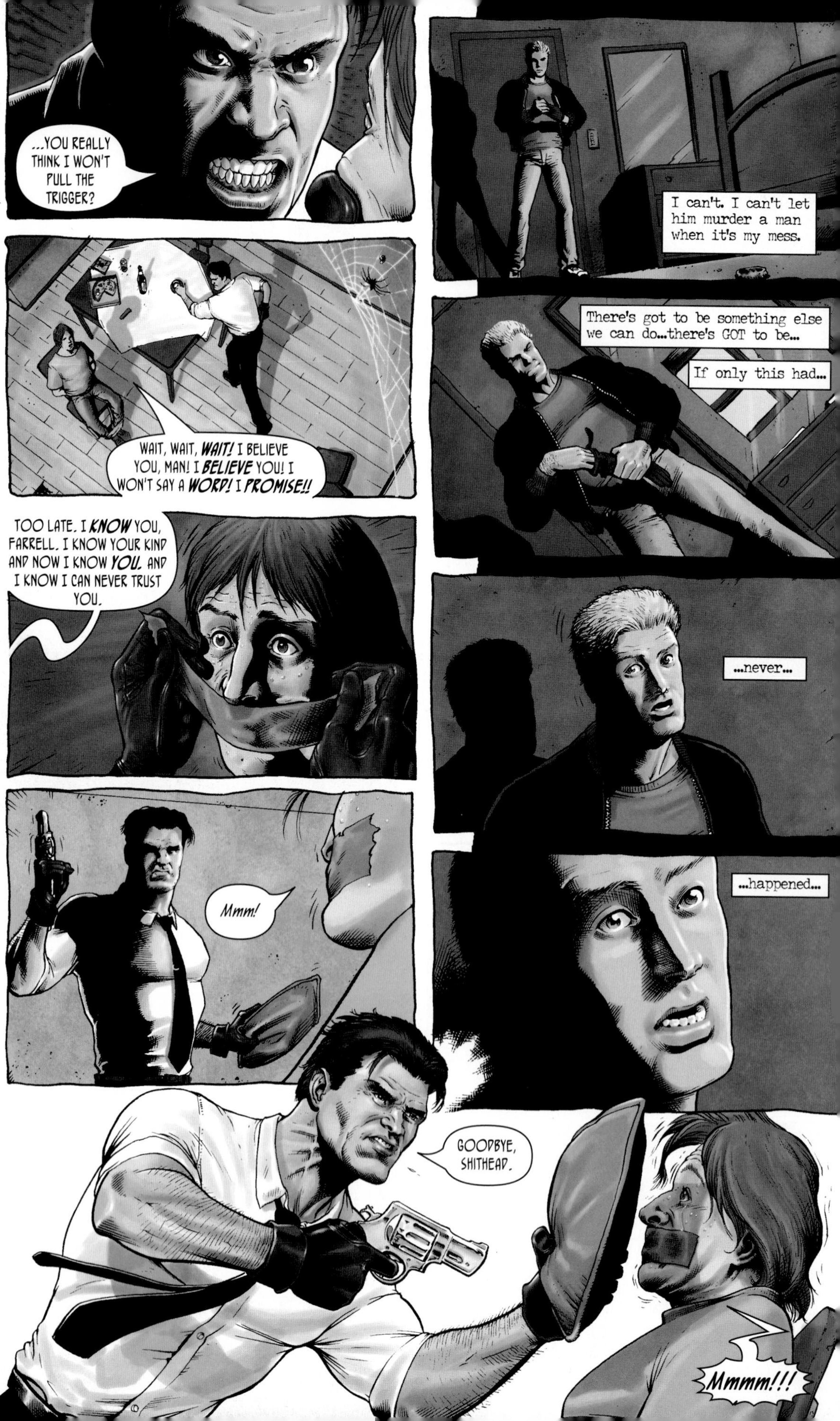
...YOU REALLY THINK I WON'T PULL THE TRIGGER?
WAIT, WAIT, WAIT! I BELIEVE YOU, MAN! I BELIEVE YOU! I WON'T SAY A WORD! I PROMISE!!
TOO LATE. I KNOW YOU, FARRELL. I KNOW YOUR KIND AND NOW I KNOW YOU. AND I KNOW I CAN NEVER TRUST YOU.
Mmm!
I can't. I can't let him murder a man when it's my mess.
There's got to be something else we can do...there's GOT to be...
If only this had...
...never...
...happened...
GOODBYE, SHITHEAD.
Mmmm!!!

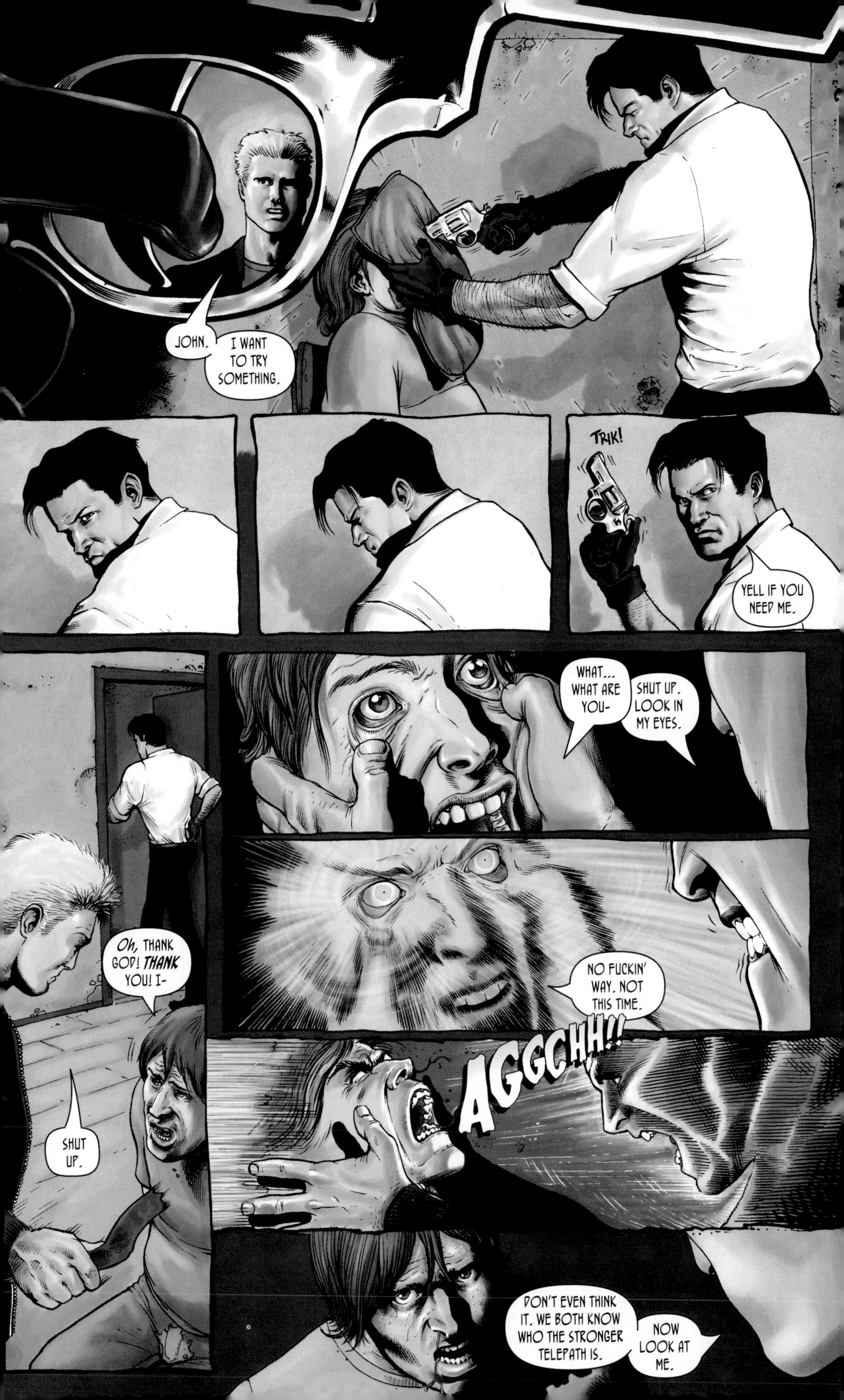
JOHN.
I WANT TO TRY SOMETHING.
TRIK!
YELL IF YOU NEED ME.
Oh, THANK GOD! THANK YOU! I-
SHUT UP.
WHAT... WHAT ARE YOU-
SHUT UP. LOOK IN MY EYES.
NO FUCKIN' WAY. NOT THIS TIME.
AGGCHH!!
DON'T EVEN THINK IT. WE BOTH KNOW WHO THE STRONGER TELEPATH IS.
NOW LOOK AT ME.

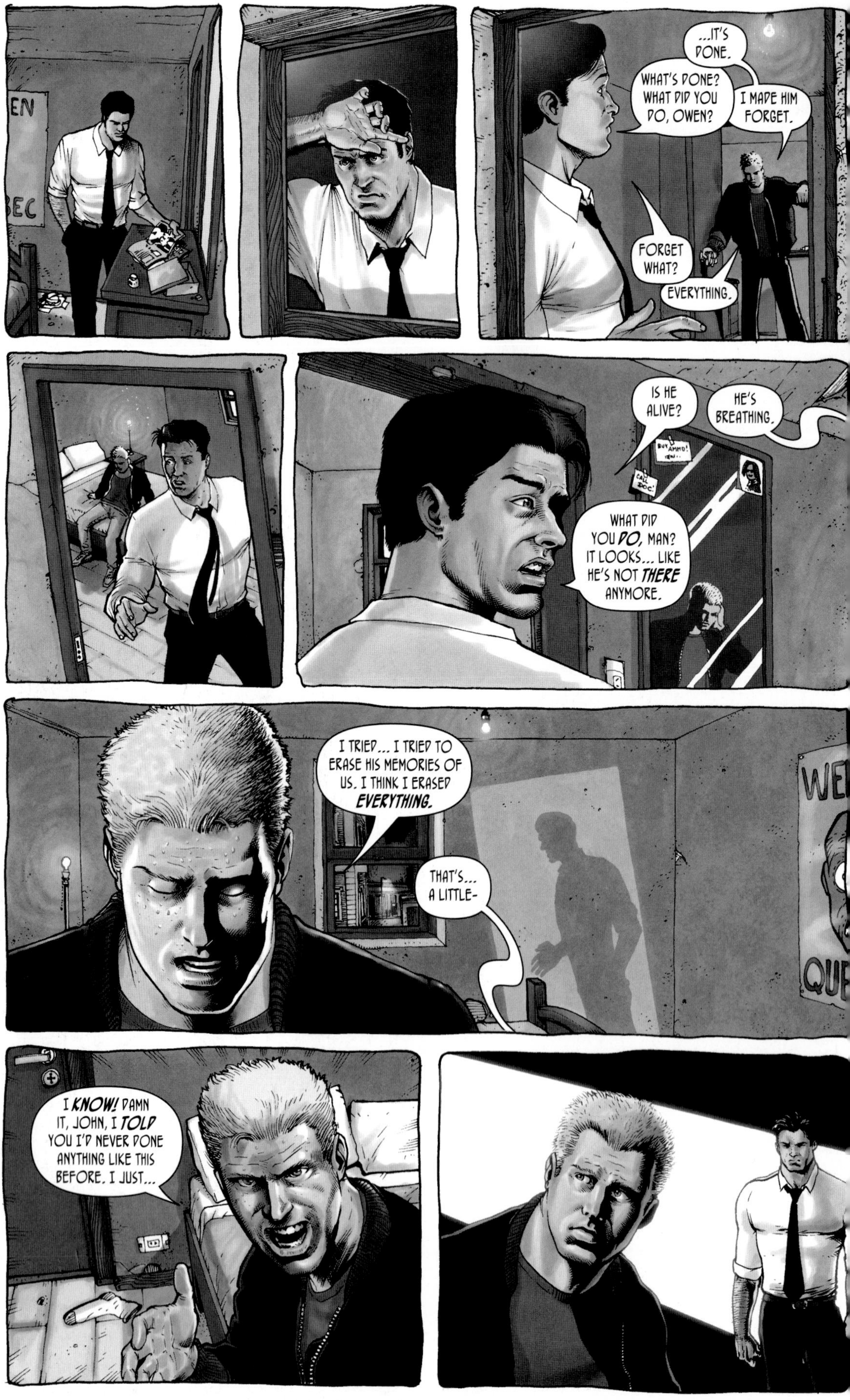
...IT'S DONE.
WHAT'S DONE? WHAT DID YOU DO, OWEN?
I MADE HIM FORGET.
FORGET WHAT?
EVERYTHING.
IS HE ALIVE?
HE'S BREATHING.
BUY AMMO!
CALL DOC!
WHAT DID YOU DO, MAN? IT LOOKS... LIKE HE'S NOT THERE ANYMORE.
I TRIED... I TRIED TO ERASE HIS MEMORIES OF US. I THINK I ERASED EVERYTHING.
THAT'S... A LITTLE-
I KNOW! DAMN IT, JOHN, I TOLD YOU I'D NEVER DONE ANYTHING LIKE THIS BEFORE. I JUST...

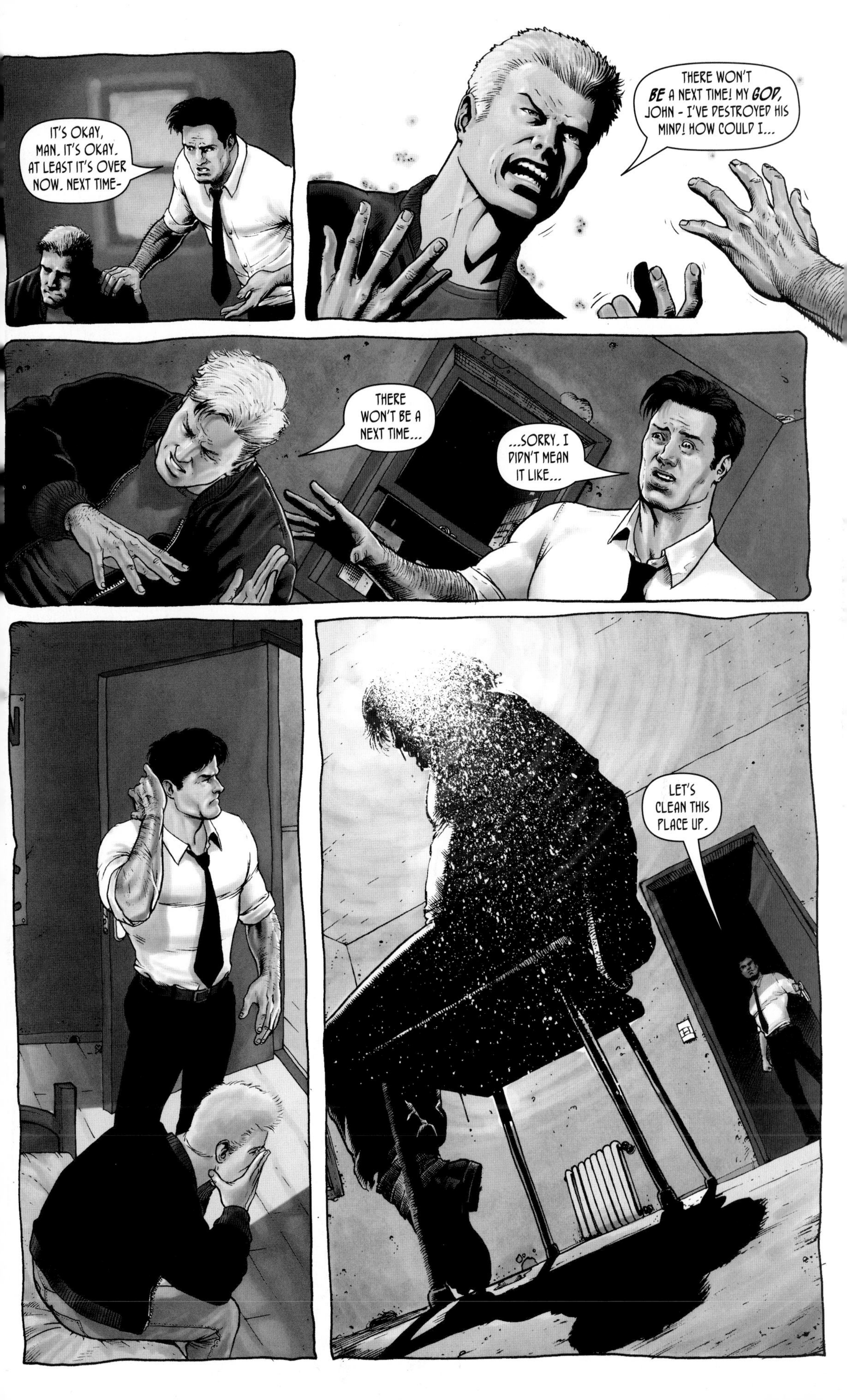
IT'S OKAY, MAN. IT'S OKAY. AT LEAST IT'S OVER NOW. NEXT TIME-
THERE WON'T BE A NEXT TIME! MY GOD, JOHN - I'VE DESTROYED HIS MIND! HOW COULD I...
THERE WON'T BE A NEXT TIME...
...SORRY. I DIDN'T MEAN IT LIKE...
LET'S CLEAN THIS PLACE UP.

DETECTIVE YOUNG?

MR KERR.

CAN WE TALK?

THIS WAY.

...

I SEE YOU'RE BACK AT WORK. FEELING BETTER?

...YEAH, A BIT.

...SO HOW'S YOUR CLIENT?

PRETTY MUCH UNCHANGED. THE DOCTORS ARE STUMPED. THEY'VE NEVER SEEN SUCH A BAD CASE OF MEMORY LOSS FROM WHAT SEEMS TO BE A FAIRLY MINOR BUMP TO THE HEAD

IT'S LIKE HE CAN'T REMEMBER ANYTHING AT ALL. HE CAN'T TALK OR WALK OR EVEN CHEW OR SWALLOW.

THEY TELL ME HIS MIND MAY "WAKE UP" SOME DAY, BUT THEY DON'T HOLD OUT MUCH HOPE. HE MAY HAVE TO LEARN HOW TO DO EVERYTHING ALL OVER AGAIN - IF HE CAN LEARN AT ALL.

THAT'S... I'M SORRY TO HEAR THAT. TRULY.

Mmm...

YOU KNOW, I THINK YOU'RE A VERY LUCKY MAN, DETECTIVE.

AFTER MR FARRELL WAS FOUND, I CALLED YOUR I.A.D. TO CHECK ON THE PROGRESS OF A COMPLAINT WE'D MADE. I WAS TOLD THEY HAD NO RECORD OF IT.

SEEMS IT GOT LOST SOMEWHERE ALONG THE WAY.

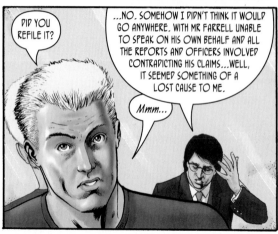

DID YOU REFILE IT?

...NO. SOMEHOW I DIDN'T THINK IT WOULD GO ANYWHERE. WITH MR FARRELL UNABLE TO SPEAK ON HIS OWN BEHALF AND ALL THE REPORTS AND OFFICERS INVOLVED CONTRADICTING HIS CLAIMS...WELL, IT SEEMED SOMETHING OF A LOST CAUSE TO ME.

Mmm...

I ALWAYS THOUGHT THE POLICE WERE THE GOOD GUYS, YOU KNOW?

I KNEW WHAT I WAS GETTING INTO AS A PUBLIC DEFENDER - I KNOW THAT 99% OF MY CLIENTS ARE GOING TO BE GUILTY. THAT'S THE JOB.

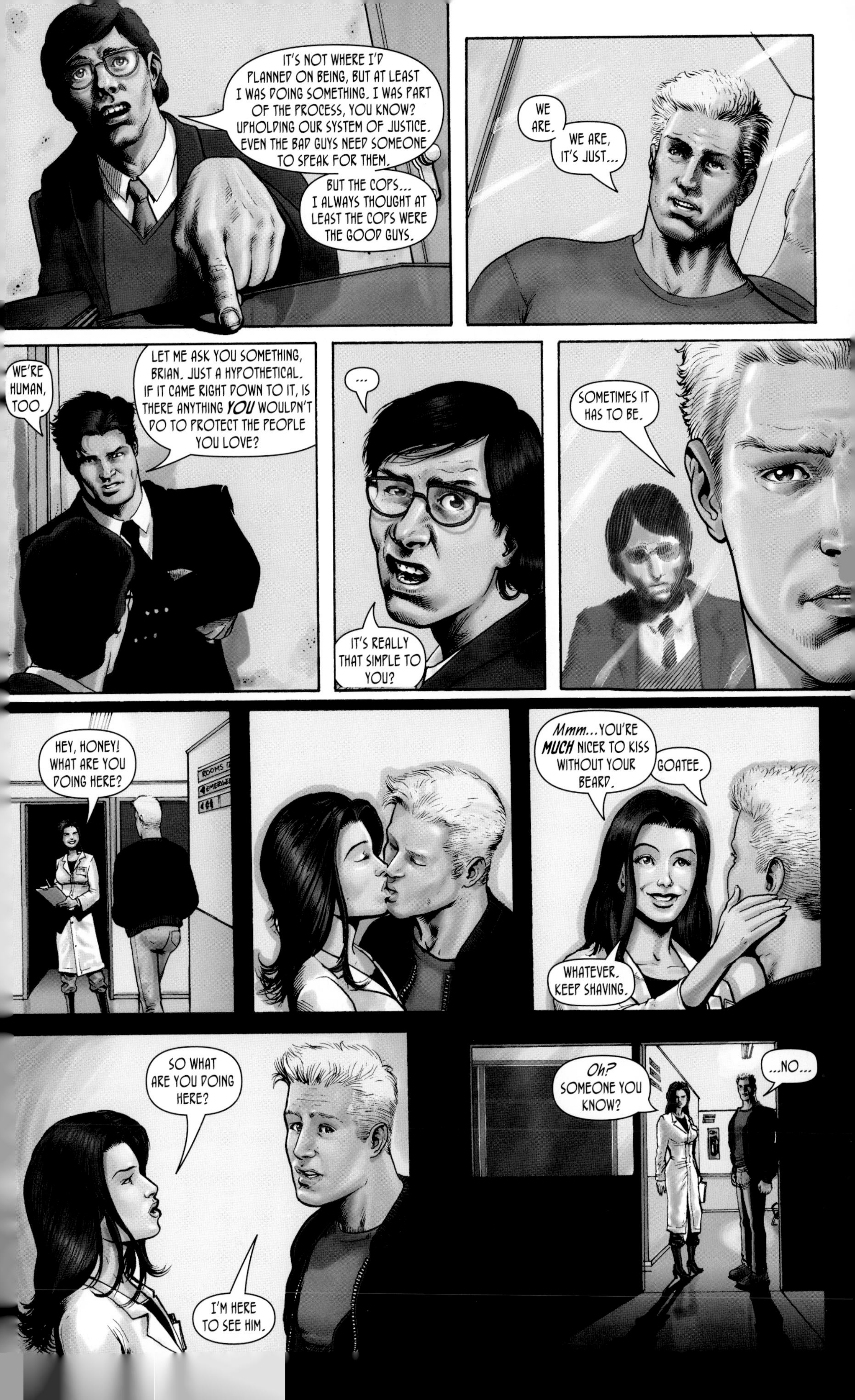
IT'S NOT WHERE I'D PLANNED ON BEING, BUT AT LEAST I WAS DOING SOMETHING. I WAS PART OF THE PROCESS, YOU KNOW? UPHOLDING OUR SYSTEM OF JUSTICE. EVEN THE BAD GUYS NEED SOMEONE TO SPEAK FOR THEM.
BUT THE COPS... I ALWAYS THOUGHT AT LEAST THE COPS WERE THE GOOD GUYS.
WE ARE.
WE ARE, IT'S JUST...
WE'RE HUMAN, TOO.
LET ME ASK YOU SOMETHING, BRIAN. JUST A HYPOTHETICAL. IF IT CAME RIGHT DOWN TO IT, IS THERE ANYTHING *YOU* WOULDN'T DO TO PROTECT THE PEOPLE YOU LOVE?
...
IT'S REALLY THAT SIMPLE TO YOU?
SOMETIMES IT HAS TO BE.
HEY, HONEY! WHAT ARE YOU DOING HERE?
Mmm...YOU'RE *MUCH* NICER TO KISS WITHOUT YOUR BEARD.
GOATEE.
WHATEVER. KEEP SHAVING.
SO WHAT ARE YOU DOING HERE?
I'M HERE TO SEE HIM.
Oh? SOMEONE YOU KNOW?
...NO...

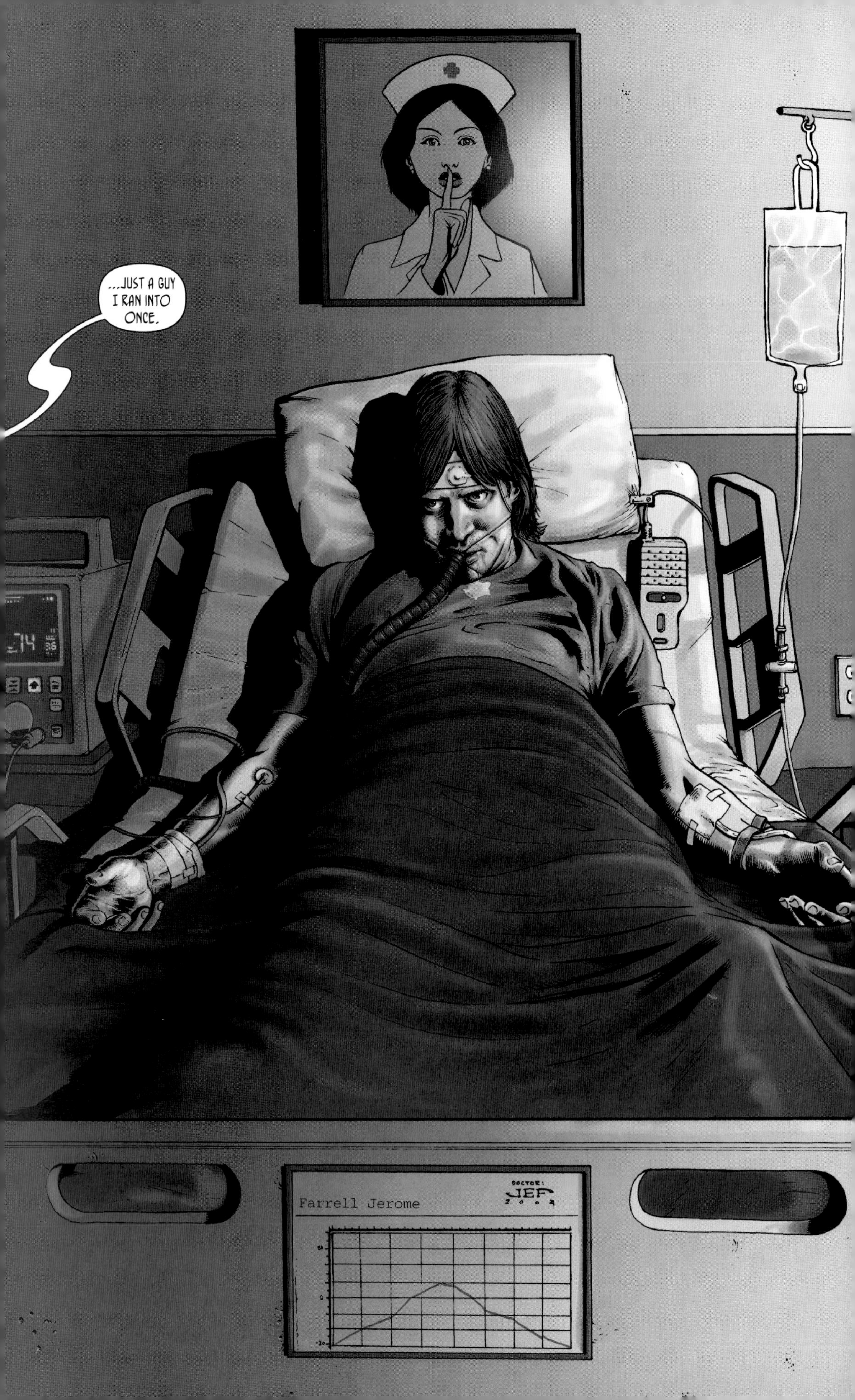
...JUST A GUY I RAN INTO ONCE.
Farrell Jerome
DOCTOR:
JEF

GLOSSARY

ADA

Assistant District Attorney.

Bond

Money paid as surety to secure a suspect's pre-trial release from prison. Generally known as "bail". Thus, being "bonded out" refers to a suspect paying bond and being released.

Class

How powerful a psychic is is defined by their class. Classes range from one, the least powerful, to nine, the most. Most psis fall into the lower classes, with only 33% categorised as class five or above.

Code 10

The police code for an emergency situation, code 10 means to activate lights and sirens (if in a patrol car) and get to the scene as quickly as possible.

DA

District Attorney.

DOJ

Department of Justice.

Empathy

Empathy is the psychic ability dealing with emotions. Empaths are commonly able to detect and (depending on the strength of the empath) alter people's emotions. Almost a subset of telepathy, empaths are common enough to rate their own type. It is illegal for an officer of a law enforcement agency to be an empath.

I.A.D.

Internal Affairs Division.

Mindraper

Possibly the most offensive term ever coined to describe telepaths.

'path

Slang for a telepath or empath, though the former usage is most common.

Perp

Perpetrator. Police slang for a criminal.

Precognition

Precognition is the ability to see the future. Psis who possess this ability are called precognitives, or more commonly, precogs. Precogs experience visions at various times and in various situations. Precognition is an unconscious ability — there are no known precogs that can control either the timing of their visions, or what they see during them.

Psychic

Psychics, or psis in common parlance, possess preternatural mental abilities of various kinds — telepathy, telekinesis, empathy and precognition being the most common.

Simons-Krueger Test

A telepathic lie detector test, the Simons-Krueger was developed by Professor Martin Simons and Dr Claudia Krueger at MIT. The Simons-Krueger involves directed questioning by a trained professional (usually an ADA) and mental probing by a telepath employed by the DOJ. The Simons-Krueger is far more reliable than a mechanical lie detector and the results are admissible in court. Because the Simons-Krueger involves mental scanning (essentially an invasion of privacy) it can only be taken voluntarily.

Telekinesis

Telekinesis is the generic name for all abilities concerned with physical movement. Telekinetics can move objects, other people and even themselves.

Tel-Emp

Tel-emp is a slang term that encapsulates telepathic and empathic abilities, or the people who possess one or the other, or both.

Telepathy

A general term for abilities that directly affect the thoughts of the subject, telepathy takes various forms, including mind reading and mind-to-mind communication. It is illegal for an officer of a law enforcement agency to be a telepath.

Unregistered

In America, all psis have to be registered. That information is indicated in their SSN and shown on driver's licenses. Those with abilities whose use could potentially constitute an invasion of privacy (empaths and telepaths primarily) are required to inform their local police department of their living and working arrangements. Some psis still slip through the cracks, but if they later come to the attention of the authorities they face severe penalties, including prison time.

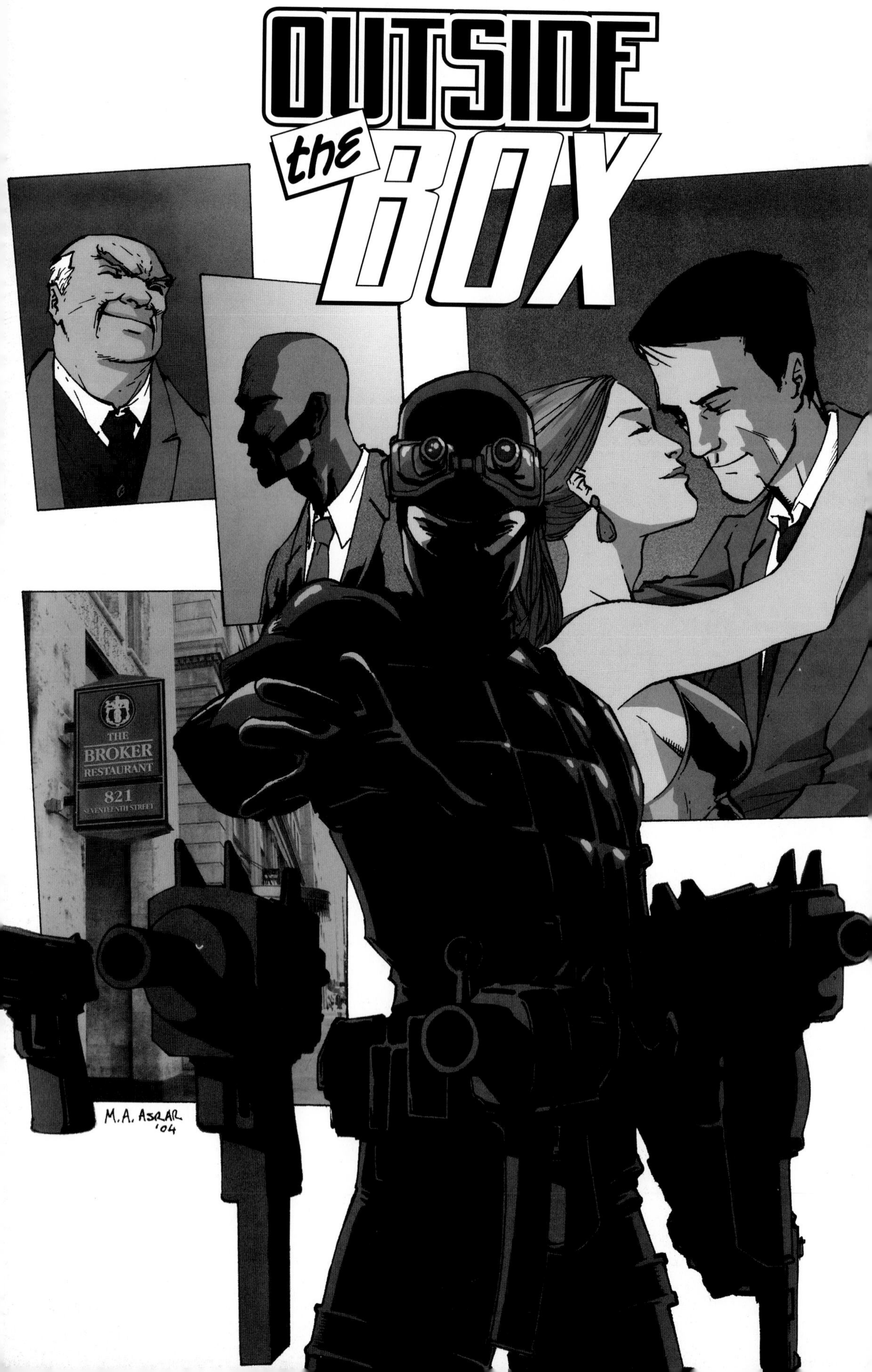
OUTSIDE the BOX
THE BROKER RESTAURANT
821 SEVENTEENTH STREET
M.A. ASRAR '04

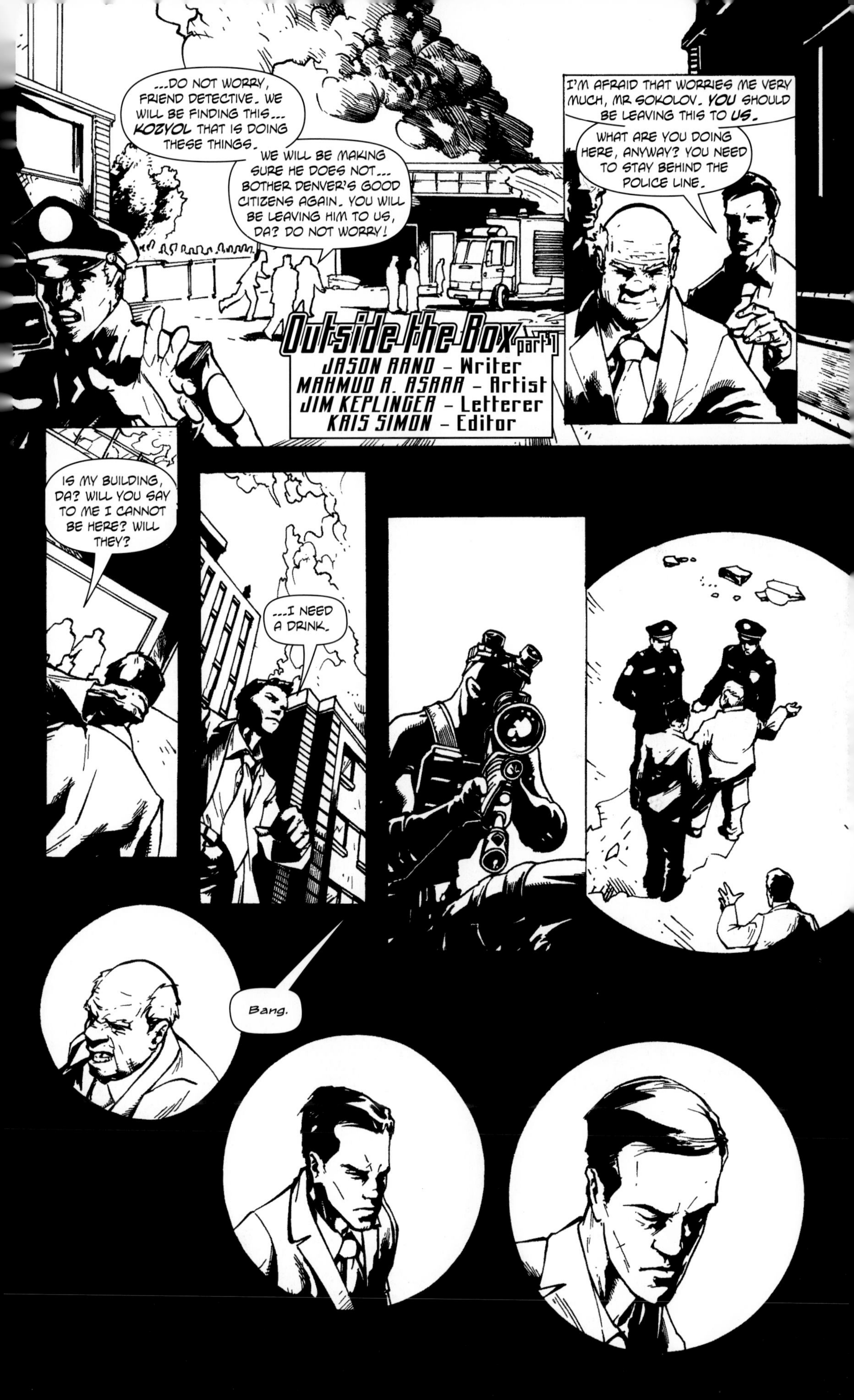
...DO NOT WORRY, FRIEND DETECTIVE. WE WILL BE FINDING THIS... KOZYOL THAT IS DOING THESE THINGS.
WE WILL BE MAKING SURE HE DOES NOT... BOTHER DENVER'S GOOD CITIZENS AGAIN. YOU WILL BE LEAVING HIM TO US, DA? DO NOT WORRY!
Outside the Box part 1
JASON RAND - Writer
MAHMUD A. ASRAR - Artist
JIM KEPLINGER - Letterer
KRIS SIMON - Editor
I'M AFRAID THAT WORRIES ME VERY MUCH, MR SOKOLOV. YOU SHOULD BE LEAVING THIS TO US.
WHAT ARE YOU DOING HERE, ANYWAY? YOU NEED TO STAY BEHIND THE POLICE LINE.
IS MY BUILDING, DA? WILL YOU SAY TO ME I CANNOT BE HERE? WILL THEY?
...I NEED A DRINK.
Bang.

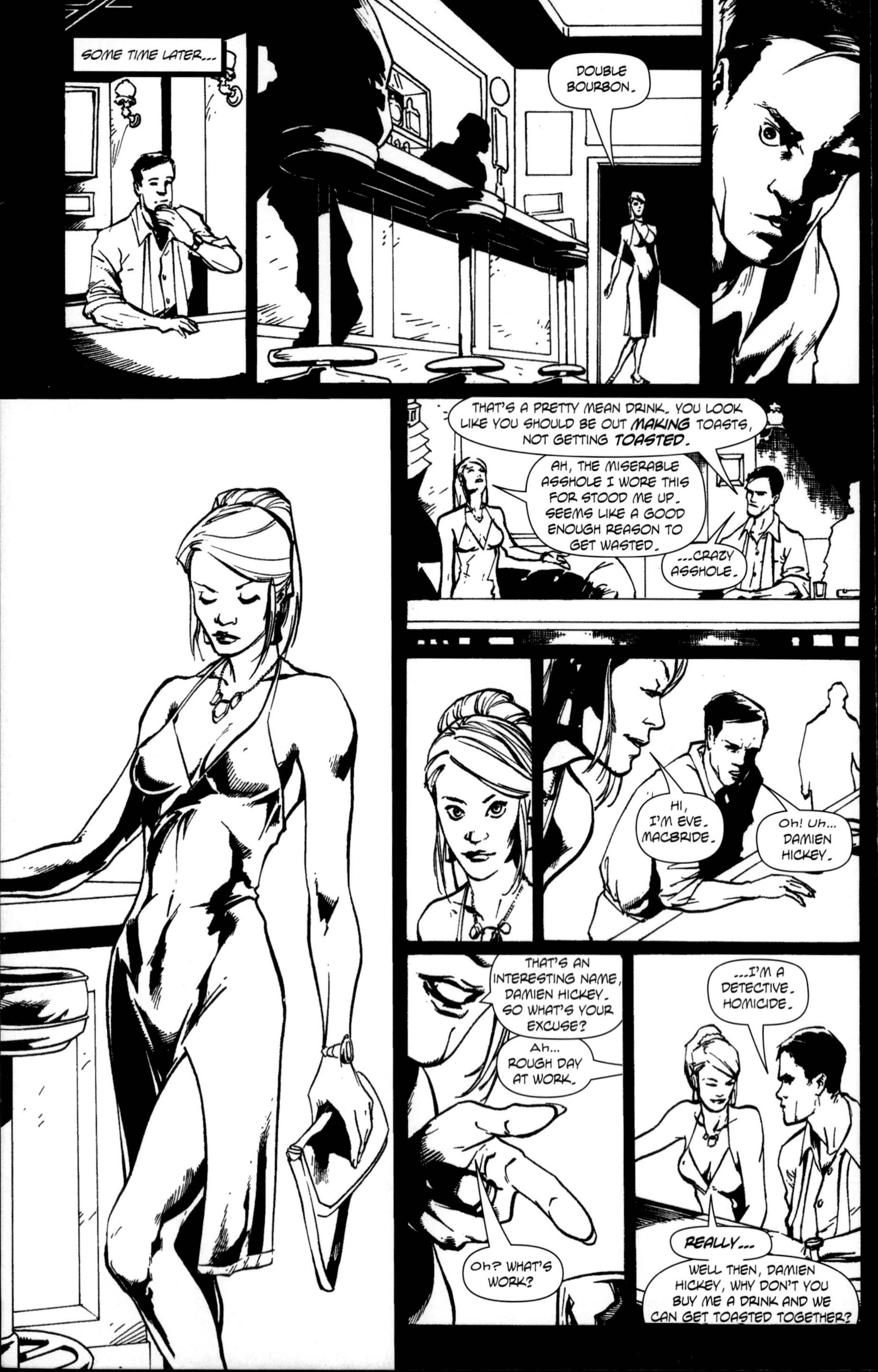
SOME TIME LATER...
DOUBLE BOURBON.
THAT'S A PRETTY MEAN DRINK. YOU LOOK LIKE YOU SHOULD BE OUT MAKING TOASTS, NOT GETTING TOASTED.
AH, THE MISERABLE ASSHOLE I WORE THIS FOR STOOD ME UP. SEEMS LIKE A GOOD ENOUGH REASON TO GET WASTED.
...CRAZY ASSHOLE.
HI, I'M EVE MACBRIDE.
Oh! Uh... DAMIEN HICKEY.
THAT'S AN INTERESTING NAME, DAMIEN HICKEY. SO WHAT'S YOUR EXCUSE?
Ah... ROUGH DAY AT WORK.
Oh? WHAT'S WORK?
...I'M A DETECTIVE. HOMICIDE.
REALLY...
WELL THEN, DAMIEN HICKEY, WHY DON'T YOU BUY ME A DRINK AND WE CAN GET TOASTED TOGETHER?

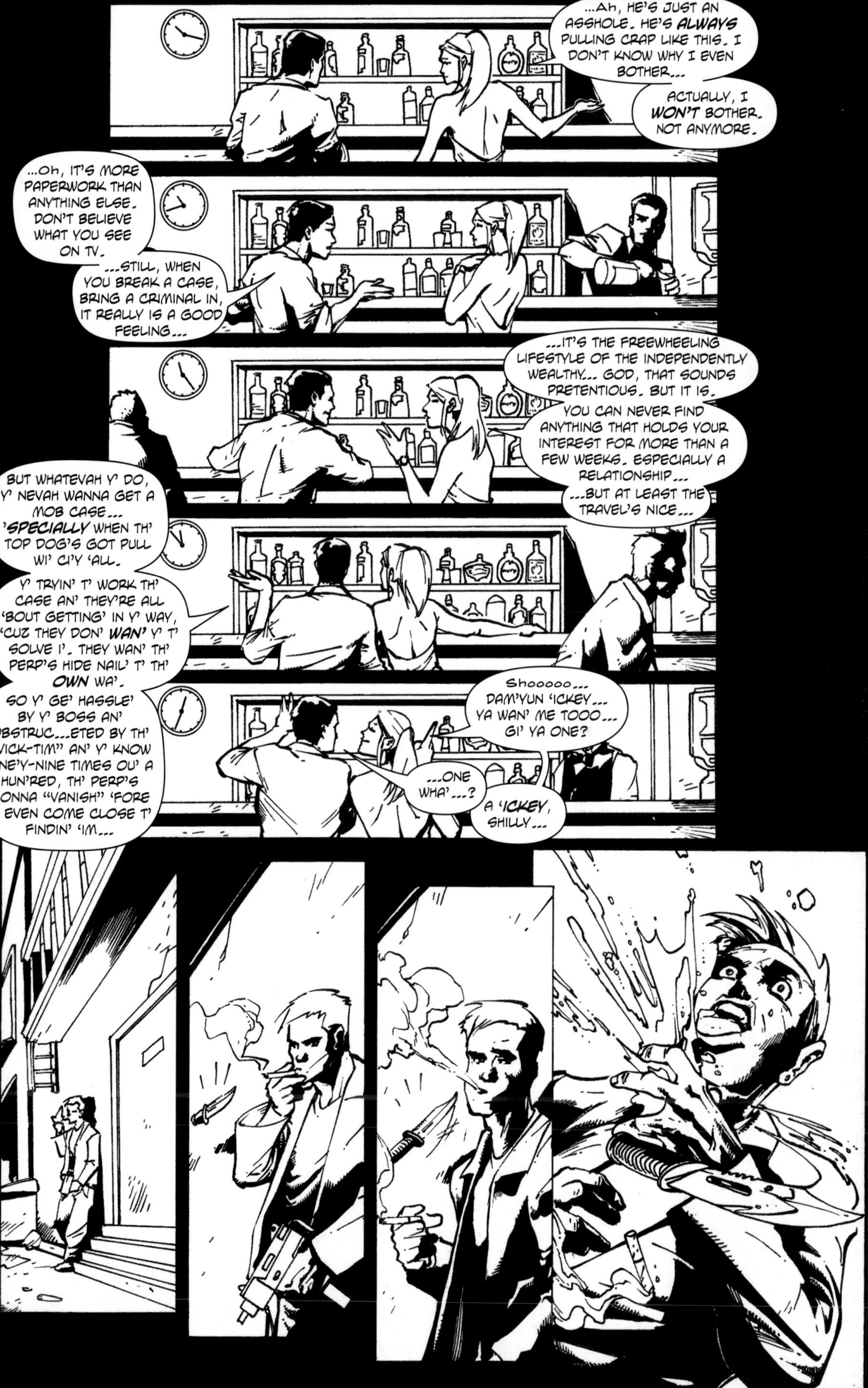
...Ah, HE'S JUST AN ASSHOLE. HE'S ALWAYS PULLING CRAP LIKE THIS. I DON'T KNOW WHY I EVEN BOTHER...
ACTUALLY, I WON'T BOTHER. NOT ANYMORE.
...Oh, IT'S MORE PAPERWORK THAN ANYTHING ELSE. DON'T BELIEVE WHAT YOU SEE ON TV.
...STILL, WHEN YOU BREAK A CASE, BRING A CRIMINAL IN, IT REALLY IS A GOOD FEELING...
...IT'S THE FREEWHEELING LIFESTYLE OF THE INDEPENDENTLY WEALTHY... GOD, THAT SOUNDS PRETENTIOUS. BUT IT IS.
YOU CAN NEVER FIND ANYTHING THAT HOLDS YOUR INTEREST FOR MORE THAN A FEW WEEKS. ESPECIALLY A RELATIONSHIP...
...BUT AT LEAST THE TRAVEL'S NICE...
BUT WHATEVAH Y' DO, Y' NEVAH WANNA GET A MOB CASE... 'SPECIALLY WHEN TH' TOP DOG'S GOT PULL WI' CI'Y 'ALL.
Y' TRYIN' T' WORK TH' CASE AN' THEY'RE ALL 'BOUT GETTING' IN Y' WAY, 'CUZ THEY DON' WAN' Y' T' SOLVE I'. THEY WAN' TH' PERP'S HIDE NAIL' T' TH' OWN WA'.
SO Y' GE' HASSLE' BY Y' BOSS AN' OBSTRUC...ETED BY TH' "VICK-TIM" AN' Y' KNOW NINE'Y-NINE TIMES OU' A HUN'RED, TH' PERP'S GONNA "VANISH" 'FORE Y' EVEN COME CLOSE T' FINDIN' 'IM...
Shooooo... DAM'YUN 'ICKEY... YA WAN' ME TOOO... GI' YA ONE?
...ONE WHA'...?
A 'ICKEY, SHILLY...

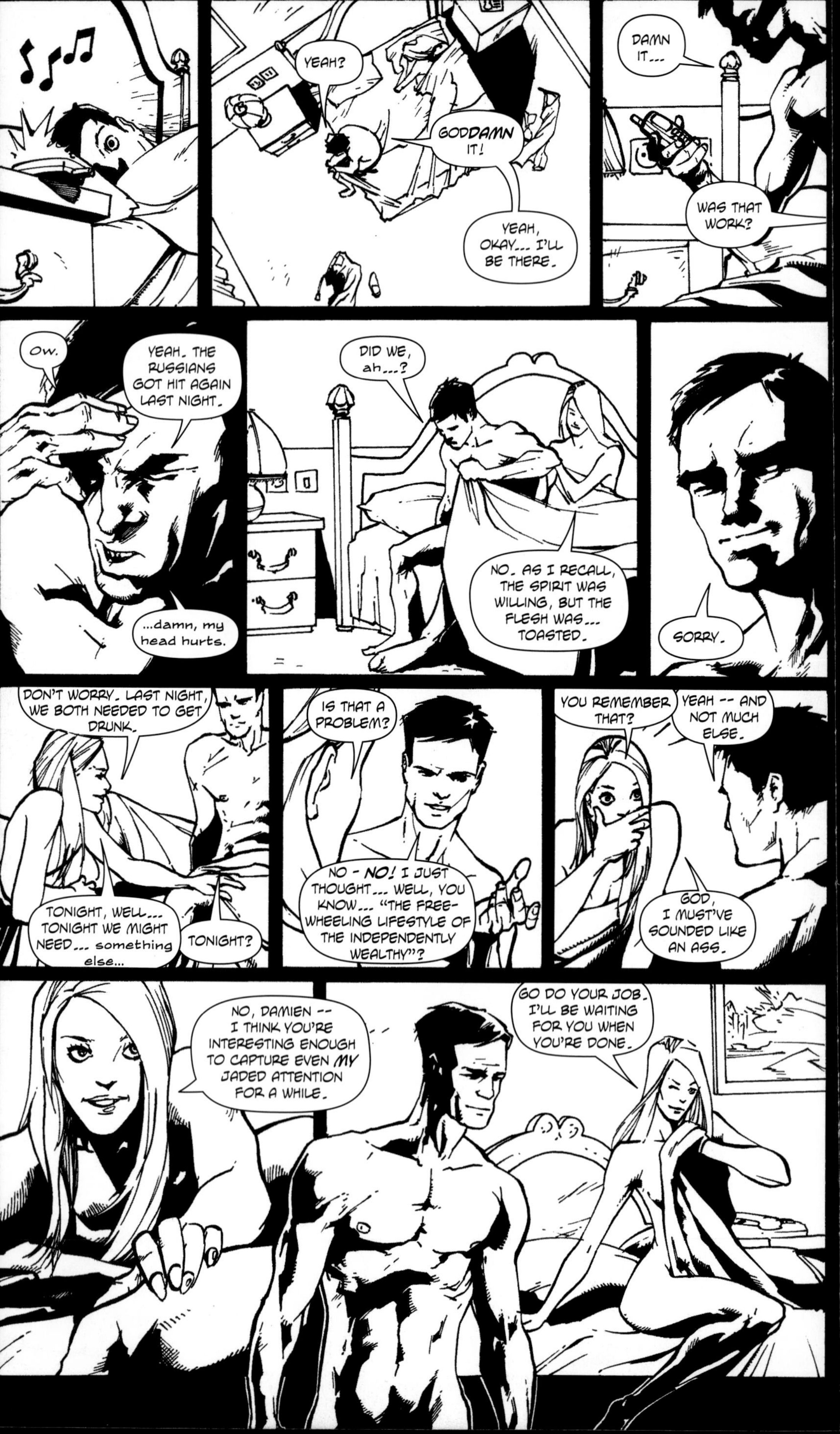
YEAH?
GODDAMN IT!
YEAH, OKAY... I'LL BE THERE.
DAMN IT...
WAS THAT WORK?
Ow.
YEAH. THE RUSSIANS GOT HIT AGAIN LAST NIGHT.
...damn, my head hurts.
DID WE, ah...?
NO. AS I RECALL, THE SPIRIT WAS WILLING, BUT THE FLESH WAS... TOASTED.
SORRY.
DON'T WORRY. LAST NIGHT, WE BOTH NEEDED TO GET DRUNK.
TONIGHT, WELL... TONIGHT WE MIGHT NEED... something else...
TONIGHT?
IS THAT A PROBLEM?
NO - NO! I JUST THOUGHT... WELL, YOU KNOW... "THE FREE-WHEELING LIFESTYLE OF THE INDEPENDENTLY WEALTHY"?
YOU REMEMBER THAT?
YEAH -- AND NOT MUCH ELSE.
GOD, I MUST'VE SOUNDED LIKE AN ASS.
NO, DAMIEN -- I THINK YOU'RE INTERESTING ENOUGH TO CAPTURE EVEN MY JADED ATTENTION FOR A WHILE.
GO DO YOUR JOB. I'LL BE WAITING FOR YOU WHEN YOU'RE DONE.

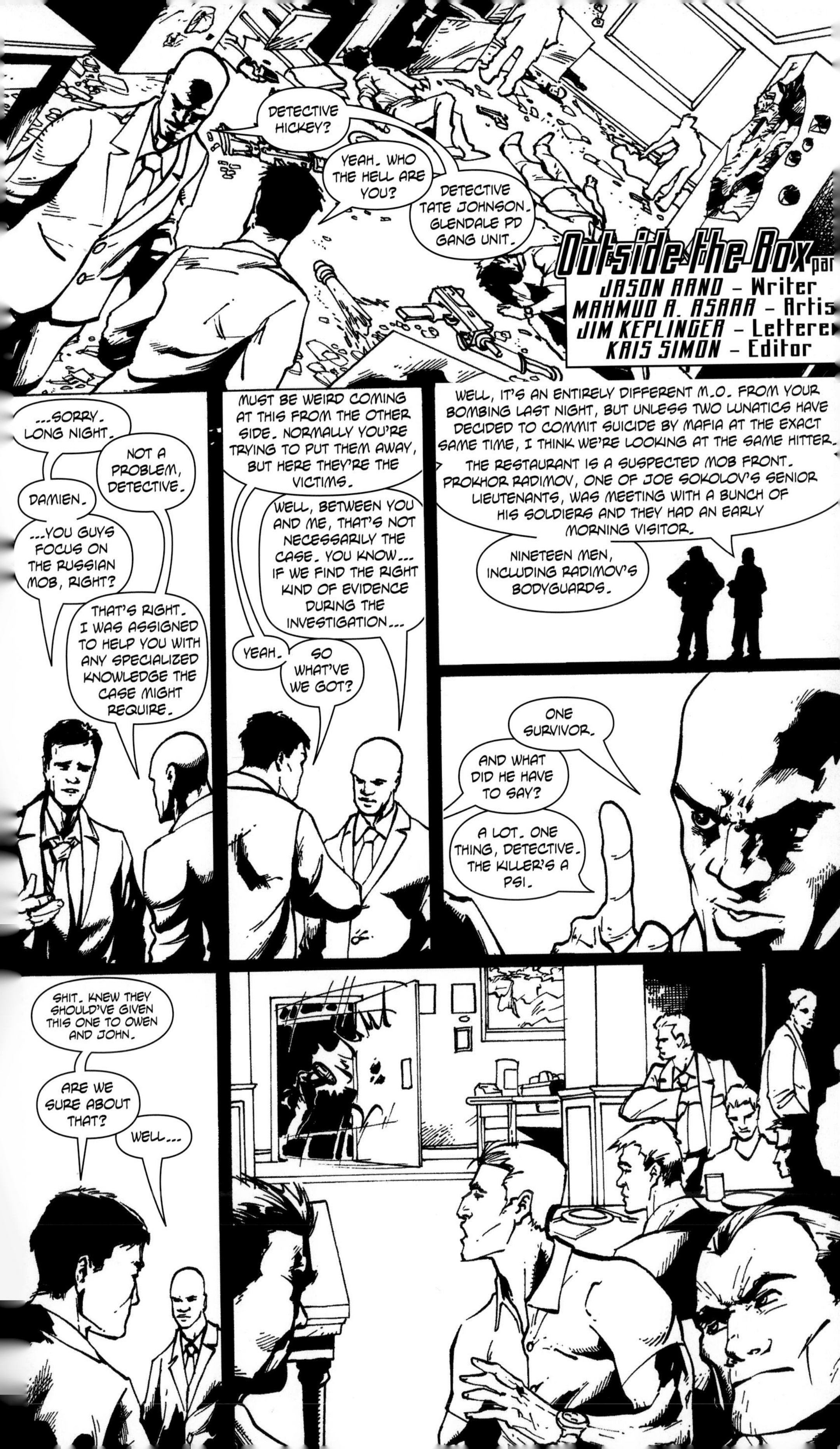

DETECTIVE HICKEY?
YEAH. WHO THE HELL ARE YOU?
DETECTIVE TATE JOHNSON. GLENDALE PD GANG UNIT.
Outside the Box par
JASON RAND - Writer
MAHMUD A. ASRAR - Artis
JIM KEPLINGER - Letterer
KRIS SIMON - Editor
...SORRY. LONG NIGHT.
NOT A PROBLEM, DETECTIVE.
DAMIEN.
...YOU GUYS FOCUS ON THE RUSSIAN MOB, RIGHT?
THAT'S RIGHT. I WAS ASSIGNED TO HELP YOU WITH ANY SPECIALIZED KNOWLEDGE THE CASE MIGHT REQUIRE.
MUST BE WEIRD COMING AT THIS FROM THE OTHER SIDE. NORMALLY YOU'RE TRYING TO PUT THEM AWAY, BUT HERE THEY'RE THE VICTIMS.
WELL, BETWEEN YOU AND ME, THAT'S NOT NECESSARILY THE CASE. YOU KNOW... IF WE FIND THE RIGHT KIND OF EVIDENCE DURING THE INVESTIGATION...
YEAH.
SO WHAT'VE WE GOT?
WELL, IT'S AN ENTIRELY DIFFERENT M.O. FROM YOUR BOMBING LAST NIGHT, BUT UNLESS TWO LUNATICS HAVE DECIDED TO COMMIT SUICIDE BY MAFIA AT THE EXACT SAME TIME, I THINK WE'RE LOOKING AT THE SAME HITTER.
THE RESTAURANT IS A SUSPECTED MOB FRONT. PROKHOR RADIMOV, ONE OF JOE SOKOLOV'S SENIOR LIEUTENANTS, WAS MEETING WITH A BUNCH OF HIS SOLDIERS AND THEY HAD AN EARLY MORNING VISITOR.
NINETEEN MEN, INCLUDING RADIMOV'S BODYGUARDS.
ONE SURVIVOR.
AND WHAT DID HE HAVE TO SAY?
A LOT. ONE THING, DETECTIVE. THE KILLER'S A PSI.
SHIT. KNEW THEY SHOULD'VE GIVEN THIS ONE TO OWEN AND JOHN.
ARE WE SURE ABOUT THAT?
WELL...

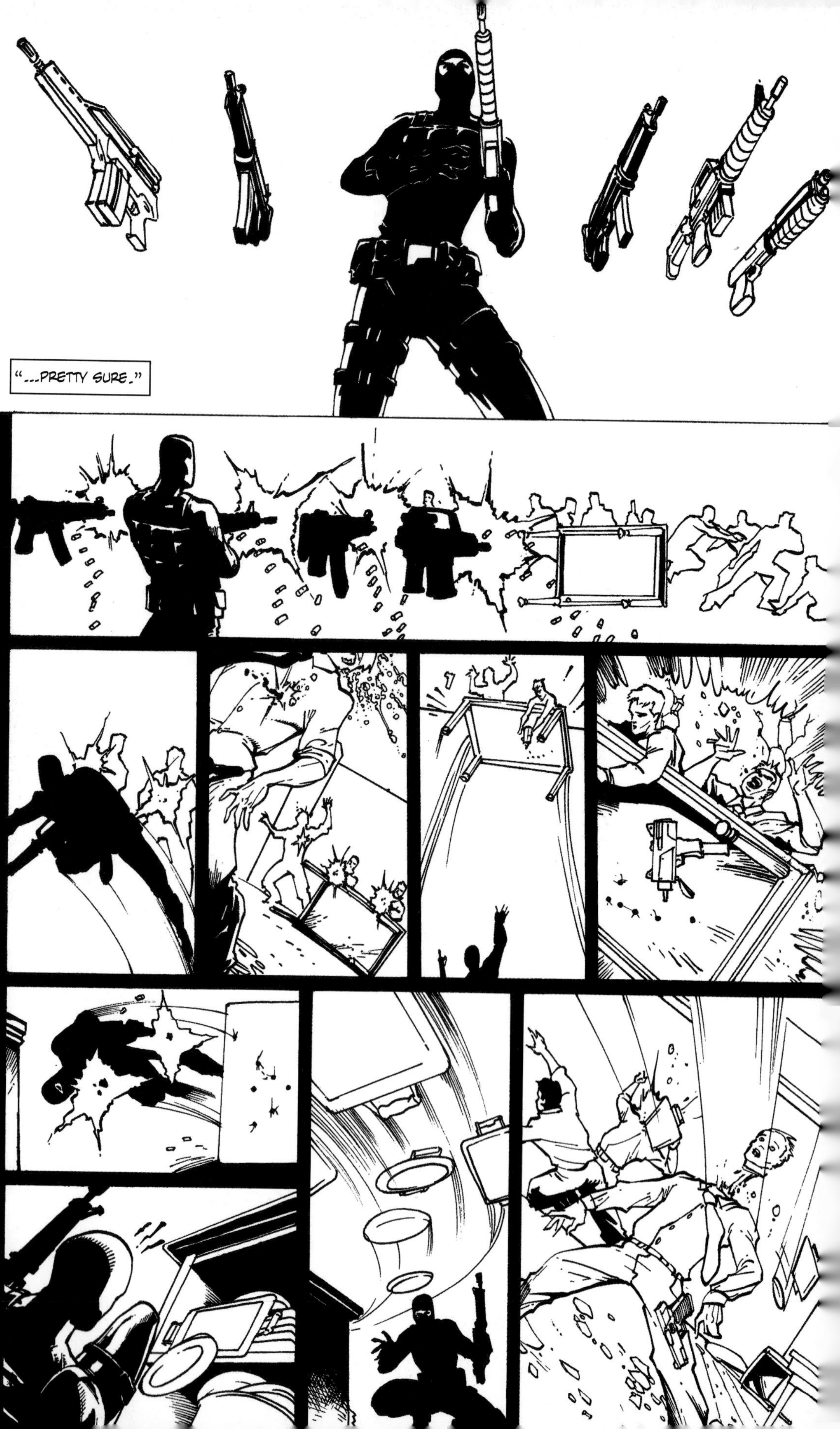
"...PRETTY SURE."

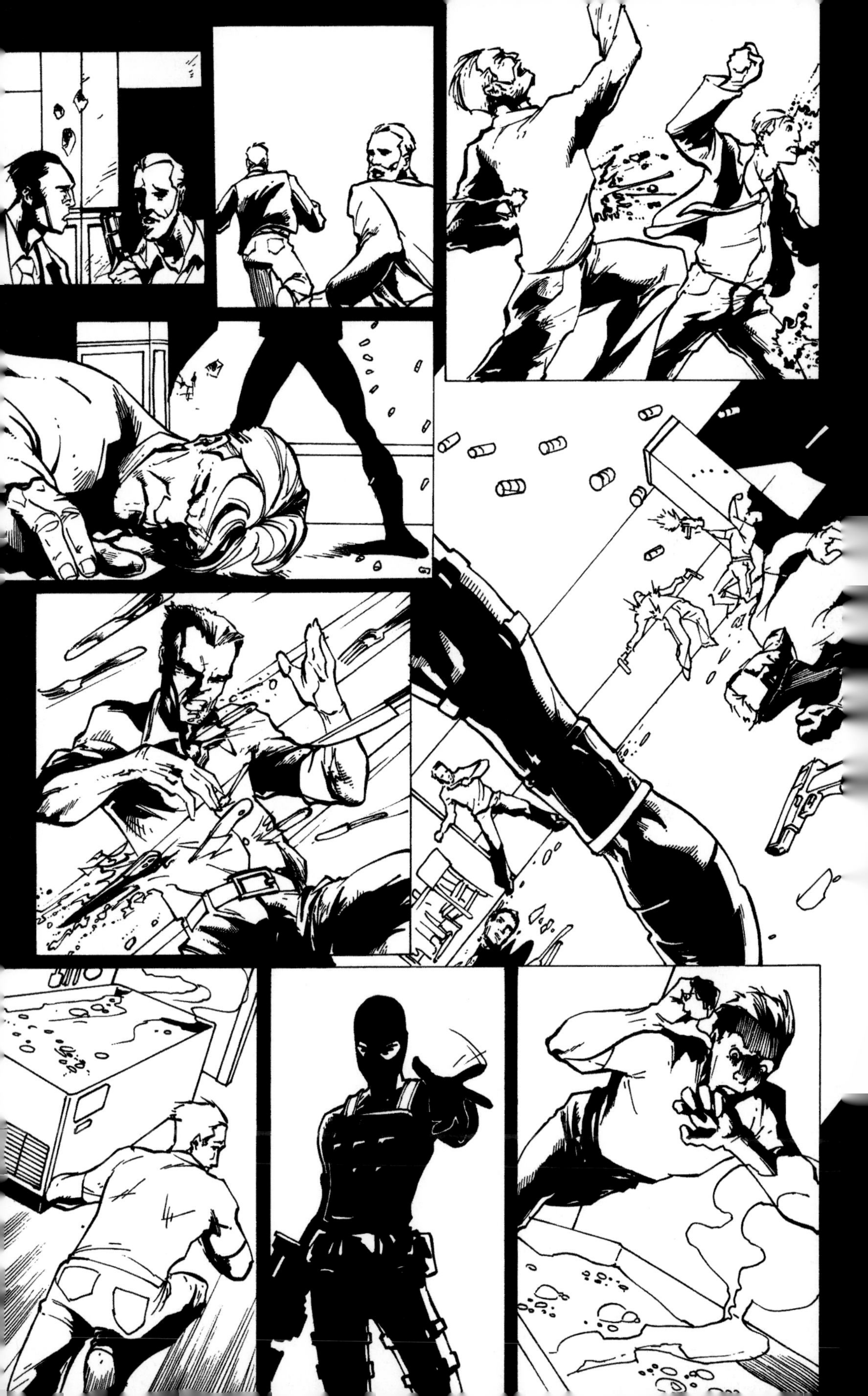

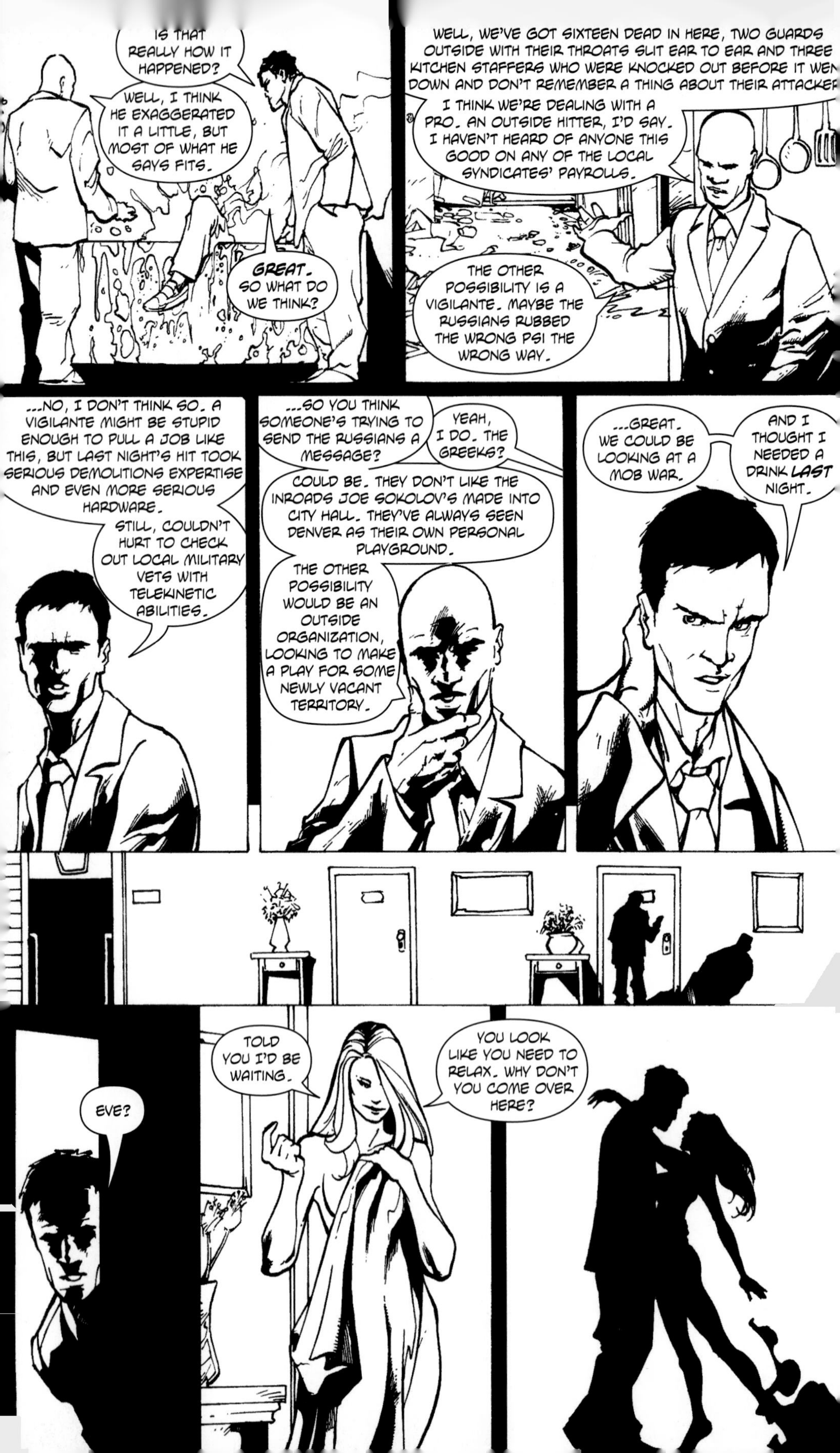
IS THAT REALLY HOW IT HAPPENED?
WELL, I THINK HE EXAGGERATED IT A LITTLE, BUT MOST OF WHAT HE SAYS FITS.
GREAT. SO WHAT DO WE THINK?
WELL, WE'VE GOT SIXTEEN DEAD IN HERE, TWO GUARDS OUTSIDE WITH THEIR THROATS SLIT EAR TO EAR AND THREE KITCHEN STAFFERS WHO WERE KNOCKED OUT BEFORE IT WENT DOWN AND DON'T REMEMBER A THING ABOUT THEIR ATTACKER.
I THINK WE'RE DEALING WITH A PRO. AN OUTSIDE HITTER, I'D SAY. I HAVEN'T HEARD OF ANYONE THIS GOOD ON ANY OF THE LOCAL SYNDICATES' PAYROLLS.
THE OTHER POSSIBILITY IS A VIGILANTE. MAYBE THE RUSSIANS RUBBED THE WRONG PSI THE WRONG WAY.
...NO, I DON'T THINK SO. A VIGILANTE MIGHT BE STUPID ENOUGH TO PULL A JOB LIKE THIS, BUT LAST NIGHT'S HIT TOOK SERIOUS DEMOLITIONS EXPERTISE AND EVEN MORE SERIOUS HARDWARE.
STILL, COULDN'T HURT TO CHECK OUT LOCAL MILITARY VETS WITH TELEKINETIC ABILITIES.
...SO YOU THINK SOMEONE'S TRYING TO SEND THE RUSSIANS A MESSAGE?
YEAH, I DO. THE GREEKS?
COULD BE. THEY DON'T LIKE THE INROADS JOE SOKOLOV'S MADE INTO CITY HALL. THEY'VE ALWAYS SEEN DENVER AS THEIR OWN PERSONAL PLAYGROUND.
THE OTHER POSSIBILITY WOULD BE AN OUTSIDE ORGANIZATION, LOOKING TO MAKE A PLAY FOR SOME NEWLY VACANT TERRITORY.
...GREAT. WE COULD BE LOOKING AT A MOB WAR.
AND I THOUGHT I NEEDED A DRINK LAST NIGHT.
EVE?
TOLD YOU I'D BE WAITING.
YOU LOOK LIKE YOU NEED TO RELAX. WHY DON'T YOU COME OVER HERE?

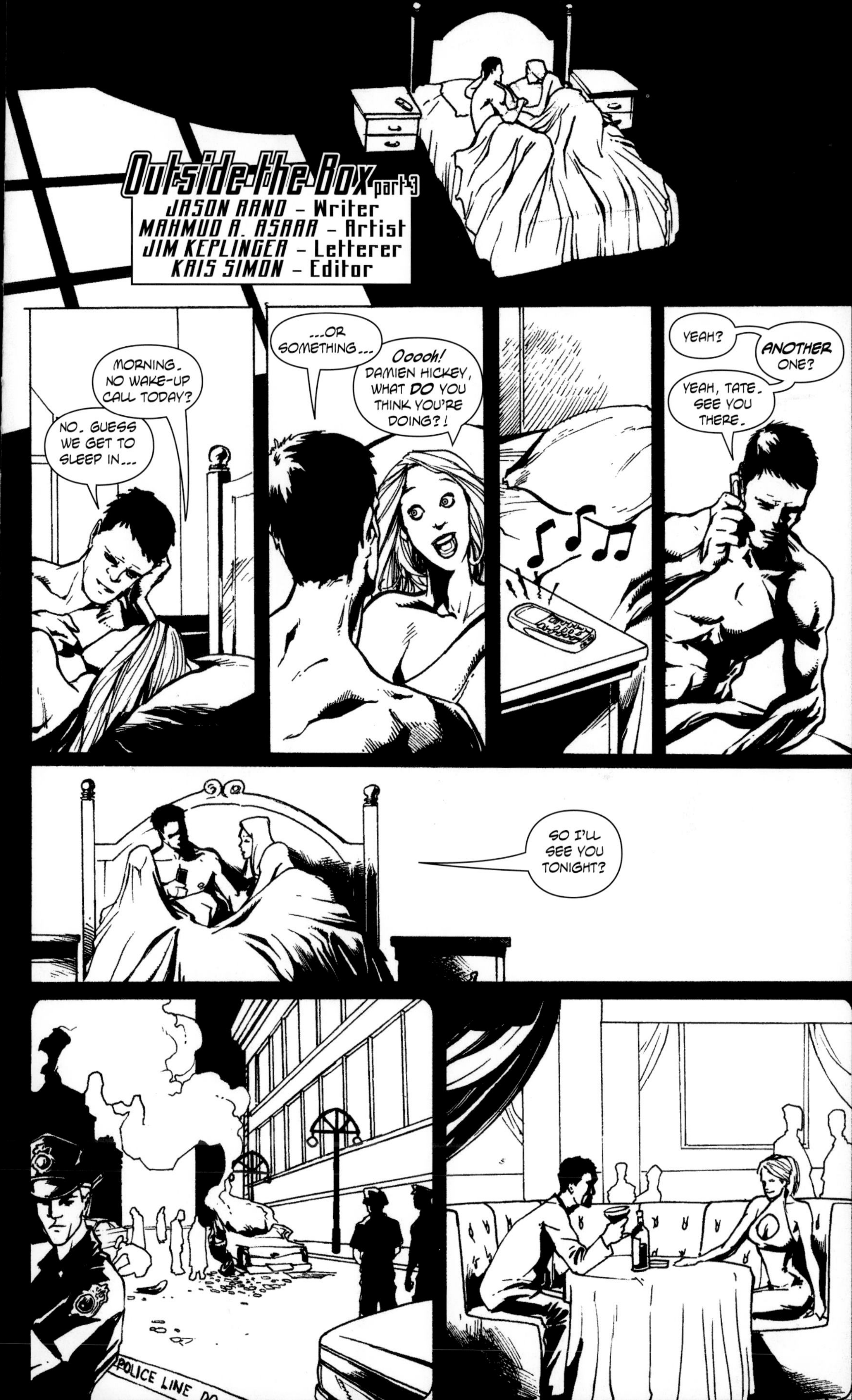
Outside the Box part 3
JASON RAND – Writer
MAHMUD A. ASRAR – Artist
JIM KEPLINGER – Letterer
KRIS SIMON – Editor
MORNING. NO WAKE-UP CALL TODAY?
NO. GUESS WE GET TO SLEEP IN...
...OR SOMETHING...
Ooooh! DAMIEN HICKEY, WHAT DO YOU THINK YOU'RE DOING?!
YEAH?
ANOTHER ONE?
YEAH, TATE. SEE YOU THERE.
SO I'LL SEE YOU TONIGHT?
POLICE LINE DO

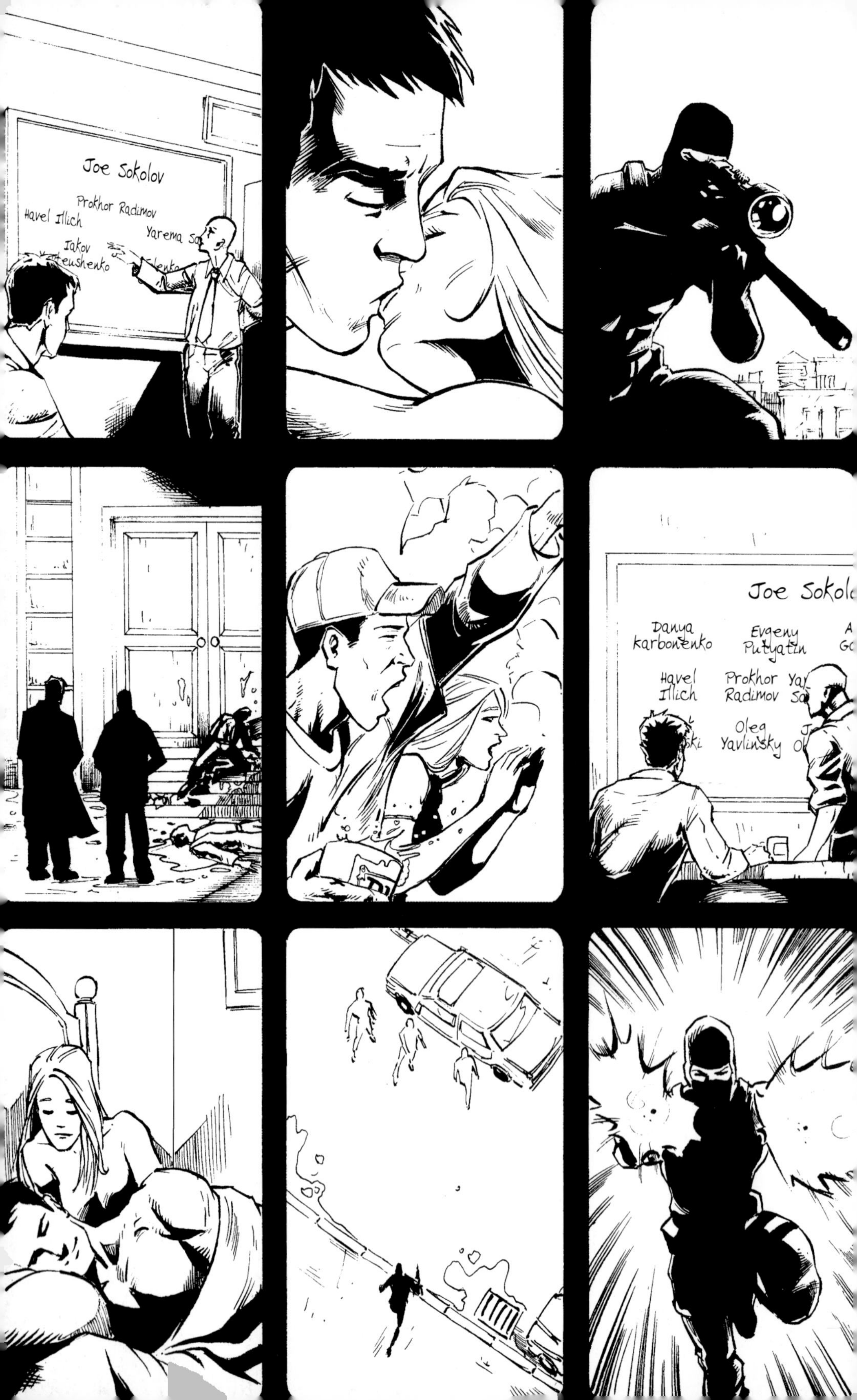
Joe Sokolov
Prokhor Radimov
Havel Illich
Iakov
Danya Karbonenko
Evgeny Putyatin
Havel Illich
Prokhor Radimov
Oleg Yavlinsky

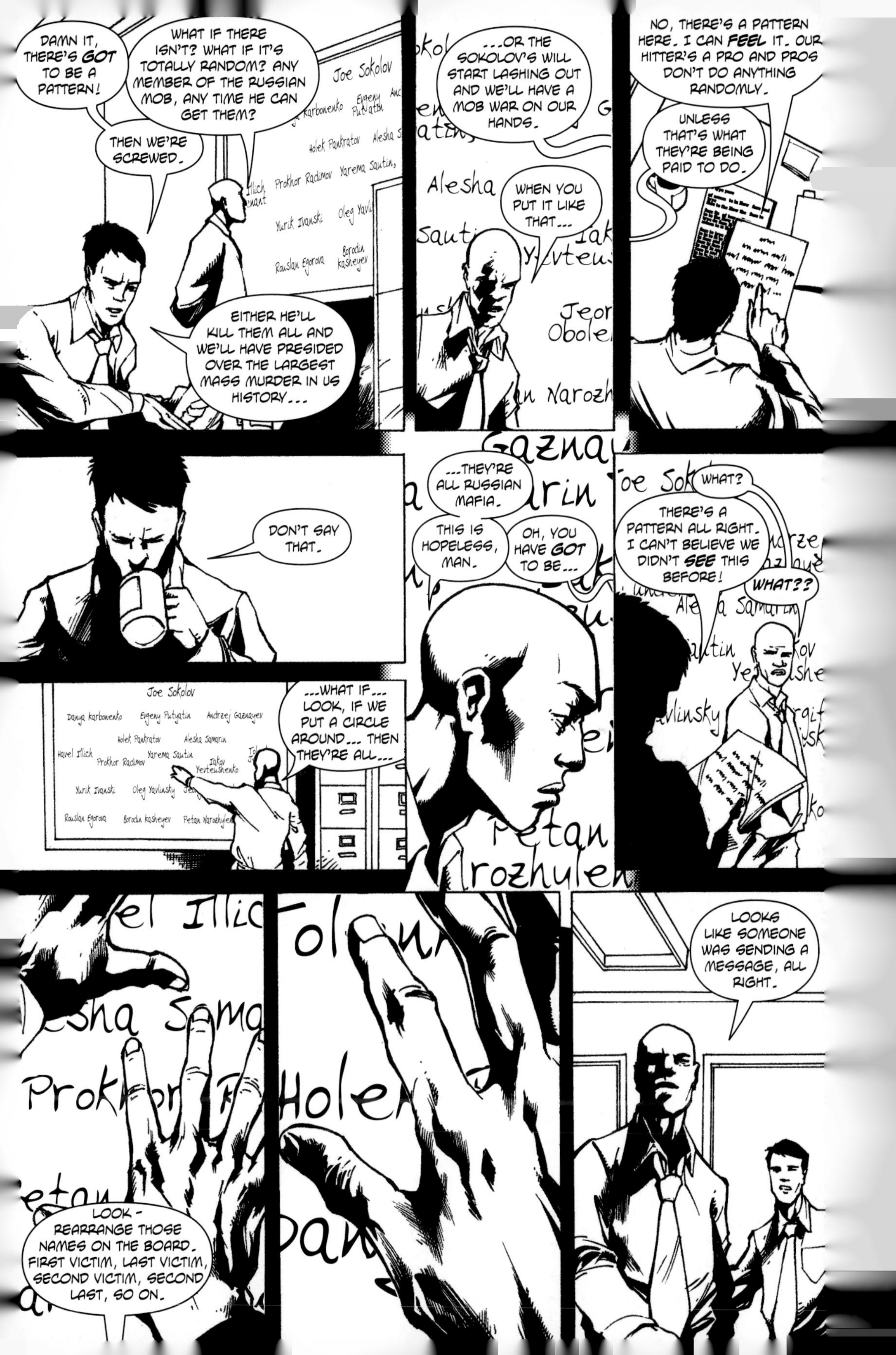
DAMN IT, THERE'S **GOT** TO BE A PATTERN!
WHAT IF THERE ISN'T? WHAT IF IT'S TOTALLY RANDOM? ANY MEMBER OF THE RUSSIAN MOB, ANY TIME HE CAN GET THEM?
THEN WE'RE SCREWED.
EITHER HE'LL KILL THEM ALL AND WE'LL HAVE PRESIDED OVER THE LARGEST MASS MURDER IN US HISTORY...
...OR THE SOKOLOV'S WILL START LASHING OUT AND WE'LL HAVE A MOB WAR ON OUR HANDS.
WHEN YOU PUT IT LIKE THAT...
NO, THERE'S A PATTERN HERE. I CAN **FEEL** IT. OUR HITTER'S A PRO AND PROS DON'T DO ANYTHING RANDOMLY.
UNLESS THAT'S WHAT THEY'RE BEING PAID TO DO.
DON'T SAY THAT.
Joe Sokolov
Danya Karbonenko Evgeny Putyatin Andrzej Gaznayev
Holek Pankratov Alesha Samarin
Havel Illich Prokhor Radimov Yarema Sautin Iakov Yevteushenko
Yurik Ivanski Oleg Yavlinsky
Ruslan Egorova Borodin Kasheyev Petan Narozhulenko
...WHAT IF... LOOK, IF WE PUT A CIRCLE AROUND... THEN THEY'RE ALL...
...THEY'RE ALL RUSSIAN MAFIA.
THIS IS HOPELESS, MAN.
OH, YOU HAVE **GOT** TO BE...
WHAT?
THERE'S A PATTERN ALL RIGHT. I CAN'T BELIEVE WE DIDN'T **SEE** THIS BEFORE!
WHAT??
LOOK - REARRANGE THOSE NAMES ON THE BOARD. FIRST VICTIM, LAST VICTIM, SECOND VICTIM, SECOND LAST, SO ON.
LOOKS LIKE SOMEONE WAS SENDING A MESSAGE, ALL RIGHT.

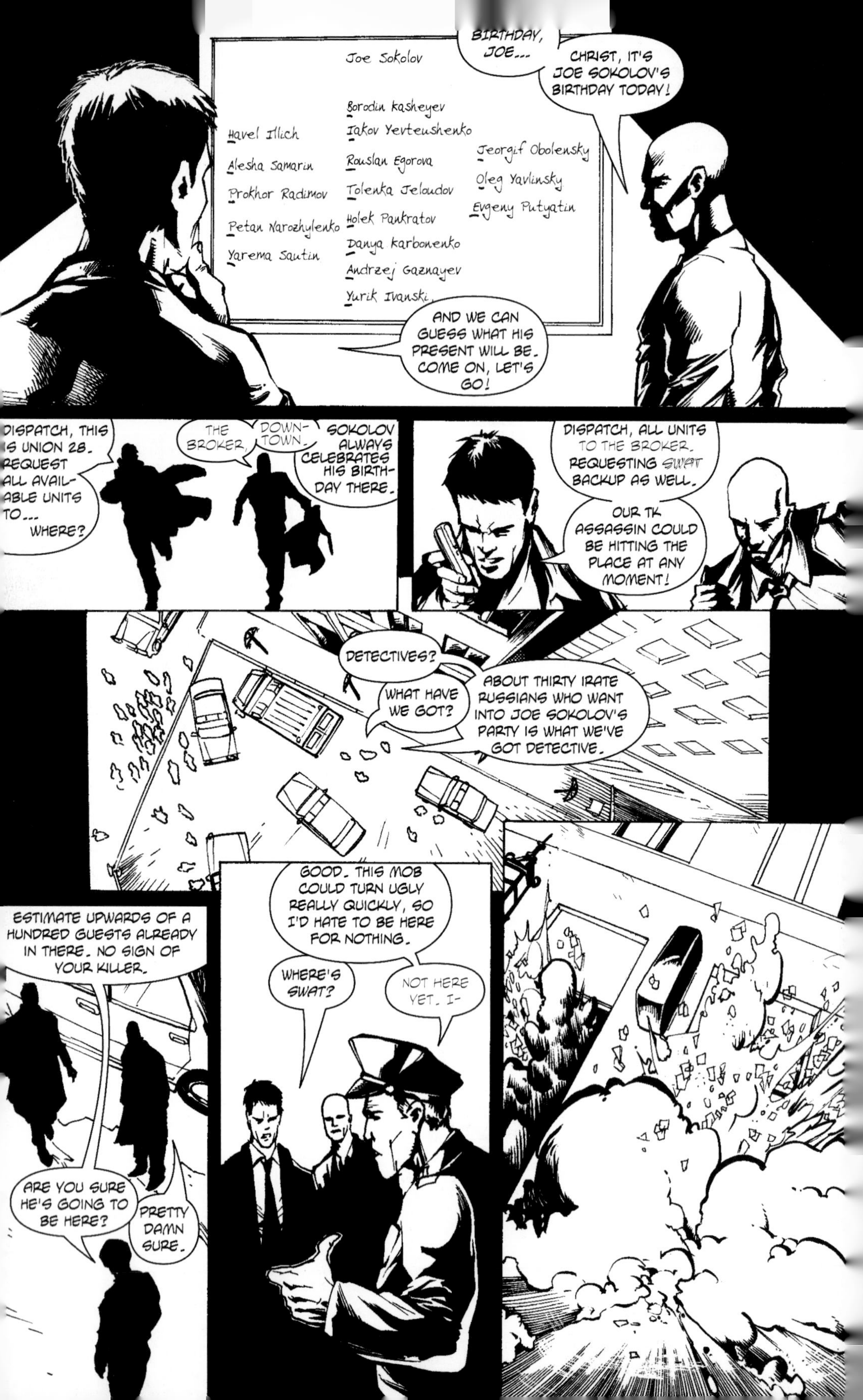
Joe Sokolov
Borodin Kasheyev
Havel Illich
Iakov Yevteushenko
Jeorgif Obolensky
Alesha Samarin
Rouslan Egorova
Oleg Yavlinsky
Prokhor Radimov
Tolenka Jeloudov
Evgeny Putyatin
Holek Pankratov
Petan Narozhylenko
Danya Karbonenko
Yarema Sautin
Andrzej Gaznayev
Yurik Ivanski
BIRTHDAY, JOE...
CHRIST, IT'S JOE SOKOLOV'S BIRTHDAY TODAY!
AND WE CAN GUESS WHAT HIS PRESENT WILL BE. COME ON, LET'S GO!
DISPATCH, THIS IS UNION 28. REQUEST ALL AVAILABLE UNITS TO... WHERE?
THE BROKER,
DOWNTOWN.
SOKOLOV ALWAYS CELEBRATES HIS BIRTHDAY THERE.
DISPATCH, ALL UNITS TO THE BROKER. REQUESTING SWAT BACKUP AS WELL.
OUR TK ASSASSIN COULD BE HITTING THE PLACE AT ANY MOMENT!
DETECTIVES?
WHAT HAVE WE GOT?
ABOUT THIRTY IRATE RUSSIANS WHO WANT INTO JOE SOKOLOV'S PARTY IS WHAT WE'VE GOT DETECTIVE.
ESTIMATE UPWARDS OF A HUNDRED GUESTS ALREADY IN THERE. NO SIGN OF YOUR KILLER.
ARE YOU SURE HE'S GOING TO BE HERE?
PRETTY DAMN SURE.
GOOD. THIS MOB COULD TURN UGLY REALLY QUICKLY, SO I'D HATE TO BE HERE FOR NOTHING.
WHERE'S SWAT?
NOT HERE YET. I-

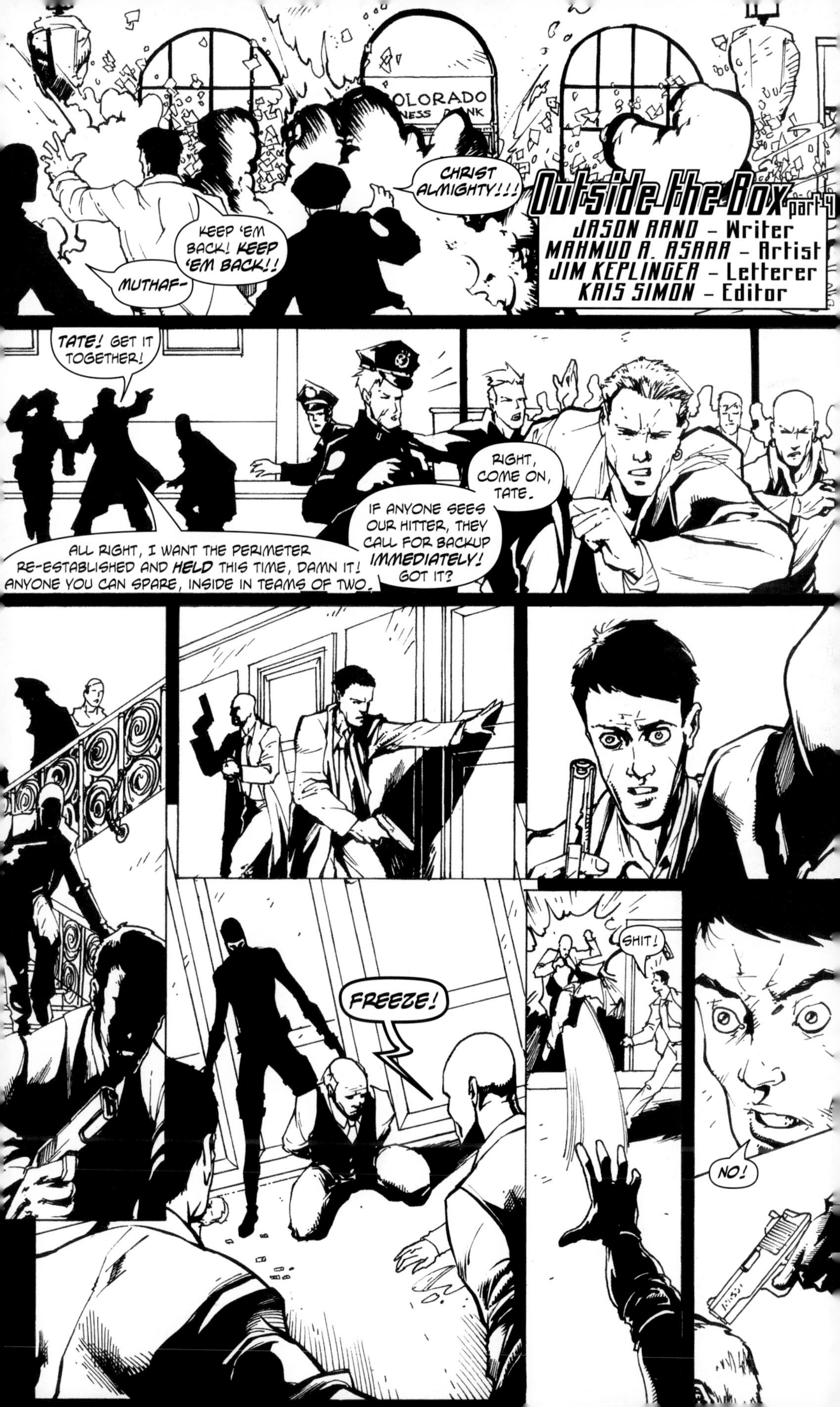

COLORADO
NESS BANK
CHRIST ALMIGHTY!!!
KEEP 'EM BACK! KEEP 'EM BACK!!
MUTHAF-
Outside the Box part 4
JASON RAND - Writer
MAHMUD A. ASRAR - Artist
JIM KEPLINGER - Letterer
KRIS SIMON - Editor
TATE! GET IT TOGETHER!
ALL RIGHT, I WANT THE PERIMETER RE-ESTABLISHED AND HELD THIS TIME, DAMN IT! ANYONE YOU CAN SPARE, INSIDE IN TEAMS OF TWO.
IF ANYONE SEES OUR HITTER, THEY CALL FOR BACKUP IMMEDIATELY! GOT IT?
RIGHT, COME ON, TATE.
FREEZE!
SHIT!
NO!

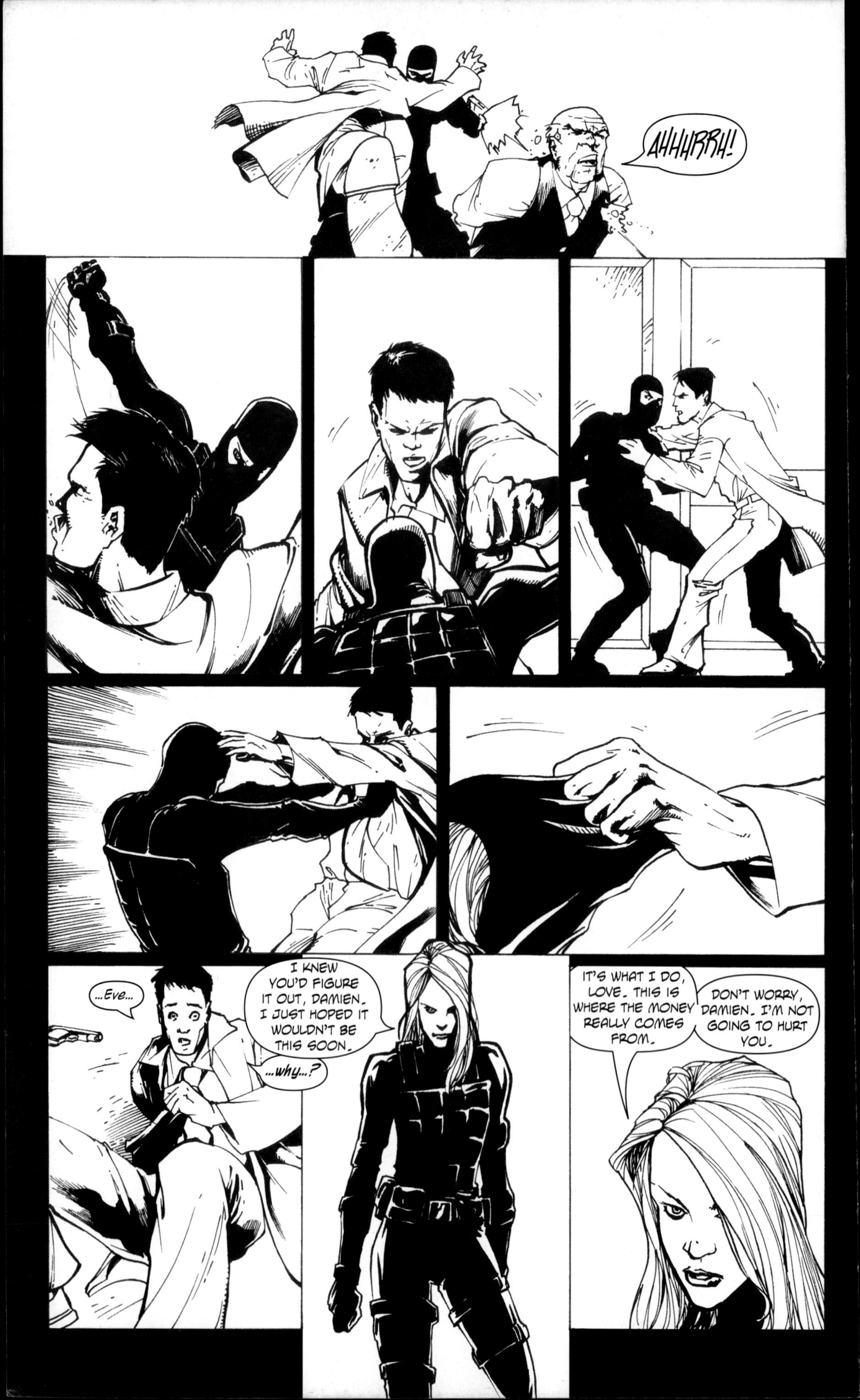
AHHHRRH!
...Eve...
I KNEW YOU'D FIGURE IT OUT, DAMIEN. I JUST HOPED IT WOULDN'T BE THIS SOON.
...why...?
IT'S WHAT I DO, LOVE. THIS IS WHERE THE MONEY REALLY COMES FROM.
DON'T WORRY, DAMIEN. I'M NOT GOING TO HURT YOU.

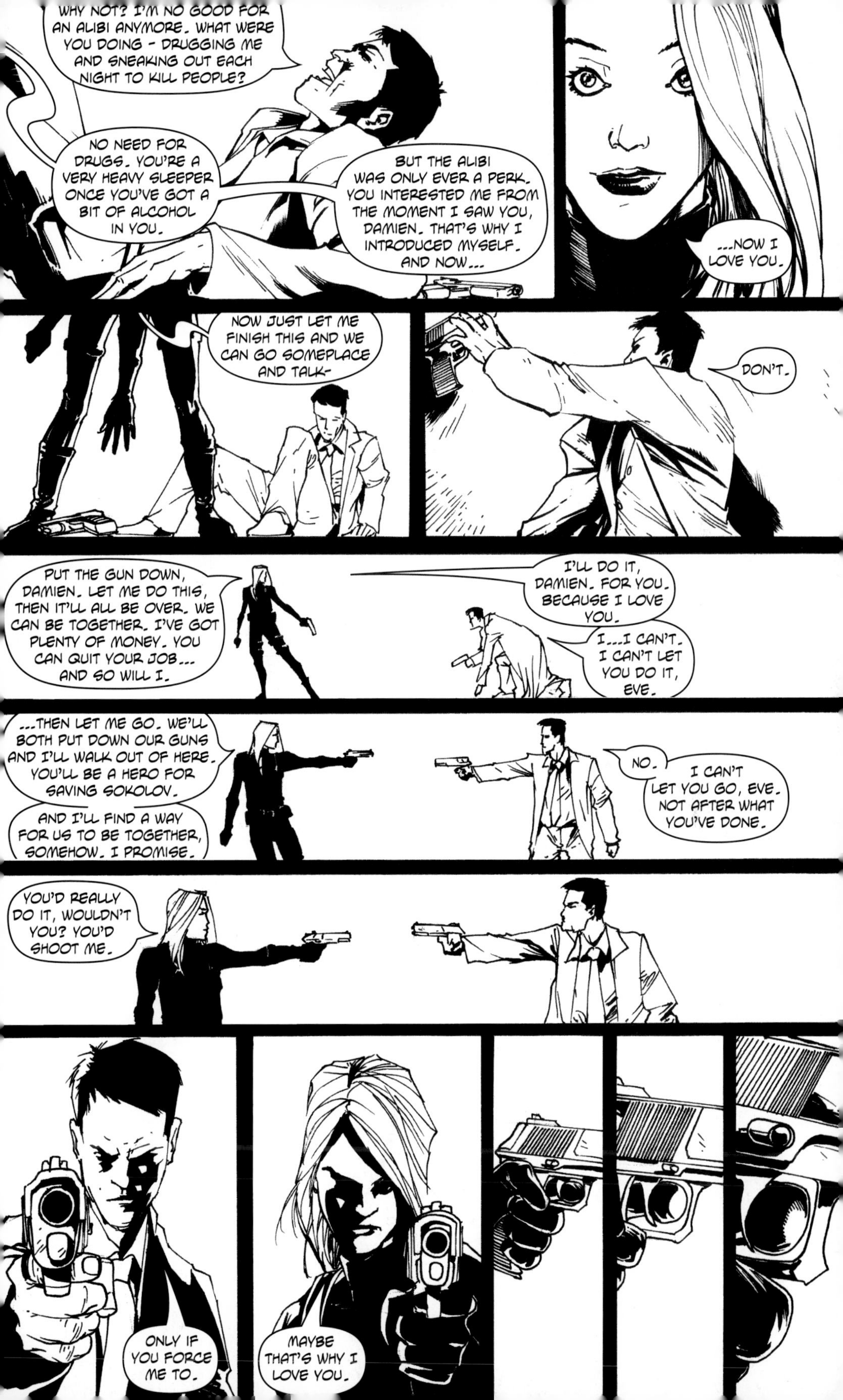
WHY NOT? I'M NO GOOD FOR AN ALIBI ANYMORE. WHAT WERE YOU DOING - DRUGGING ME AND SNEAKING OUT EACH NIGHT TO KILL PEOPLE?
NO NEED FOR DRUGS. YOU'RE A VERY HEAVY SLEEPER ONCE YOU'VE GOT A BIT OF ALCOHOL IN YOU.
BUT THE ALIBI WAS ONLY EVER A PERK. YOU INTERESTED ME FROM THE MOMENT I SAW YOU, DAMIEN. THAT'S WHY I INTRODUCED MYSELF. AND NOW...
...NOW I LOVE YOU.
NOW JUST LET ME FINISH THIS AND WE CAN GO SOMEPLACE AND TALK-
DON'T.
PUT THE GUN DOWN, DAMIEN. LET ME DO THIS, THEN IT'LL ALL BE OVER. WE CAN BE TOGETHER. I'VE GOT PLENTY OF MONEY. YOU CAN QUIT YOUR JOB... AND SO WILL I.
I'LL DO IT, DAMIEN. FOR YOU. BECAUSE I LOVE YOU.
I...I CAN'T. I CAN'T LET YOU DO IT, EVE.
...THEN LET ME GO. WE'LL BOTH PUT DOWN OUR GUNS AND I'LL WALK OUT OF HERE. YOU'LL BE A HERO FOR SAVING SOKOLOV.
AND I'LL FIND A WAY FOR US TO BE TOGETHER, SOMEHOW. I PROMISE.
NO.
I CAN'T LET YOU GO, EVE. NOT AFTER WHAT YOU'VE DONE.
YOU'D REALLY DO IT, WOULDN'T YOU? YOU'D SHOOT ME.
ONLY IF YOU FORCE ME TO.
MAYBE THAT'S WHY I LOVE YOU.

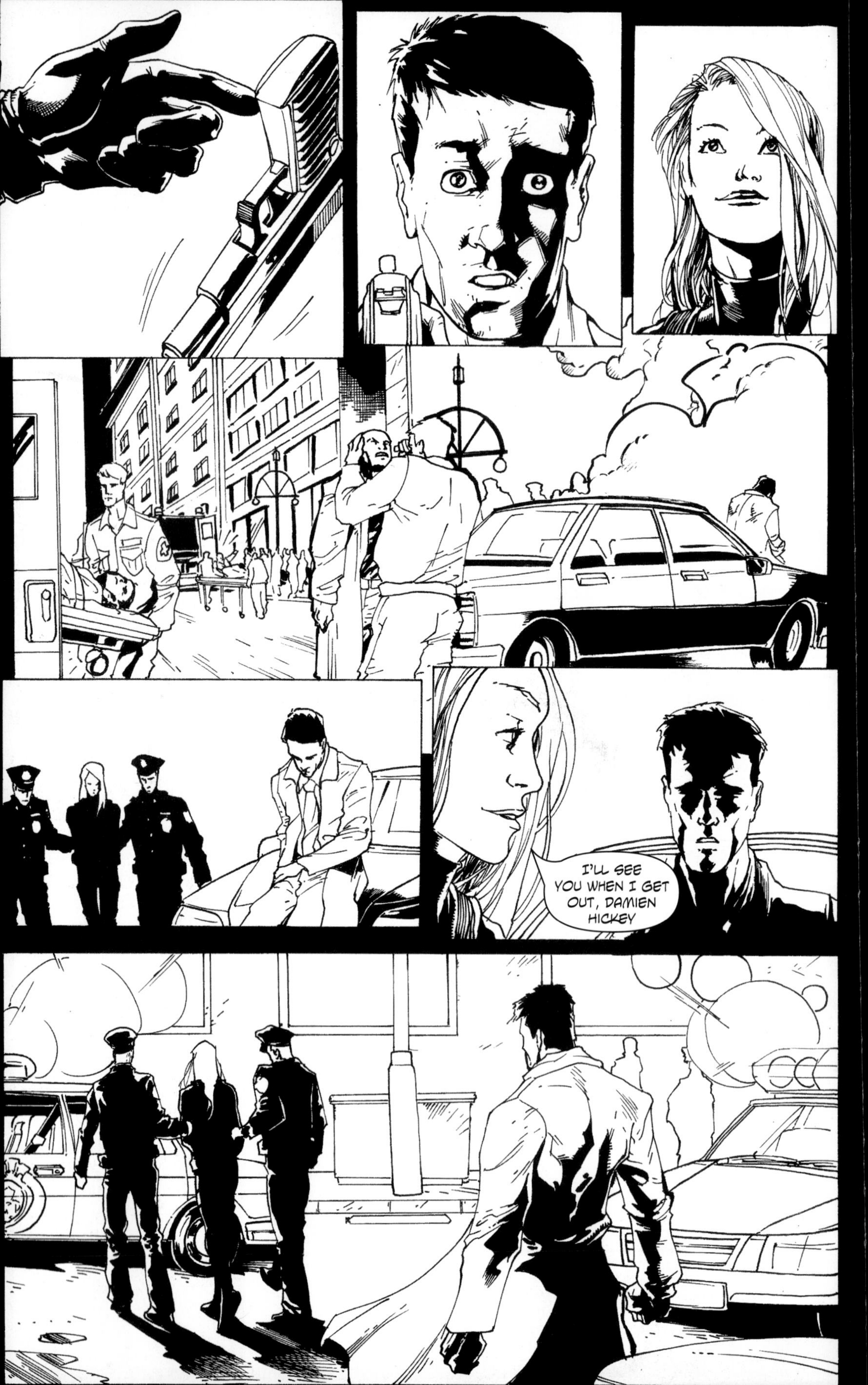
I'LL SEE YOU WHEN I GET OUT, DAMIEN HICKEY

COVER ME!

The long journey from the original proposal cover to the final image on #1.

Creating appealing covers is never an easy task, and we were no exception to the rule. It took a lot of time and effort to come up with the final cover you see on Small Gods #1.

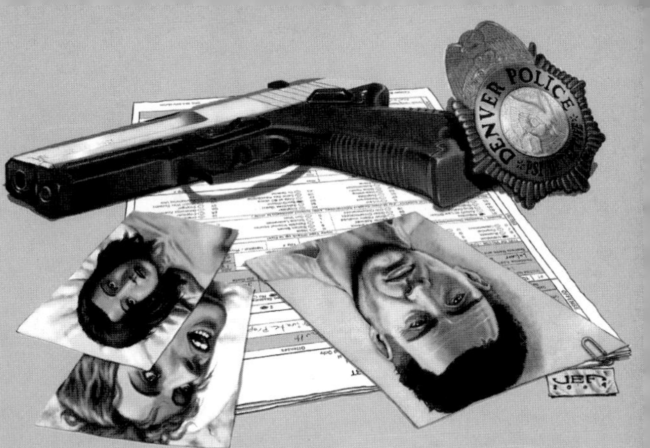
DENVER POLICE

Original proposal cover

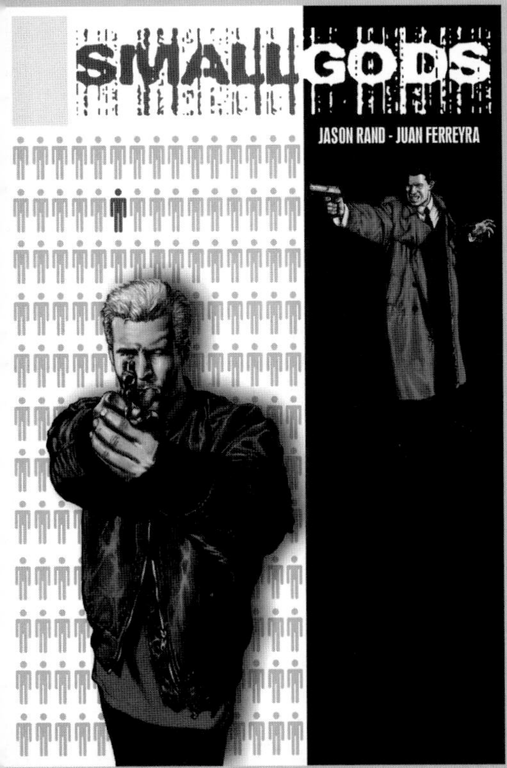
SMALLGODS
JASON RAND - JUAN FERREYRA

Second proposed cover after acceptance at Image

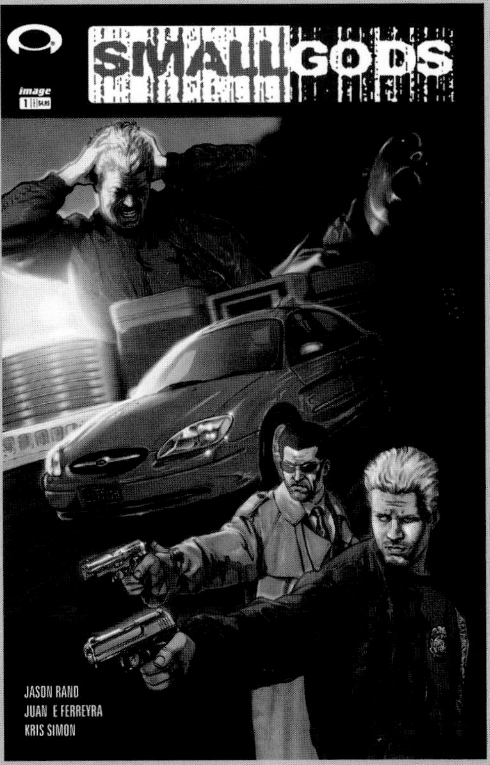
SMALLGODS
image
JASON RAND
JUAN E FERREYRA
KRIS SIMON

Further cover designs

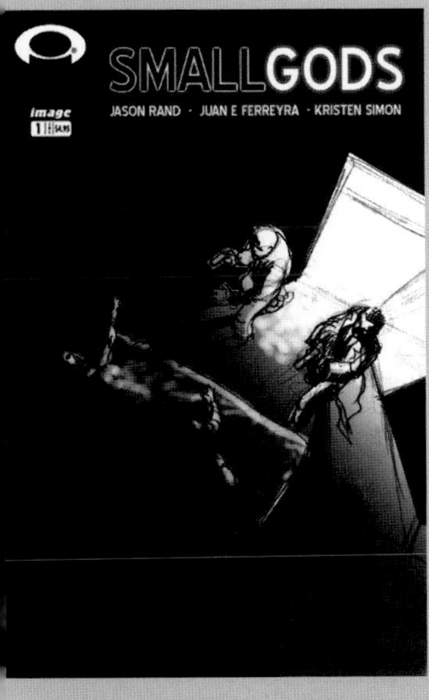
SMALLGODS
image
JASON RAND · JUAN E FERREYRA · KRISTEN SIMON

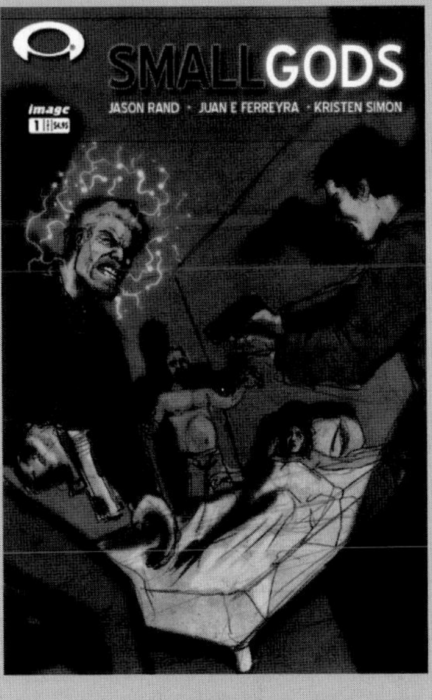
SMALLGODS
image
JASON RAND · JUAN E FERREYRA · KRISTEN SIMON

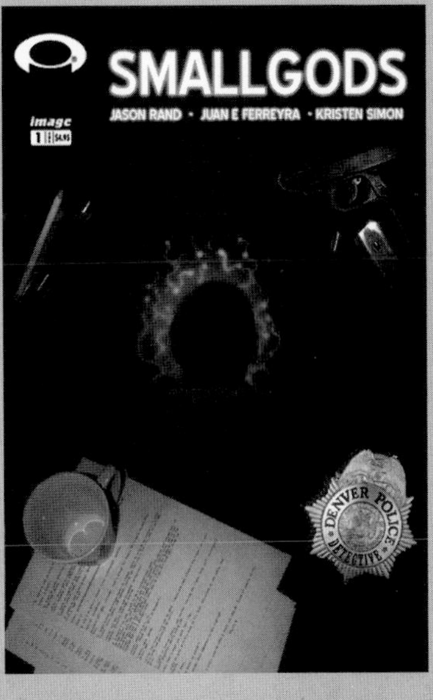
SMALLGODS
image
JASON RAND · JUAN E FERREYRA · KRISTEN SIMON
DENVER POLICE
DETECTIVE

From script to final page

The typical process of creating a page for Small Gods starts with Jason's script (issue 1, page 18 included below). Kris edits and corrects any problems, then sends it off to Juan to be drawn.

Page 18 – 8 panels

Page 18, Panel 1
Owen wakes. This is an extreme close up of his face as his eyes snap open. He's lying on his back, staring up at the ceiling. His expression is a mix of shock, fear and relief that it's just a vision. It's morning now, so don't forget to give him some stubble.

Page 18, Panel 2
Bird's eye view. Beneath us, Owen pushes himself up in bed and looks around, supporting himself on his elbows or widely spread hands.
Your call as to which – he just needs to be up enough to look around without looking silly. He's wearing boxers and nothing else, although he's mostly covered by a sheet and a couple of blankets. The covers are slightly tangled – he's been a bit restless. Dani's not there and it should be obvious she hasn't been there all night – the covers on her side are still tucked in at the top, there's no imprint of her head on her pillow etc. It's early – just after 5am – so it's still dark, possibly with a hint of dawn light coming in off the balcony. Owen's clothes from the previous day are piled on the floor on his side of the bed.

Page 18, Panel 3
Split panel. Top part - Owen rolls to his right, flopping onto his stomach. He reaches out his left hand as he does, grabbing the phone from his bedside table. His head is turned to the left, towards the phone. Use this shot to show the time on the clock-radio – 5:07am. Our POV is on a level with Owen's head and just below the clock-radio and close enough to the bed and bedside table to put the clock-radio right in the foreground of the panel.

Bottom part - Extreme close up on Owen's hand and the phone as he punches in a number – Meyer's number.

Page 18, Panel 4
Still lying on his stomach, Owen speaks into the phone. This shot is from the same angle as panel 4, but zoom in closer, so the bedside table is cut out of the panel.
1. OWEN: JOHN?
2. OWEN (2): …YEAH, I KNOW IT'S EARLY. I'M SORRY.
3. OWEN (3): …I HAD ANOTHER ONE.
4. OWEN (4): …YEAH, TWO IN TWO DAYS. I KNOW.

Page 18, Panel 5
All the panels on this page should be fairly small, to give the impression that Owen's hurrying along – he's more animated; feeling more alive today – as he says in a few panels, he's feeling more himself than he has for days. Owen rolls onto his back. He continues to speak into the phone, while covering his eyes with his free hand. This is a close up, looking down on him from directly over his head.
5. OWEN (5): …BANK JOB. LATER TODAY. THEY SHOOT ONE OF THE GUARDS.
6. OWEN (6): …YEAH, WELL THIS ONE'S DIFFERENT I KNOW WHICH BANK IT IS… AND I EYEBALLED THE PERPS.

Page 18, Panel 6
Same shot. Owen slowly starts to grin.
7. OWEN (7): …THAT'S RIGHT. I CAN ID 'EM ALL. SO GET UP – WE'VE GOT A LOT OF WORK TO DO.
8. OWEN (8): I'LL SEE YOU IN A FEW.

Page 18, Panel 7
Owen eats his breakfast in a hurry – cold cereal and milk. He's sitting on the sofa and leaning forward, watching TV as he eats. He's shaved now, just leaving his goatee. We're looking up at him from about waist level, with the cereal bowl just in front of us. He's lifting a spoonful of cereal to his mouth.
9. CAPTION: BY THE TIME I'M REALLY AWAKE, I'M FEELING MORE LIKE MYSELF THAN I HAVE IN DAYS.
10. CAPTION (2): THIS TIME…THIS TIME I CAN DO SOMETHING ABOUT IT.

Page 18, Panel 8
Owen drives to work. He's wearing his sunglasses – the sun is starting to come up now. He's listening to the radio and tapping his fingers against the steering wheel in time to the music. Give us an angle that shows the police station in the background as he drives towards it.
11. CAPTION (3): ALL WE HAVE TO DO IS WAIT FOR THE PERPS TO TURN UP AND PICK THEM UP.
12. CAPTION (4): EASY.
13. CAPTION (5): GOT A LOT TO DO BEFORE THAT, THOUGH. LOT TO DO.

After reading the script Juan draws a fast sketch on a sheet of A4 paper with the basic angles and panel layouts. He often also lays out basic balloon placement.

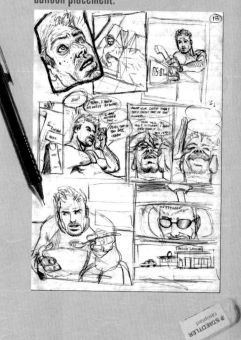

After comments and approval from Jason, Juan pencils the page on a 10" by t15" board.

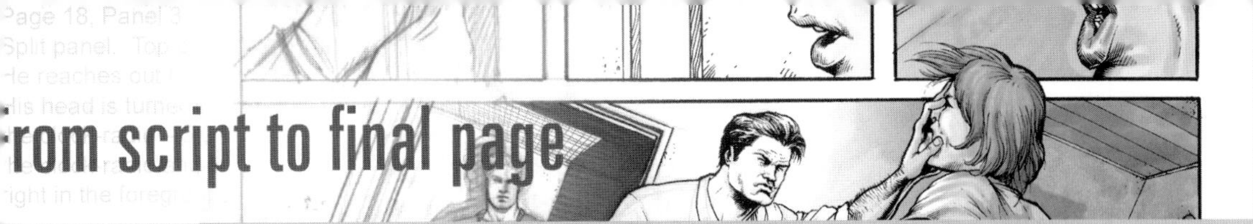

Page 18, Panel 3
Split panel. Top

rom script to final page

he page is then inked traditionally, most commonly with brush and india k. Juan also uses a pigment ink pen for some backgrounds.

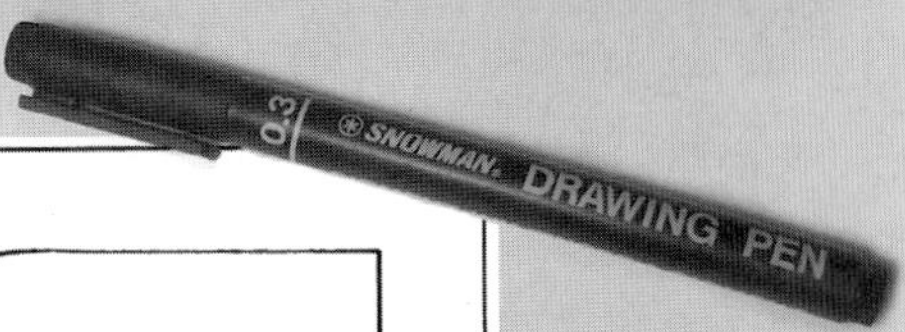

0.3
SNOWMAN DRAWING PEN

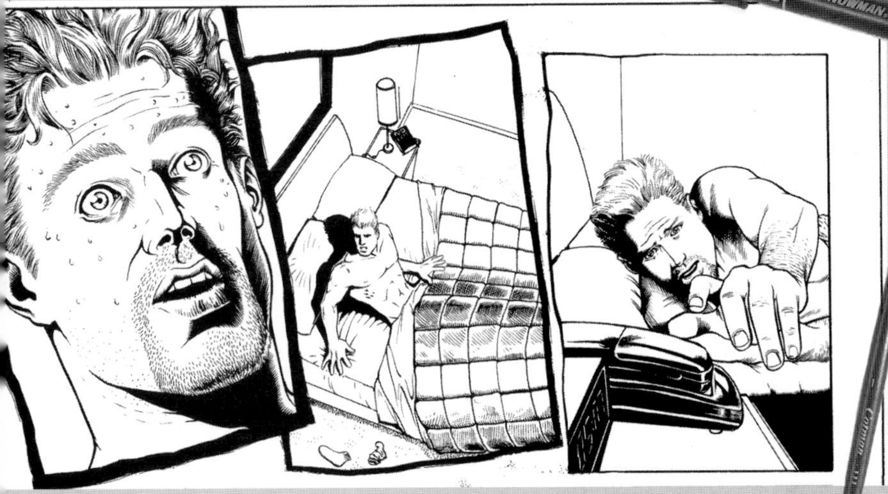

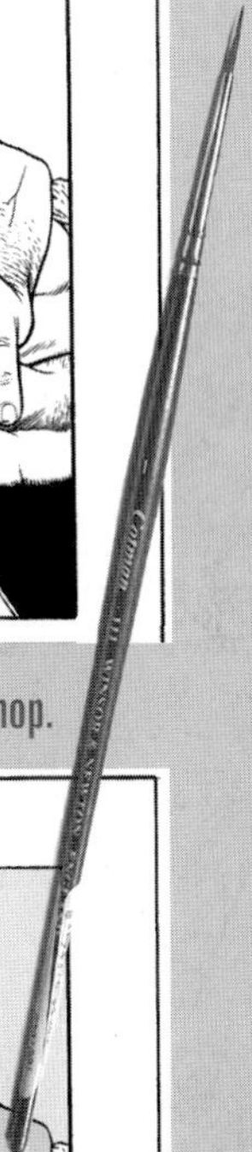

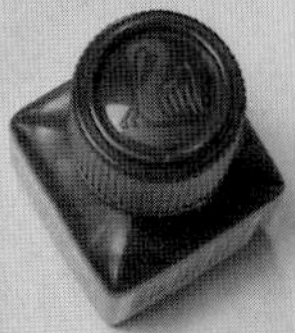

lext the page is scanned into the computer to allow flat greys to be added tin Adobe Photoshop.

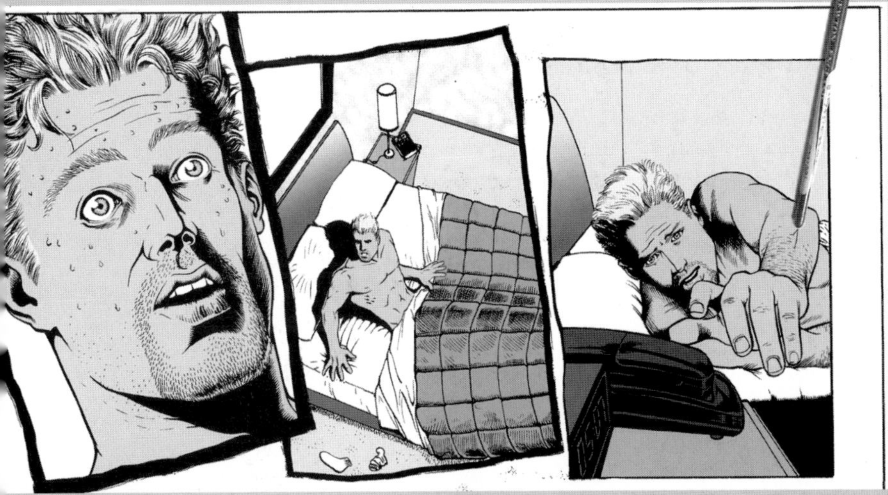

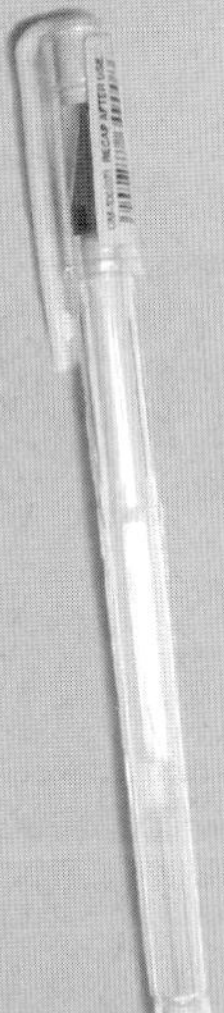

The final stage before lettering is to give the page different tones, adding volume to the figures as well as certain lighting elements. This is done using a Wacom Tablet (digital pen) on different layers in Photoshop.

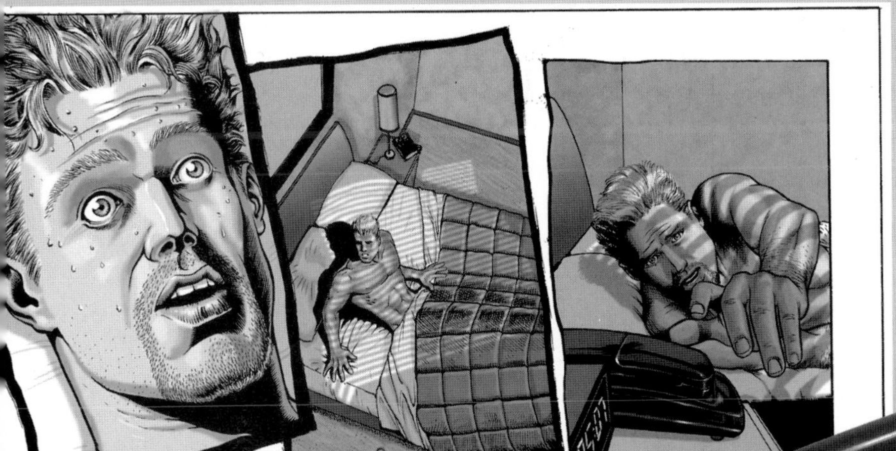

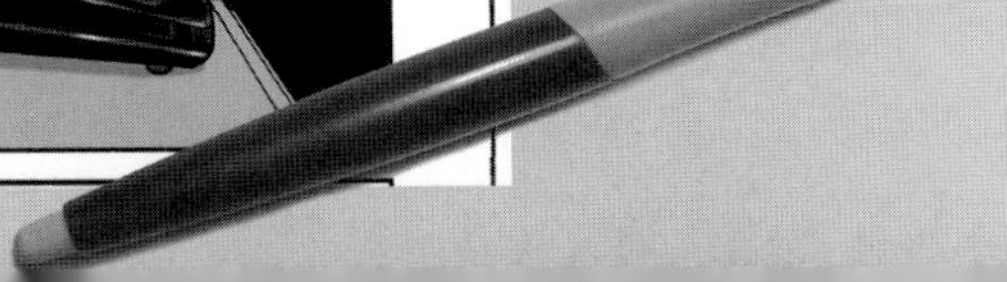

IDENTIKIT

Sketches! Everyone loves sketches and like any new series, we have plenty of them.
Here are some of our favourites.

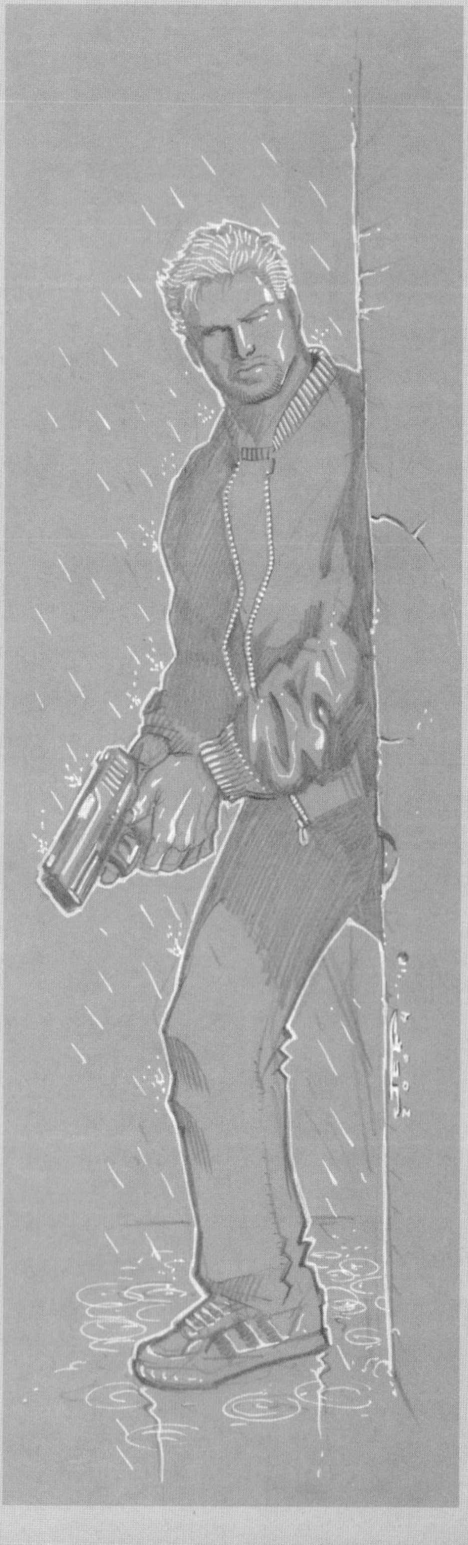

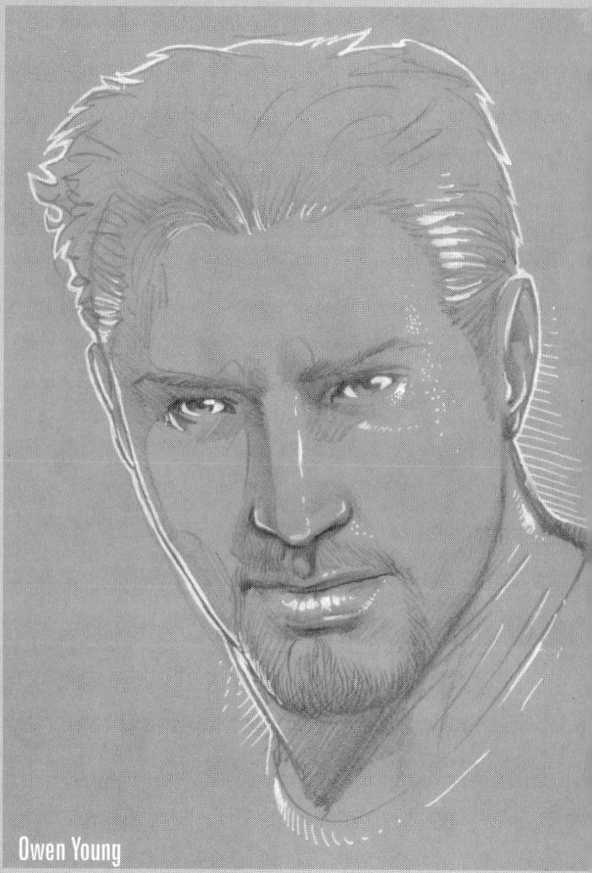

Owen Young

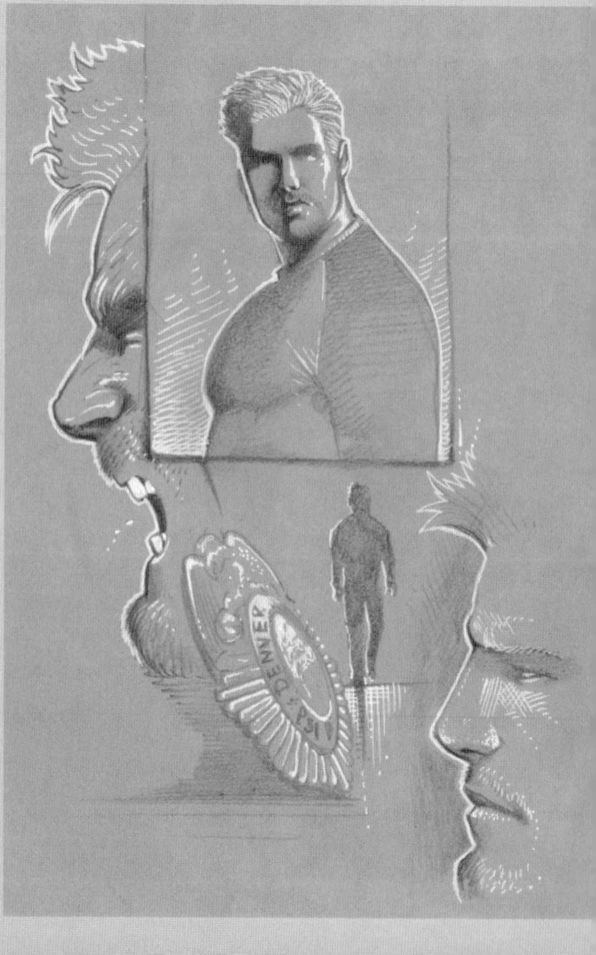

DENVER

IDENTIKIT

John Meyer

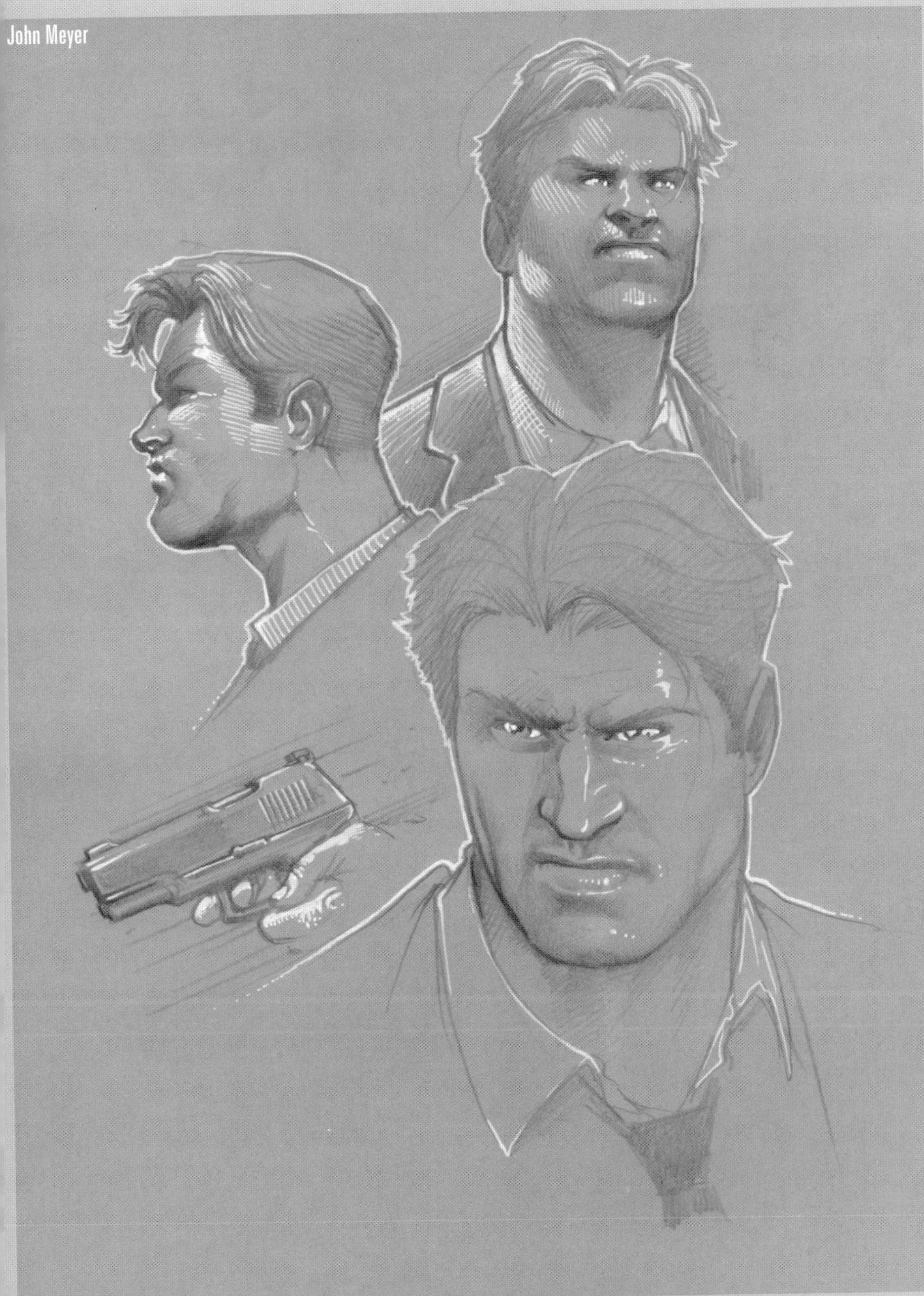

IDENTIKIT

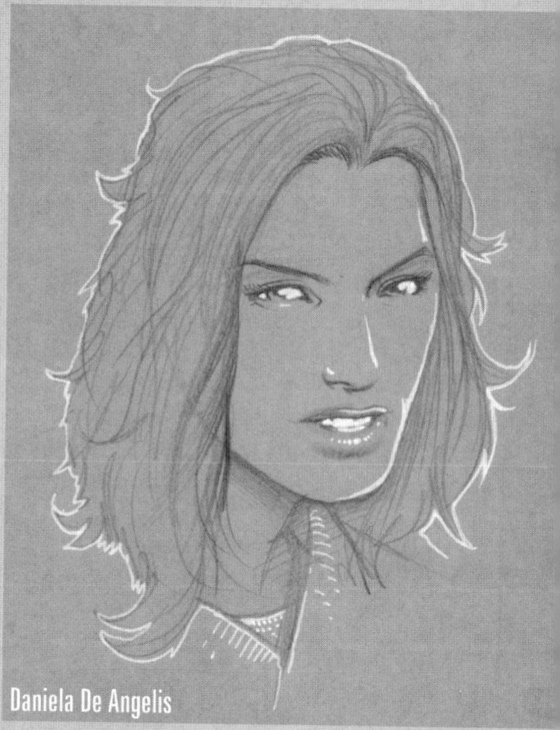
Daniela De Angelis

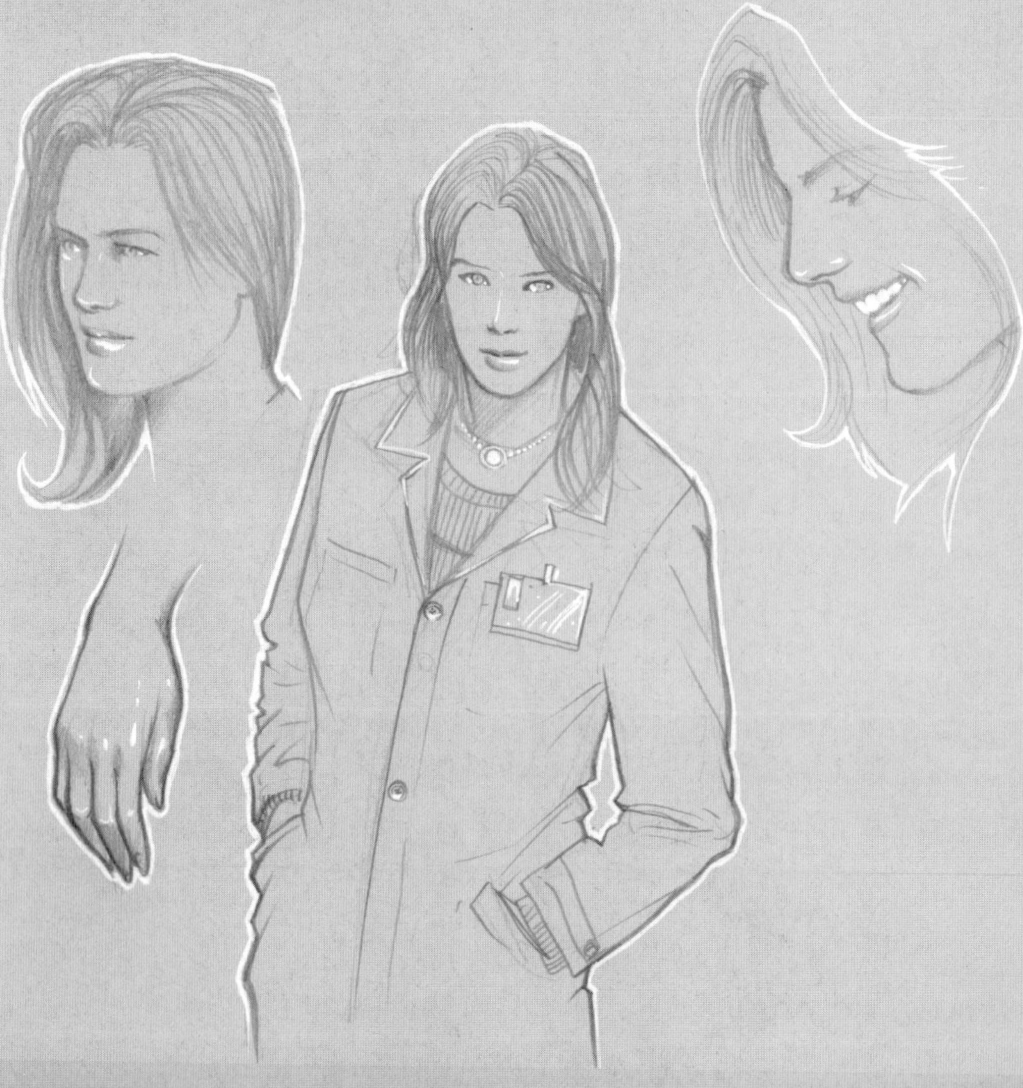

IDENTIKIT

Jodi Asamori-Lane

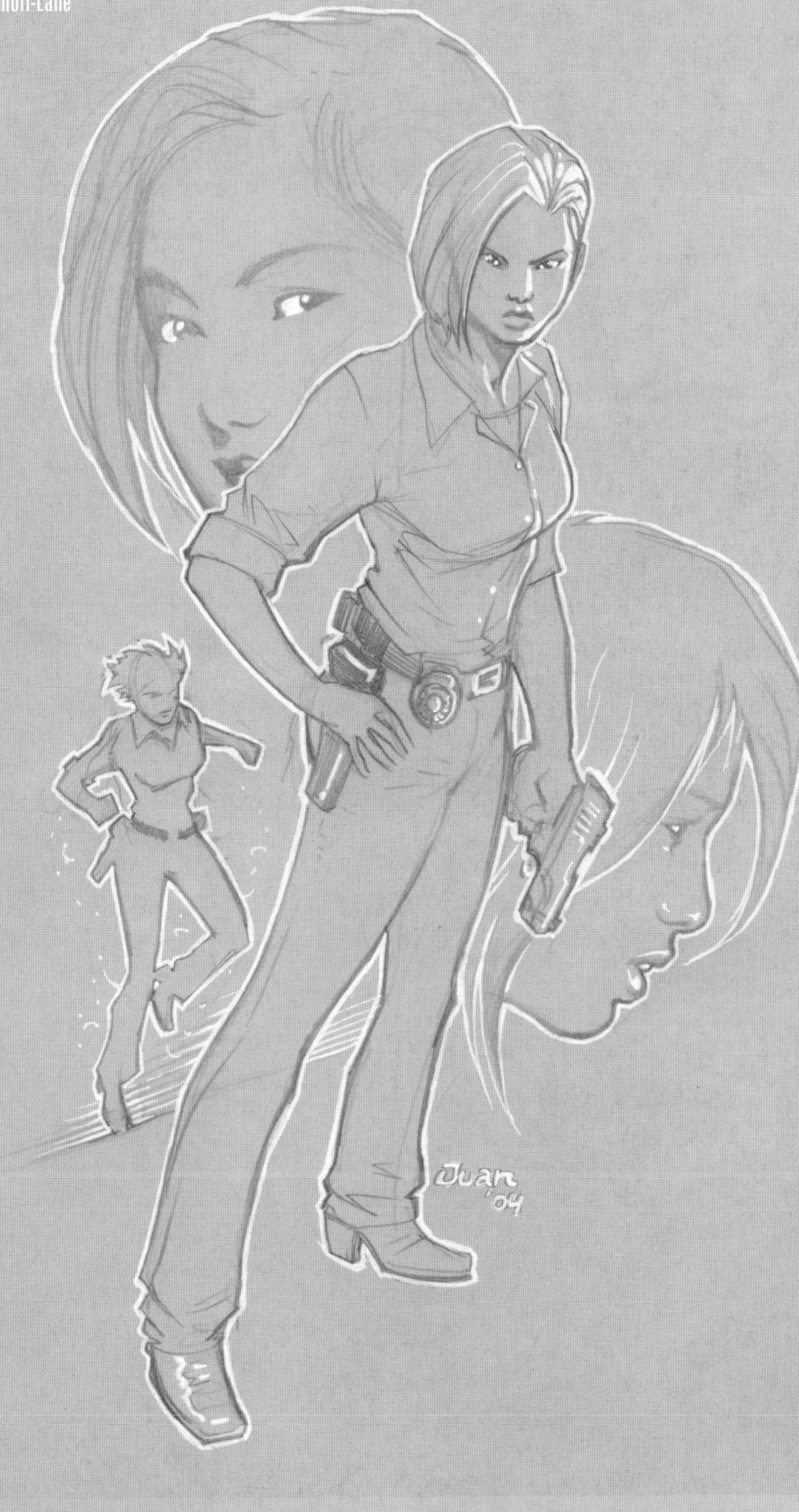
Juan
'04

IDENTIKIT

Jerry Farrell

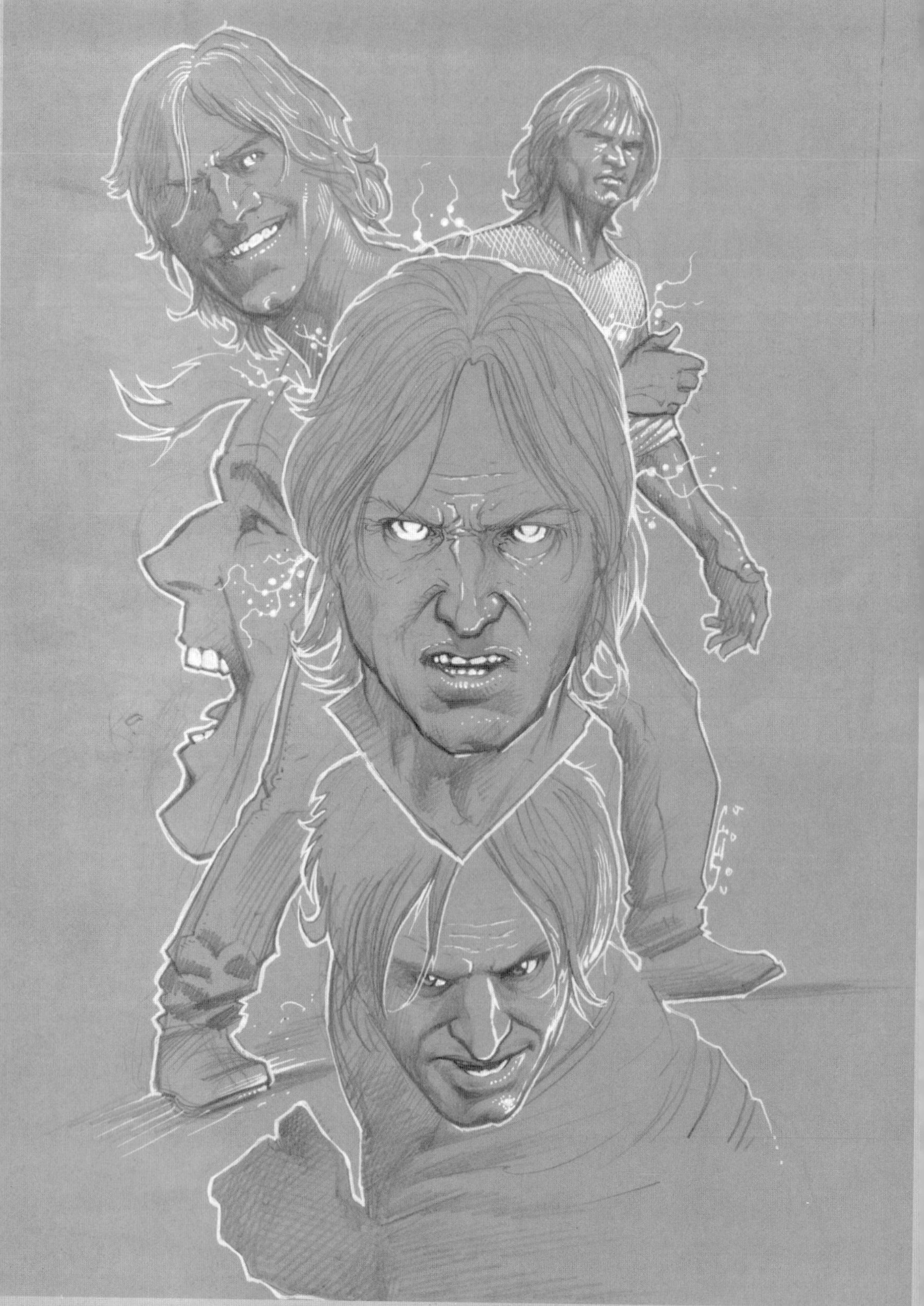

small gods™

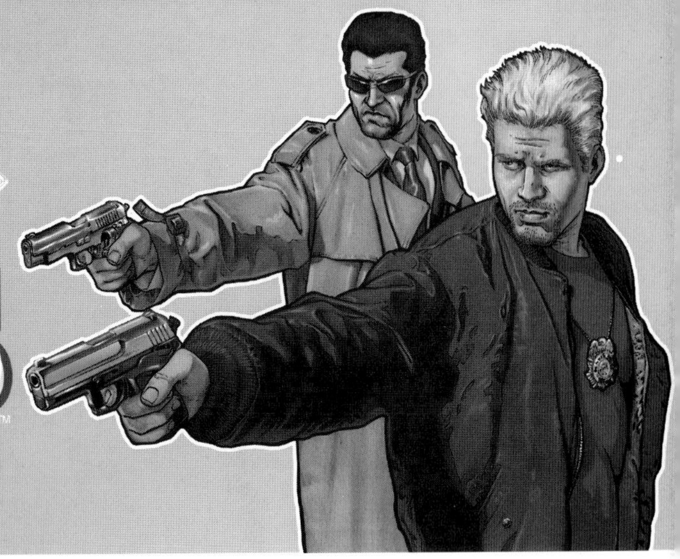

KILLING GRIN

JASON RAND writer

JUAN E. FERREYRA artist

JUAN & EDUARDO FERREYRA grey tones

MAHMUD A. ASRAR back-up artist

JIM KEPLINGER letterer

KRISTEN SIMON editor

JOSEPH SQUIRE technical advisor

Small Gods created by Jason Rand

Cover illustration & gallery art by Juan E. Ferreyra

Small Gods logo by Jim Keplinger

Collected edition design by Juan E. Ferreyra

MORE GREAT TITLES FROM IMAGE COMICS

FOR THE COMIC SHOP NEAR YOU CARRYING COMICS AND COLLECTIONS FROM IMAGE COMICS, PLEASE CALL TOLL FREE: 1-888-COMIC-BOOK.

ARIA VOL. 1 HC
ISBN# 158240139X
DEC01589

AVIGON
ISBN: 1-58240-182-9
STAR11946

BLACK FOREST
ISBN: 1-58240-350-3
JAN041286

CITY OF SILENCE
ISBN# 1582403678
DEC041603

CLOUDBURST
ISBN# 1582403686
APR041390

DARKNESS VOL. 1:
COMING OF AGE
ISBN# 1582400326
DEC041607

DIORAMAS
ISBN# 1582403597
FEB041312

A DISTANT SOIL VOL I
THE GATHERING
ISBN: 1-887259-51-2
STAR07382

DROWNED
ISBN# 1582403791
MAY04 1413

HAMMER OF THE GODS:
MORTAL ENEMY TP
ISBN# 158240271X
DEC041624

HEAVEN LLC.
ISBN: 1-58240-351-1
JAN041297

HEAVEN'S WAR GN
ISBN# 1582403309
DEC041626

KABUKI, VOL I
CIRCLE OF BLOOD
ISBN: 1-88727-9-806
STAR12480

MAGE VOL. 1 HC
ISBN# 1582403562
FEB041329

PARADIGM VOL. 1:
SEGUE TO AN
INTERLUDE TP
ISBN# 1582403198
DEC041662

SAVAGE DRAGON VOL 1:
BAPTISM OF FIRE TP
ISBN# 1582400474
DEC041682

SEI:
DEATH AND LEGEND GN
ISBN# 1582403341
SEP031300

WALKING DEAD VOL. 1
ISBN# 1582403589
DEC041722

WALKING DEAD VOL. 2
ISBN# 1582404135
AUG041586

WITCHBLADE VOL. 1 ORIGIN
ISBN# 1887279652
DEC041724

WONDERLAND
ISBN# 1582404151
AUG041588

IMAGECOMICS.COM
DIRECT SALES

7 09853 00259 8   00111

SMALL GODS, VOL. 1: KILLING GRIN